Creative Form Drawing

with children aged 6–10 years

Workbook 1

Angela Lord

Hawthorn Press

Hawthorn Press

Published by Hawthorn Press, Hawthorn House,
1 Lansdown Lane, Stroud, Gloucestershire, GL5 1BJ, UK
Tel: (01453) 757040 Email: info@hawthornpress.com
Website: www.hawthornpress.com

Design by Lucy Guenot
Printed by Melita Press. Malta.
Reprinted by Short Run Press Ltd, Exeter 2021.
Printed on environmentally friendly chlorine-free paper sourced from renewable forest stock.

British Library Cataloguing in Publication Data applied for.

ISBN 978-1-907359-98-9

Creative Form Drawing
with children aged 6–10 years

Workbook 1

Angela Lord

Hawthorn Press

Contents

Introduction

Form drawing was introduced into the Waldorf School curriculum by Rudolf Steiner, working together with many groups of teachers in central Europe and Britain about one hundred years ago (1919–1924).

Some of our contemporary educational problems could be solved through introducing this subject into a broader school context. Form drawing addresses diverse capacities through the nature of its containing a variety of aspects, each having specific educational benefits.

We will overview several of these in this introduction, and then consider how teachers, parents and therapists can learn this beneficial and fascinating subject so as to pass it on to their classes and children.

The true aim of education is not primarily to gather information for the sake of it, but to awaken genuine capacities of perception, judgement, creativity, and reliability in relation to life and living. Form drawing contributes in a meaningful way to healthy education. Let us consider how this happens.

Integrating sensory experience

In our present screen-orientated culture many children are experiencing 'reality confusion', and poor sensory integration, or dyspraxia. A 4-year-old child, when going for a walk, was overheard asking 'Mummy, are we in the real world now?'

When a form drawing lesson is experienced by children, with each stage assimilated and completed carefully, they have undergone an integrated process engaging several senses (sight, hearing, touch) combined with physical movement, co-ordination and balance. Each stage of the lesson is relevant and meaningful, and addresses the three different aspects of the child, namely thinking, feeling and willing. Children learn to think through doing, through activity, through the engagement of their whole bodily constitution with the surrounding world, through meaningful and appropriate experiential learning processes.

Computerised learning removes the child from healthy learning experiences, for example by supplying finished results, rather than step-by-step processes which unfold through stages that are inter-related in a relevant and living way. A type of soul poverty results. Children are given access to information without their being able to 'enter into' an integrated soul (psychological) and physical bodily engagement.

The creative engagement which form drawing processes offer are an antidote to the potential damage which computerised learning can have on the child. Real learning in the real world takes the place of an artificially construed mode of learning existing in an unreal, synthetic world.

Spatial orientation

The child's capacity to develop an integrated sense for spatial orientation – upwards, downwards; left, right; centre, periphery – is supported in the practice of form drawing. Children who are experiencing any difficulties in orientating themselves in movement co-ordination will benefit from the integrated process of:

1. observing the teacher drawing
2. moving the form in space
3. drawing the form in the air
4. drawing in their books.

These four steps are important as the sequence provides the following experiences for the children. We'll consider them in more detail.

1. Observation of movement through watching the teacher while he/she draws on the blackboard. The children are following the lines as the teacher draws. They are exercising subtle eye movements through focussed observation of a process, rather than reading completed texts or words.

2. Transferring the drawn form into a three-dimensional spatial experience through movement. What the children's eyes have seen becomes bodily movement in space.

   The large full-body movement requires:
   - planning – the children must think beforehand where they are going
   - imagination – the children must imagine the line before they walk it
   - purpose – the children need to know how far they walk in one direction before changing direction.

   In the large spatial movements (i.e. walking the forms) children are gaining first-hand direct experiences of:
   - spatial directions – forwards, backwards; left; right; diagonal
   - spatial movements – straight lines; curves; circles
   - spatial relationships – centre, periphery; angles; distance; size; proportion; arrangement.

3. Drawing forms in the air brings the form closer to them. They can imagine shapes of forms as they move their hands. Engaging both the left and the right arms, either separately or simultaneously, integrates bodily co-ordination and stimulates both left and right sides of the brain (a simple brain-gym exercise). If children need quietening down, or a more focusing process, they can draw small forms with their index fingers.

4. Drawing in their books.The large movements are condensed and focussed on the page, making movement visible. They are organising lines and surfaces in relevant, aesthetic and meaningful ways.

Handwriting

Form drawing is a significant pre-requisite for developing hand-writing skills. It provides all of the fine-motor skills, co-ordination and practical exercises which are necessary for writing. Children who have experienced form drawing will find that the transition to clear and legible handwriting is a straight-forward and natural progression. The step from handwriting to reading then follows accordingly.

Rudolf Steiner recommended that handwriting should precede learning to read. The following quotation provides the rationale for this.

'... writing is a concern of the whole being of a child. It becomes an activity of the arms and hands in particular, permeating these with spirit and exercising the whole person... Reading is merely a pursuit of the head, a one-sided activity. Therefore a teacher who develops insight into the nature of the human being will be careful to develop writing out of painting and drawing, and only after the child is able to write down what he or she inwardly experiences as a word or sentence. A child speaks, and can then write down what he or she is saying. Only then has the time come to teach reading.

Reading is easy to teach if writing has first been developed to a relatively perfect stage. Only when the child has worked over in his own being, in the motory and movement systems, the content of what is written and read; when he or she has inwardly participated in the actual development and content of the reading material, are they ready for the one-sided activity of reading.'

What do teachers need to do?

1. Become familiar with all aspects of the lesson and practise doing them:
   - moving the forms in space
   - moving the forms with one arm, then the other, then both arms
   - drawing the forms in the air with index fingers
   - drawing the forms in the air with the nose.
2. Practise drawing the forms on the blackboard.
3. Practise drawing the forms in a non-lined book.
   - The teacher's confidence and certainty with the forms and the teaching process will be readily conveyed to the children. These steps, practised before the lesson, enable the teacher to experience first-hand how form drawing works.
   - Lesson preparation becomes a refreshing and enlivening process, rather than adding to a mounting pile of paperwork.
4. Once the principles have been assimilated and understood, teachers can create new forms for their class and for individual children who may need certain aspects reinforced or extended.

Making assessments

- Observe the class carefully and discreetly throughout the lesson.
- If children are experiencing any difficulties a process can be repeated.
- Don't single out young children (6–7 years) individually, but treat them within the class as a whole. From Class 3 (8–9 years) onwards, children can be given individual suggestions as the teacher walks around the classroom to observe their work.
- Allow a time process to take place. Children have different constitutions, personalities and capacities. Faster children can draw a second form (perhaps more slowly and more carefully!). Slower children can complete their forms for homework or during spare time at school. Advanced children can create their own form related to the one in the lesson.
- More complex learning difficulties may require further assistance. Refer to the suggestions at the end of Parts One, Two and Three.

What to look for

- Movement co-ordination in space. Observe how their feet move; their ease with spatial directions or their hesitancy. Are they confident? Unsure? Going in the wrong direction?
- Movements in drawing in the air. Can they trace the whole form? Carefully and clearly? Or haphazardly?
- Are they reversing left and right movements? This is quite common, and will be corrected quite naturally in the form drawing lessons.
- Are their forms in their books accurate? Are there any weaknesses? Are they engaged and focussed when they are drawing?

The importance of repetition, rhythm and consistency

Form drawing lessons create familiarity, security and consistency. Children will not become bored through repeating the processes in the lesson structure as each lesson brings a new form, new experiences and fresh content. At the same time however, in this book, the developmental steps are carefully related in that new forms relate to previous ones. This is important. Continuity and consistency help to build certainty and security in the child. A focussed, inwardly engaged concentration develops, rather than the nervous, easily distracted hyper-active tendencies prevalent in some children at present.

Conclusion

Healthy child development is supported through meaningful, inter-related experiences, which are appropriate for their particular age group. The structuring of this book provides the forms which children need at particular times of their growth. Young children (aged 6–7 years) will be engrossed in the doing, in the activity itself. Children aged 8 upwards will begin to develop an aesthetic sense, to make discerning judgements and to self-evaluate. Some children need the security and authority which the teacher provides in the given forms. Other children will enjoy the challenges of creating their own original drawings.

In this way form drawing is both prescriptive, definitive and creatively predictable, as well as allowing interpretation, free expression and individuality to flourish.

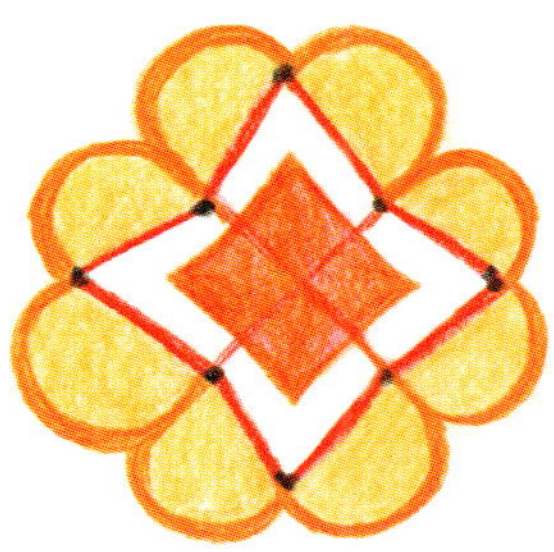

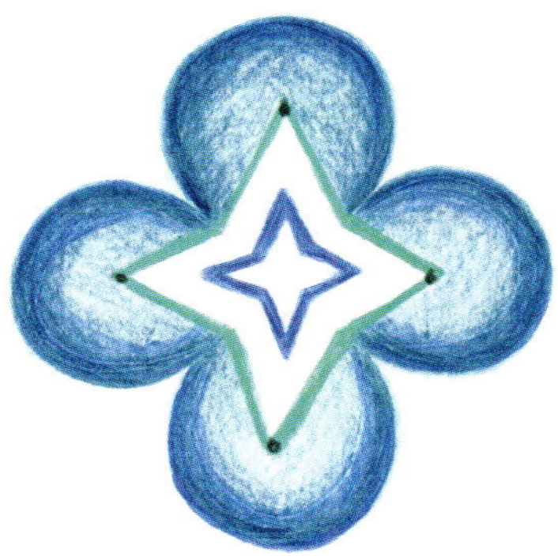

Using this book

Teaching methods

The first part of this book deals with the practical aspects of teaching form drawing, and outlines an integrated pedagogic approach. The suggestions ensure that a well-balanced, well-rounded educational process is possible, to foster children's learning in a healthy way. The methodology of form drawing is based upon educating children beyond mere 'head learning' or cleverness. It is designed to incorporate movement of the whole body, bringing meaningful co-ordination as well as fine-motor skills, and to provide a secure foundation for learning, in gradual steps, through increasingly complex, intricate and challenging forms.

Teachers themselves need to practise the forms beforehand, so that their authority and certainty is conveyed to the children. Form drawing should be absorbing, fascinating and enjoyable. When the teacher (or parent) finds enthusiasm and interest in this subject, a love of 'learning through doing' is conveyed directly to the children.

Learning processes and exercises

Each section in Parts One, Two and Three is based upon developmental stages according to the children's age, and in relation to the Waldorf School approach regarding the numbering of the classes (e.g. Class One, Class Two, and so on). This is intended as a guideline. What is important is the actual sequencing of how each stage relates to the next, as each new step is built upon the preceding one in a natural, integrated and carefully considered process to provide the children with an inter-connected, readily assimilated healthy learning process.

The beginning of each Part lists the skills which the children in each age group are developing. These developmental skills will vary, according to the individual child. They provide teachers (and parents) with a reference for assessing a child's learning progress, and a way of gauging the specific skills that form drawing is developing at each particular phase.

Then follows a list of actual experiences, i.e. the principles contained within the exercises, or 'what the children are learning'. These key phrases provide a synopsis for the content of the exercises and will help the teacher know what is being learned.

Drawing size

The illustrations in this book do not indicate the size of the children's drawings. Children should draw large forms, filling the whole page.

Teaching methods

In the classroom

1. The teacher draws the form (in one direction only) on the board while the children are watching.

2. The children stand up and draw the form in the air with their arm and hand. This can be done several times over, with movements in both directions, and with both arms (up/down; left/right; clockwise or anticlockwise). Each child should have sufficient room to move in large, uncramped gestures. The atmosphere should be quiet and concentrated.

3. The children can also 'draw' the forms in the air with their heads, following their noses.
   - In Class Two (or towards the end of Class One) some children might like to come up and draw their own form on the board, copying the teacher's form. This can be done one at a time in front of the class, or in groups of three or four at the same time. It is important never to judge or correct – just let the form 'be'. The board will be crowded with forms (as far as the children can reach) – a wonderful social experience!

4. Classes One, Two and Three can also 'move the forms in space' by walking them in the classroom, school hall or in the playground. Many possibilities can be explored with the children moving individually, in pairs and in groups. Interweaving and crossing forms; forms which differ inwardly and outwardly; intersecting lines; circles; squares and stars can be moved in groups, with one child moving at a time.
   - Moving the forms with the whole body is an essential and integral aspect to the learning process, requiring careful supervision on the part of the teacher. Forms need to be moved carefully so that the expansive spatial experience can be transferred through the whole bodily experience into the reduced form drawn in their books. This 'living into' a form on a large scale supports spatial orientation and co-ordination; observation and awareness of other children; ability to follow instructions; and provides a vital learning process which engages the whole child.
   - The teacher will need to assess the class beforehand as some children need to move in this expansive way before drawing in their books; other children may need to 'settle down' to drawing directly after the hand drawing in space. The class may vary from one day to another and it is necessary that the teacher assesses their need to find the best and most appropriate method. Some classes need to 'breathe out', especially if many children are not walking to school and need physical exercise; other classes may need to settle down indoors to focus quietly.

5. The children draw the form into an unlined book of plain white paper using large crayons or large coloured pencils. The children can sit or stand (depending on their choice). They need to draw in a relaxed uncramped process, moving their fingers, hand and arm gently but firmly. They are then able to live into the universal principle that 'all form is movement come to rest'.

6. Rubbing out with a rubber (eraser) is not necessary. The same form can be drawn over several times until it is balanced. The children should feel relaxed in this process and trust that they can 'self-correct'. An attitude of 'there are no mistakes, but processes' is important, and the teacher can support this approach by using comments such as: 'the form is coming', 'it's on its way', 'it's nearly there'.

7. Learning happens in different ways and on different levels. Observing, moving, focussing, concentrating, self-correcting, adapting, re-creating, co-ordinating and socially interacting are all essential ingredients of a learning process. They can all be incorporated into the form drawing lessons.

Using colours

The forms can be copied several times using different colours. As forms become more complex different colours can be used for intersecting lines, for varying lengths of line, for combinations and for metamorphosis (or transformation) forms. Remember that the experience of movement is important and this is experienced in the line itself. Colours enhance the sensitively felt expression of movement in the line, rather than emphasising the surface areas. Some children might colour-in their forms, in a spontaneous way. This is neither encouraged nor discouraged but the teacher tactfully emphasises the line itself, bringing the child's focus to the movement of drawing and to following the line with their eyes.

Adjacent colours

Colour sequences can be used in a progressive order related to the rainbow sequence in the colour circle. For example: red, orange, yellow; or green, blue, violet; or red, violet, blue, and so on. These adjacent colours create a harmonious and pleasing experience of colour and enhance forms which are more complex. They can be very satisfying aesthetically. Children may discover these themselves, but the teacher can also provide such examples on the blackboard with coloured chalks.

Contrasting colours

Combining colours which have strong contrasts defines a form more clearly. Structural aspects of the forms can be enhanced by using the complementary colours:

Red + Green

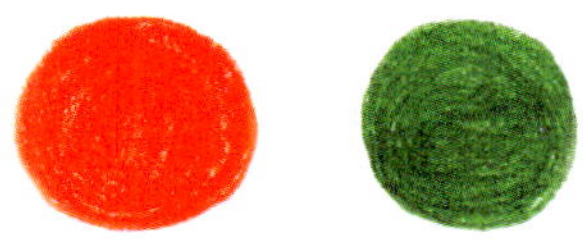

Orange + Blue

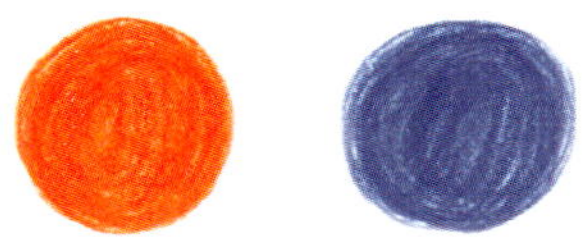

Purple + Yellow

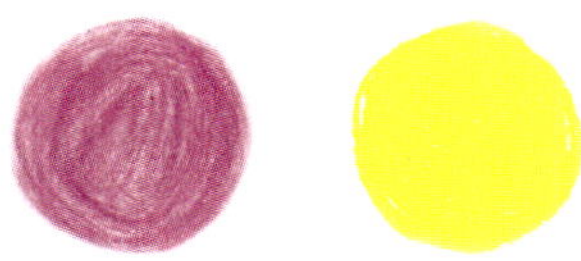

The children might also enjoy choosing colours which are bright and active in connection to the forms that are lively (red, orange, yellow) and quieter passive colours for the forms that are more flowing (green, blue, purple).

Vocabulary and language skills

I have included a descriptive vocabulary in relationship to the various forms. It can be immensely satisfying to the children to express their experiences, feelings and observations related to their work, and they will often need new words to describe their discoveries. The children will also bring their own verbalisation to what they are perceiving, and this should flow spontaneously and quite naturally. Some children may prefer to assimilate quietly and inwardly, so descriptions should not be forced or analytical. The teacher can use the vocabulary with the whole class in a 'free' way, towards the end of a lesson. Always allow time for learning processes to settle to avoid intellectualising, so some descriptions may only arise after two or three lessons. It's also not necessary to associate the forms with objects ('it looks like a…'). This may happen, of course, but it's not necessarily sought for. Language skills will develop from the actual experiences of doing the form drawing, its aesthetic qualities and its dynamic nature.

Timetabling

Form drawing can be taken as a main lesson for two to three weeks on a daily basis and repeated two to three times a year; or as a weekly lesson throughout the year. The children will very quickly compose their own forms which can be done during the lesson time. Class Two onwards can continue drawing forms at home, as set homework.

Children who are quick at completing any classroom subject can be encouraged to take out their form drawing books and to work on creating their forms. If they can be quietly engaged in this, then they won't be bored or disruptive whilst other children are still finishing their work.

Home schooling

6 to 10 year olds

- Draw the form on a blank sheet of paper with the child (or children) watching.
- The child draws the form several times in the air in both directions. This can be done together with the parent. They can also 'draw' with their head, following their noses.
- They copy the form into their books (as outlined above).
- They can also walk the form both indoors, and outdoors in a garden or park, together with siblings, friends, parents or their teacher.
- Children aged 8, 9 and 10 can create many of their own forms, related to the examples given.

Part One

Class One

6–7 years old

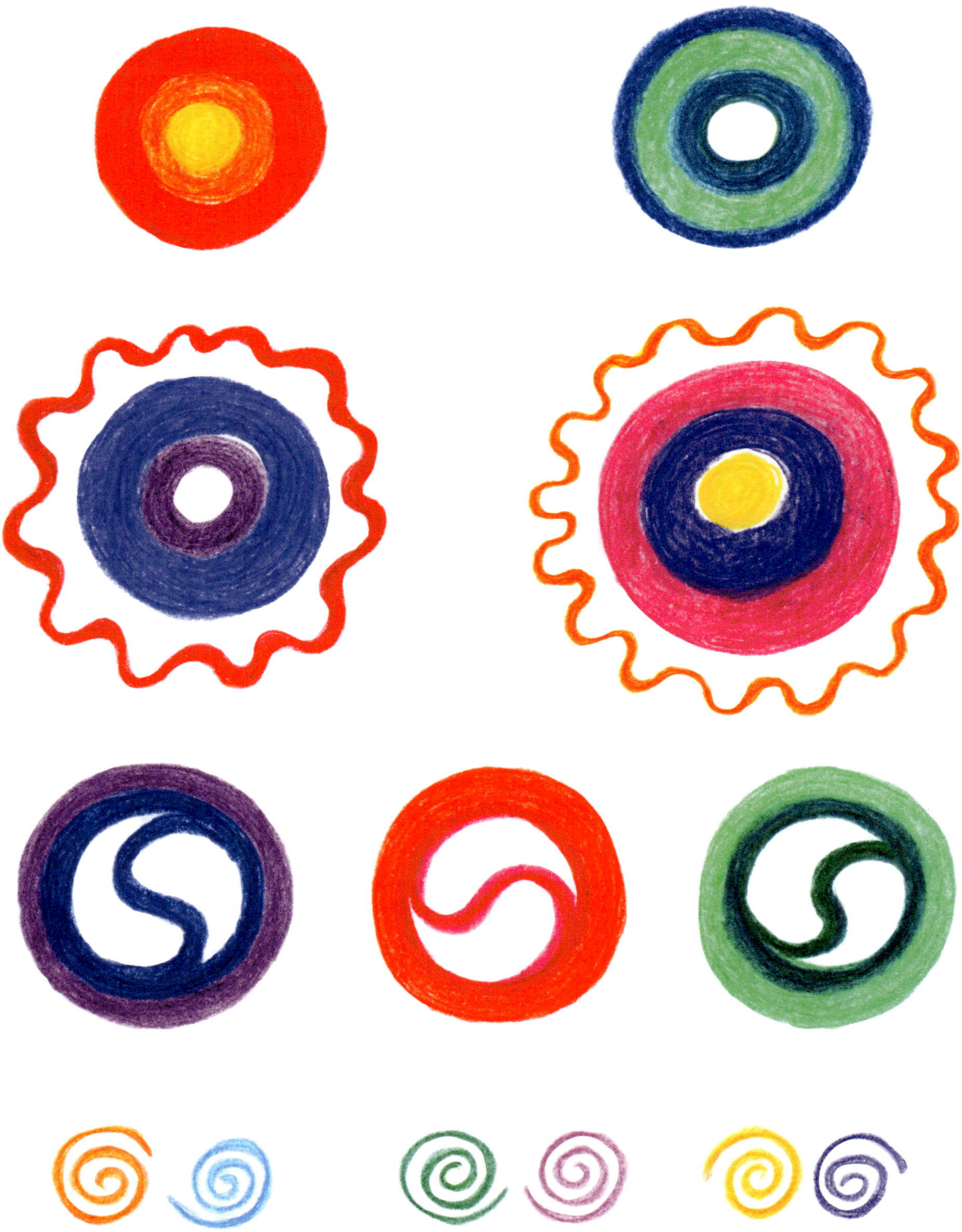

Exercises suitable for Class One (6–7 years) are developed in order to support:

- Hand and eye co-ordination
- Dexterity of the hand
- Preparation for handwriting skills
- Observation skills
- Ability to compare
- Sensitivity to contrasting forms
- Spatial orientation
- Inner sense of balance

The examples which are included here provide a foundation for experiencing:

- Proportion
- Relation
- Contrast
- Movement
- Sequence
- Strength and security in the single form
- Artistic feeling in the rhythmically repeated forms
- Comparing straightness and roundness
- Developing the principles of straight lines and curved lines into more complex forms

The first lesson: Introducing the first two forms

The very first forms are simply a straight line and a curve drawn side by side:

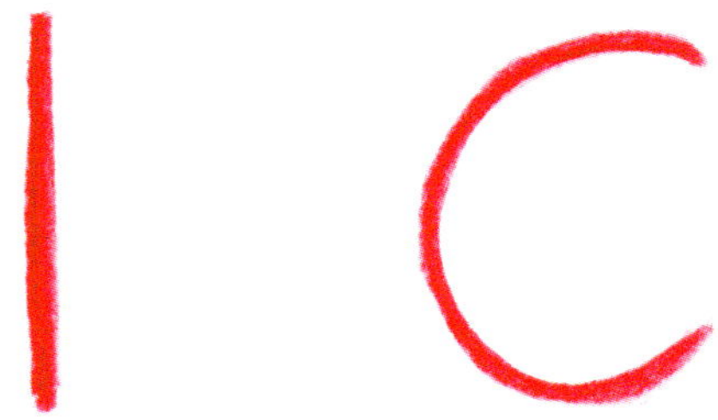

The teacher draws these in front of the children, large enough for them to see clearly. Although simple, the straight line and the curve are the fundamental foundations of all drawn forms. It is important that the children see, feel and experience the differences in these two gestures. Drawing the forms in the air and moving them in space enable the children to 'live into' these archetypal forms.

Note that the forms will be drawn on the board in one direction:

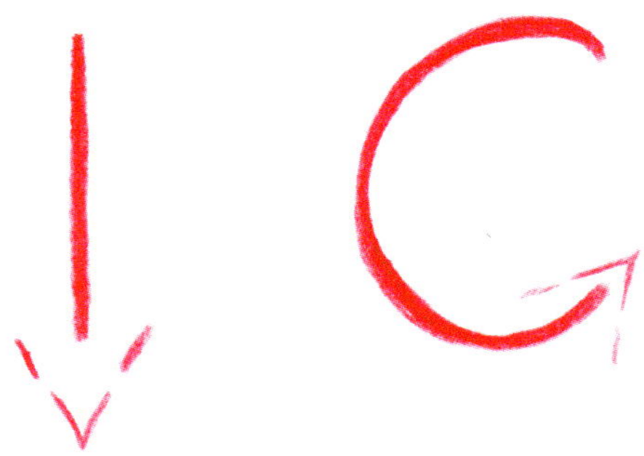

But the children will walk them in the opposite direction so that they are walking forwards in order to develop certainty and balance in spatial orientation.

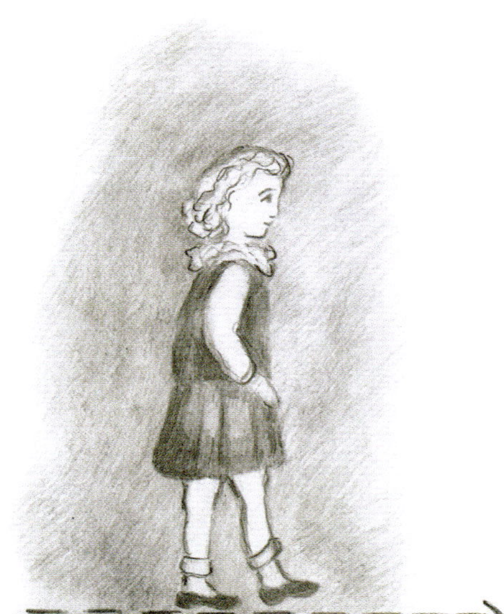

Then they can turn and follow the forms in both directions and draw them in both ways.

The forms are drawn from above, downwards.

The children imagine a straight line.
They walk the line, feeling it inwardly.
Then they turn and follow the line back again.

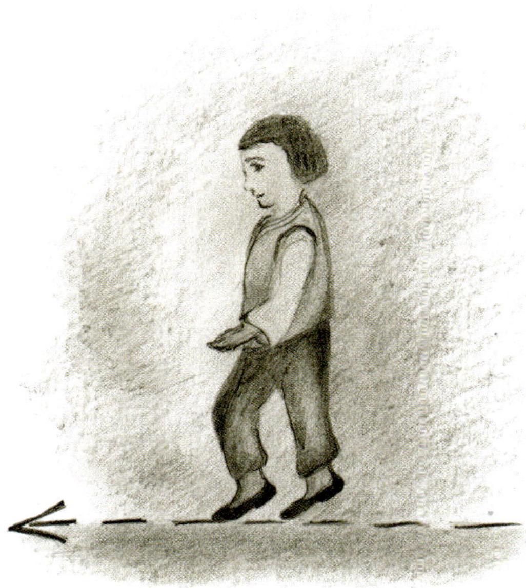

The children can also 'draw' the forms 'with their noses'. Sitting at their desks, the head is moved slowly and gently upwards and downwards, as they imagine their nose drawing the form. First, the straight line, and then the curve, both upwards and downwards. Then the two forms are drawn in their books:

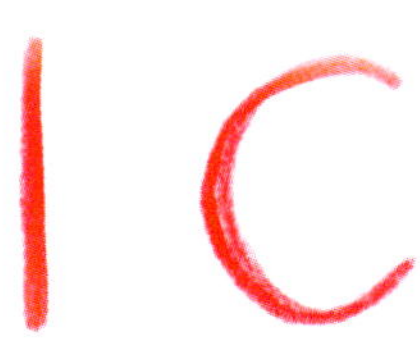

Followed by different patterns:

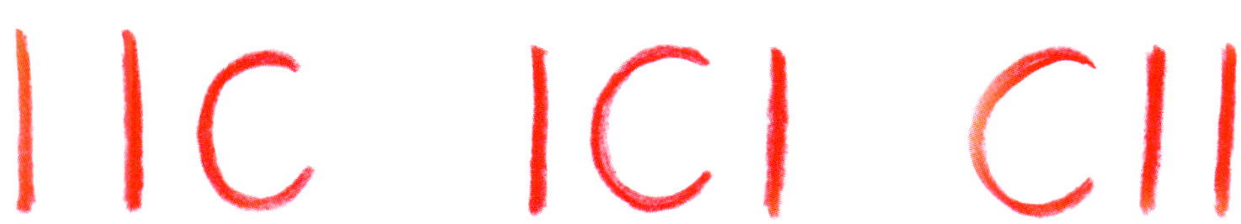

The children can listen to the sounds which their pencil makes. They will hear a difference between the straight line and the curve. Subsequently the forms can be drawn over several times, both upwards and downwards.

In the next lesson the curve can be turned in the other direction:

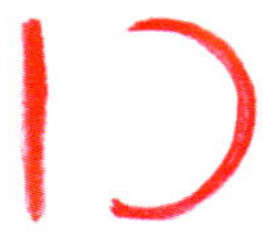

Followed by different patterns:

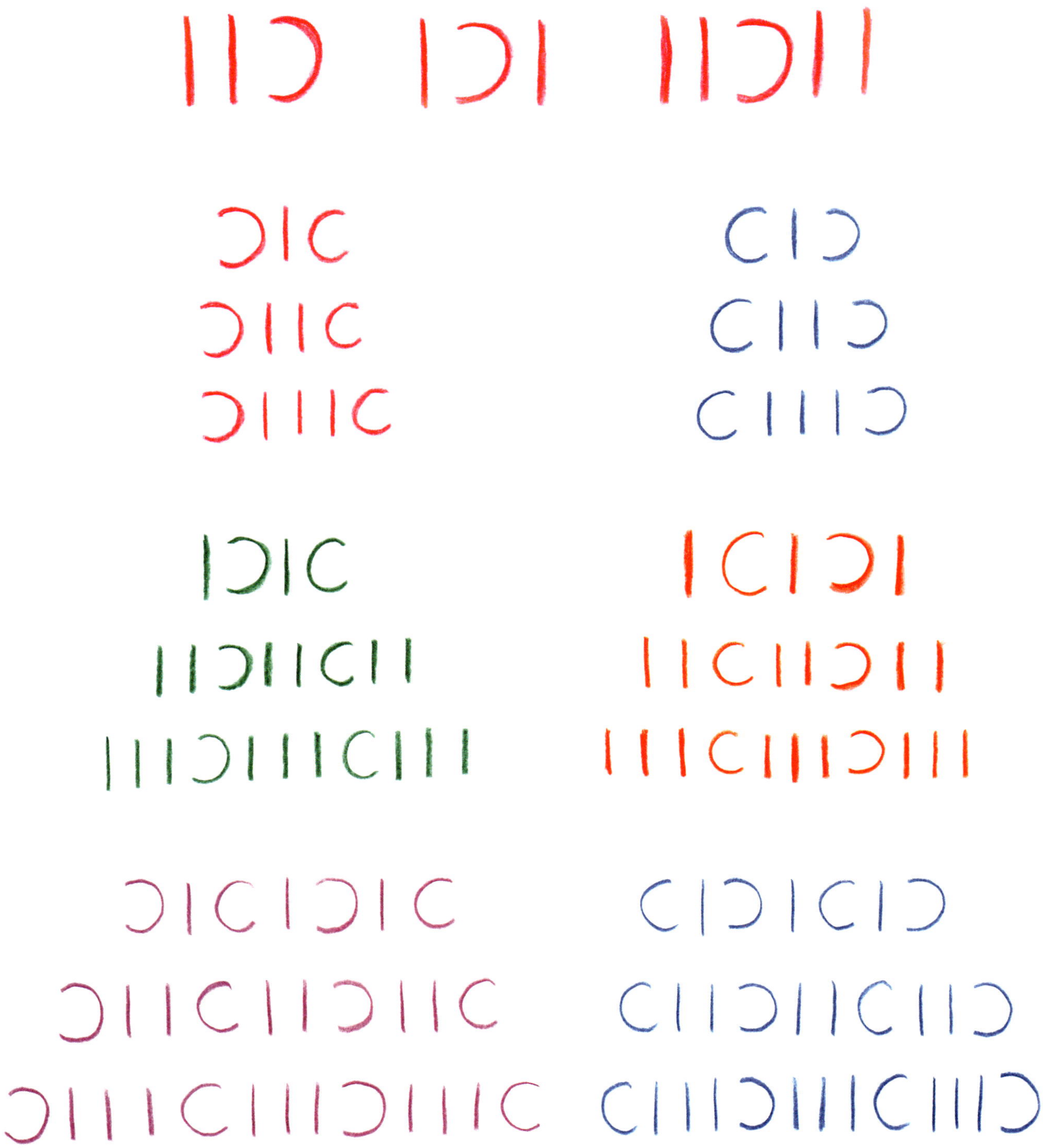

The teacher can draw a variety of patterns on the blackboard and encourage the children to complete them, both on the board and in their books.

NOTE: The patterns follow set rhythms – they are not arbitrary, but develop in related sequences. The children experience:

- order
- rhythm
- security
- relation
- artistic feeling
- sequence
- contrast.

Variations in size can be explored, by extending the length of the vertical line:

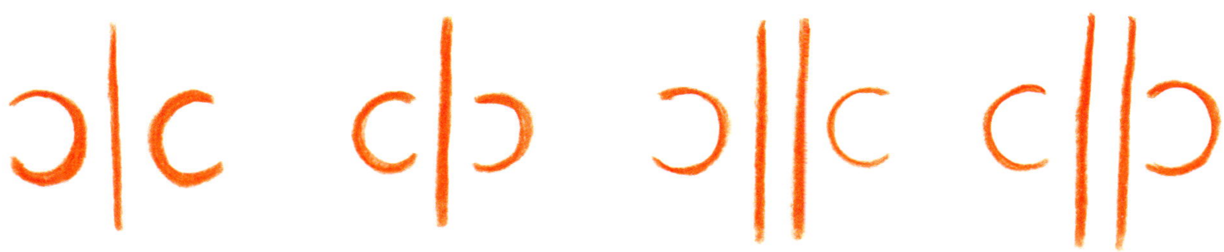

Straight lines

Patterns can be drawn using only straight lines.

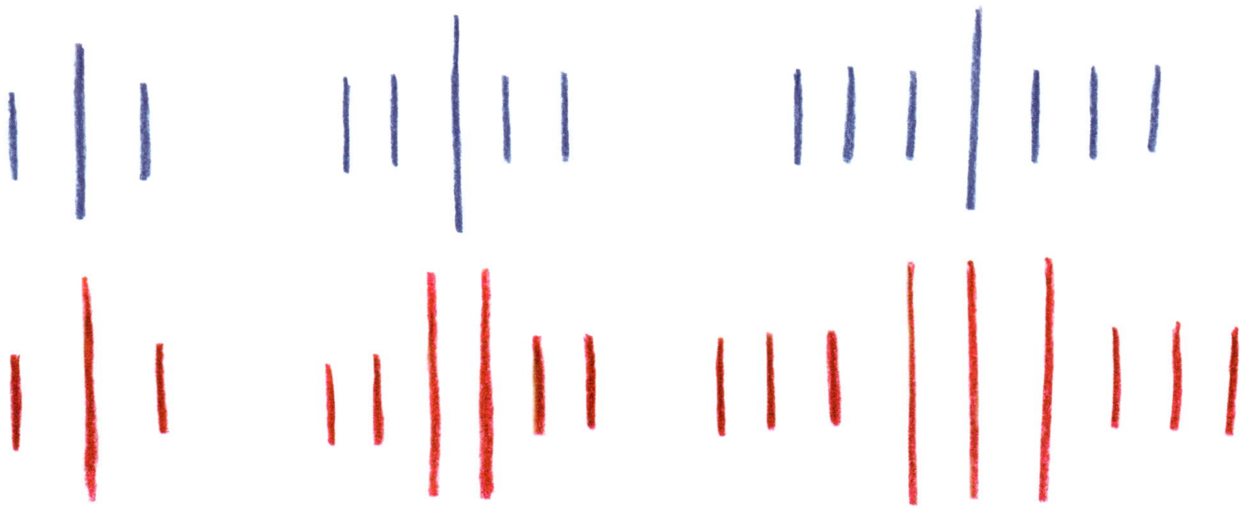

The children can step these patterns with shorter and longer steps, for example: short, long, short. Short, short, long, short, short.

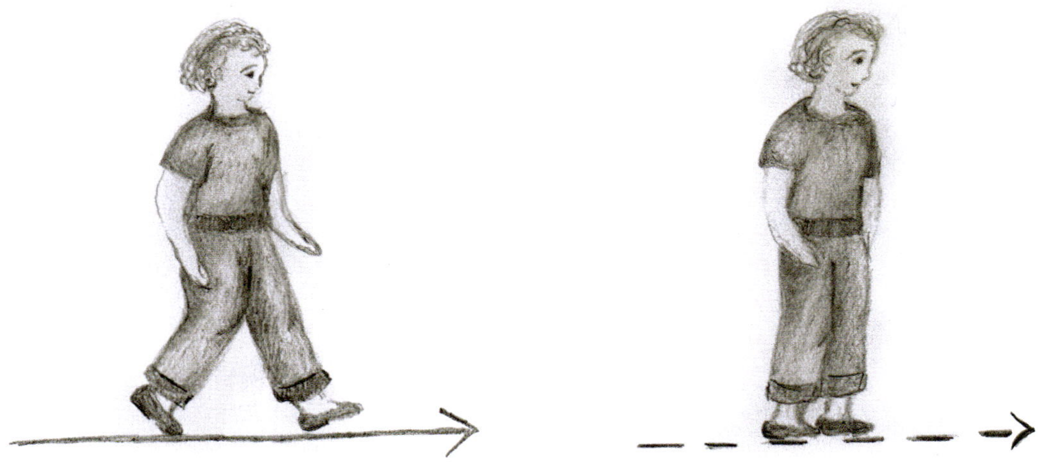

Further patterns can be drawn by placing progressively shorter lines in a sequence:.

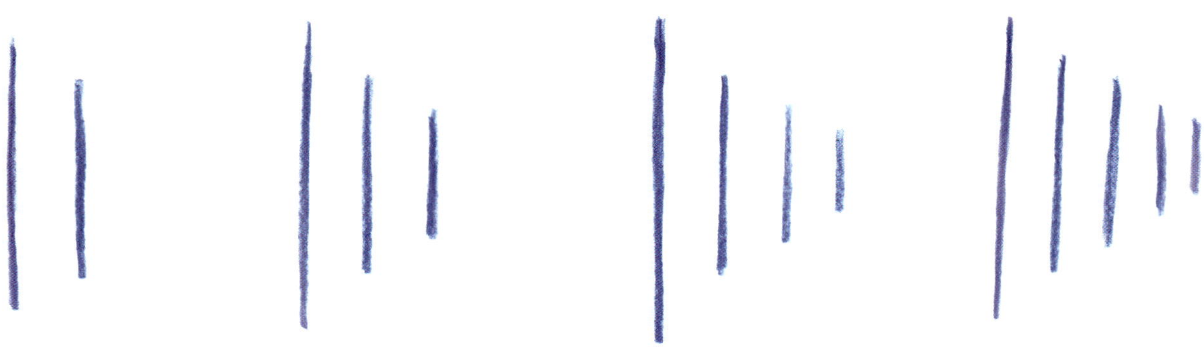

And progressively longer lines in a sequence:

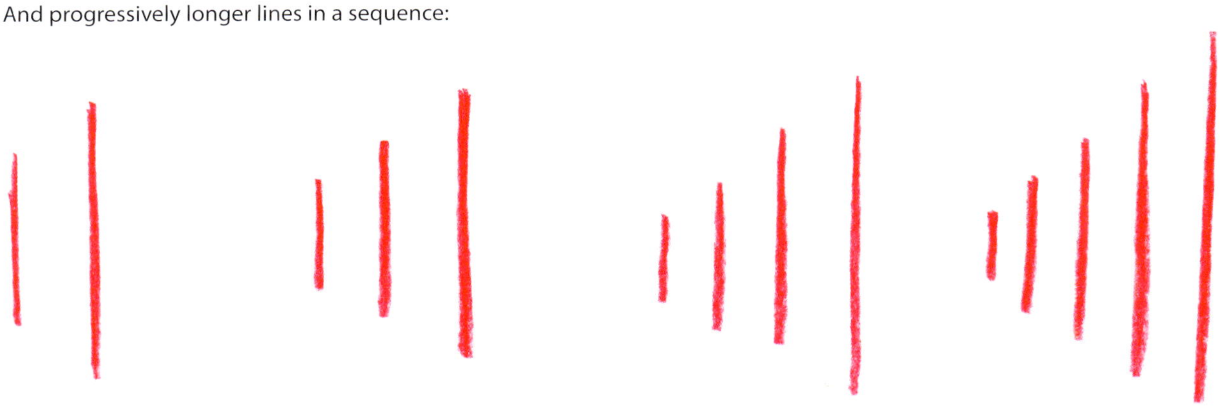

The children can then draw a balanced form:

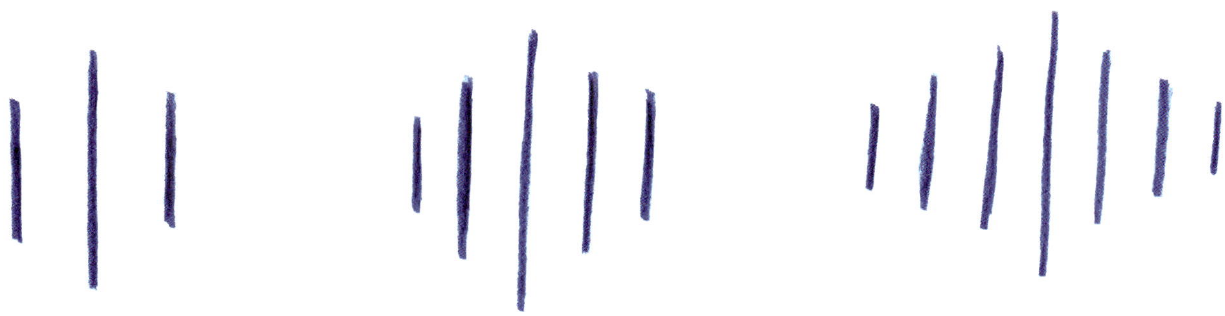

It does not matter whether the lines are absolutely accurate in length. The children will gradually correct and balance their own work, and they should not feel that their drawing is 'right or wrong'. They can enjoy drawing the forms several times and make their own discoveries.

The line-forms can also be drawn horizontally.

Long, growing shorter:

Short, growing longer:

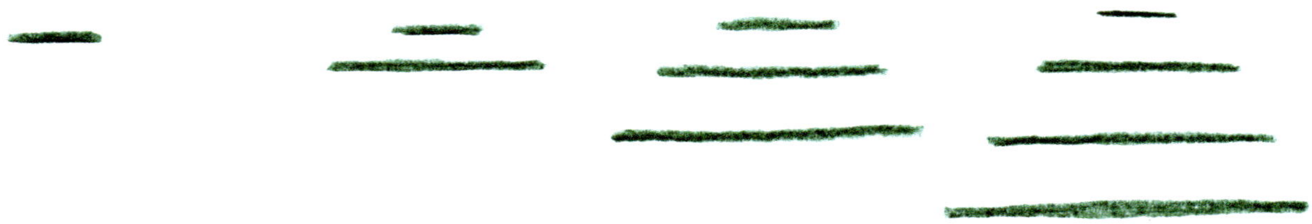

Or drawing them going in the opposite direction, downwards.

The lines can be drawn in both directions, from left to right, then right to left. This gives an extra experience of movement and spatial awareness.

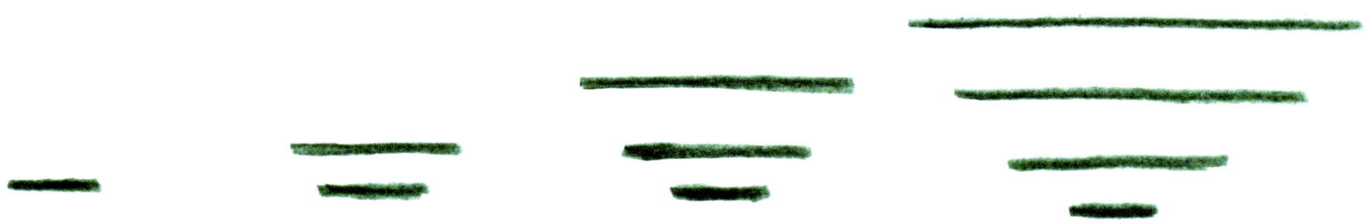

For these forms the vocabulary can include:
Left, right, above, below, longer, shorter, vertical, horizontal, in the centre; on one side, on both sides; length, spacing, downwards, upwards.

Curves

Now we can return to the curve in a new way.

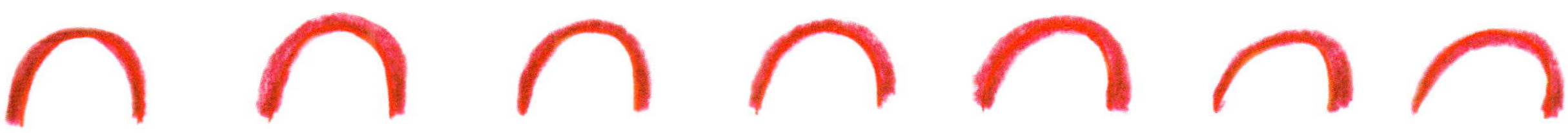

In different sizes:

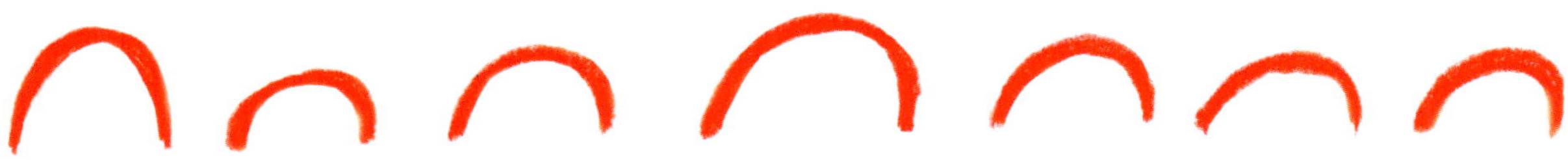

Starting little, growing larger:

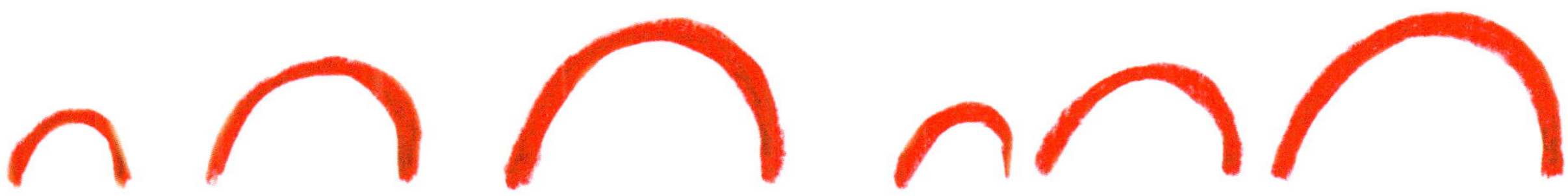

Or starting larger and getting smaller:

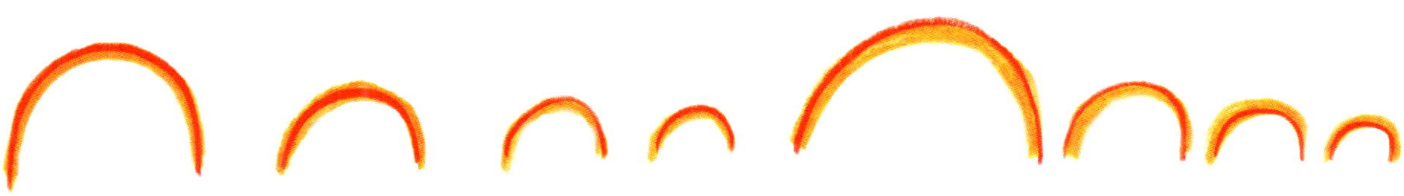

We can even put them inside each other!

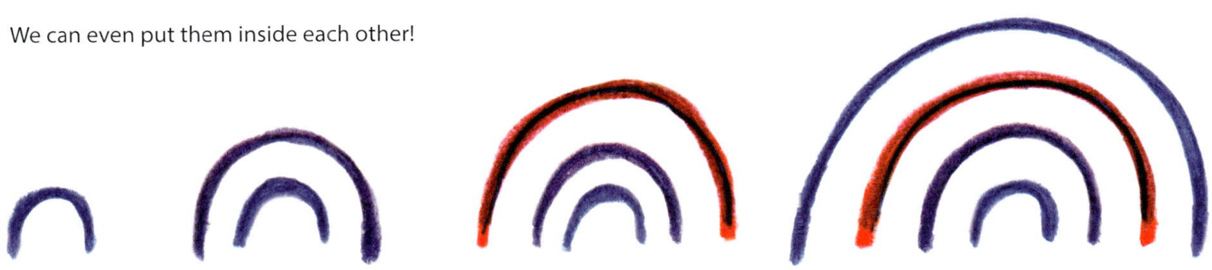

For these sequences the children can use different colours.

The curves can go another way around:

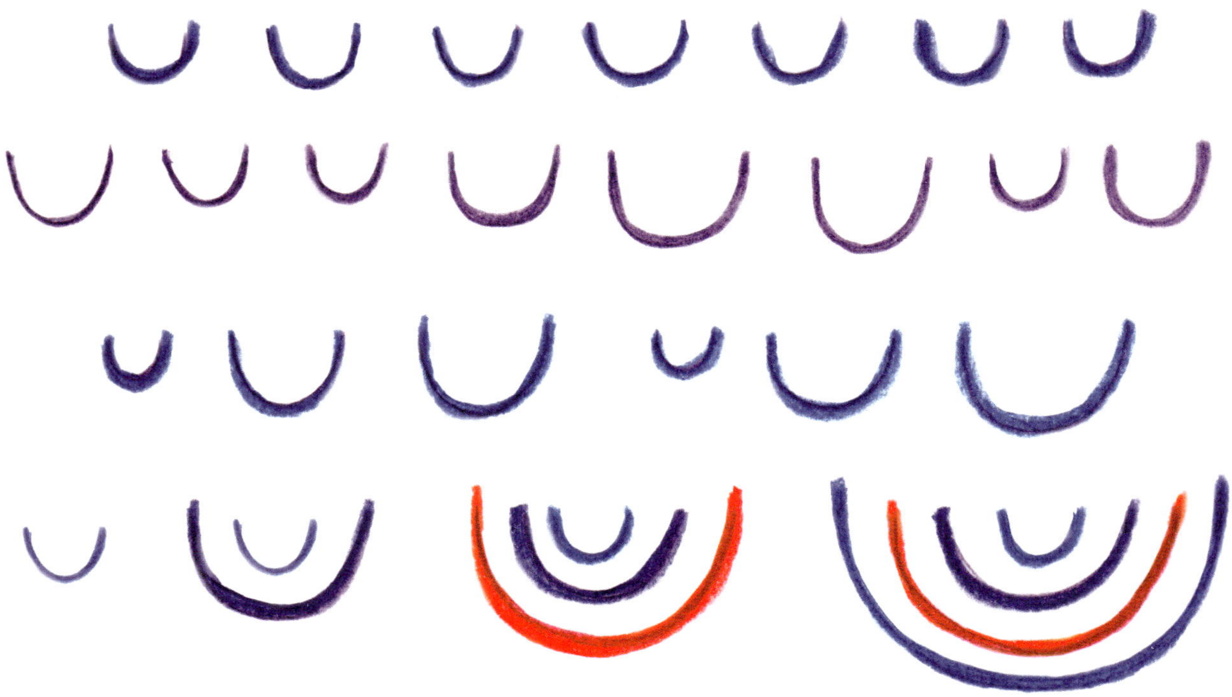

The curves can also go sideways:

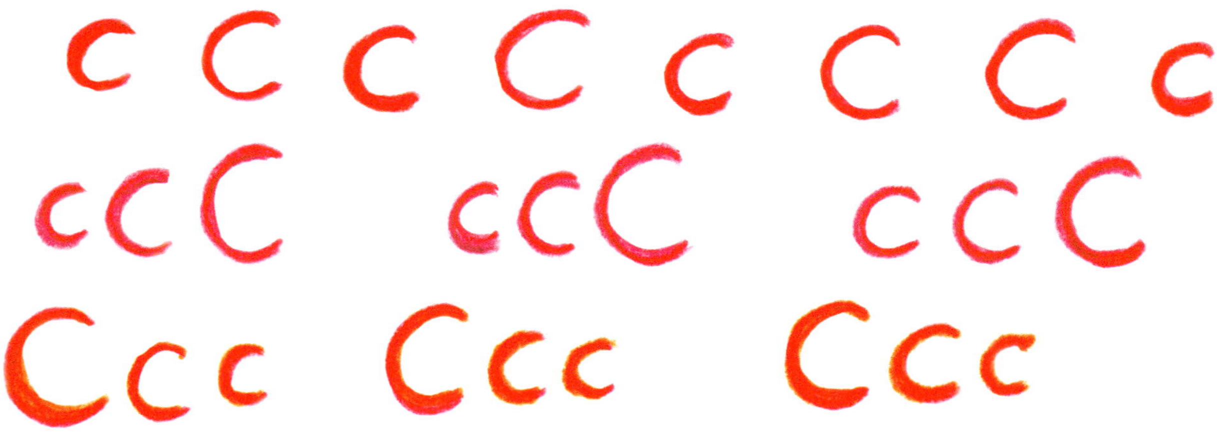

And inside each other

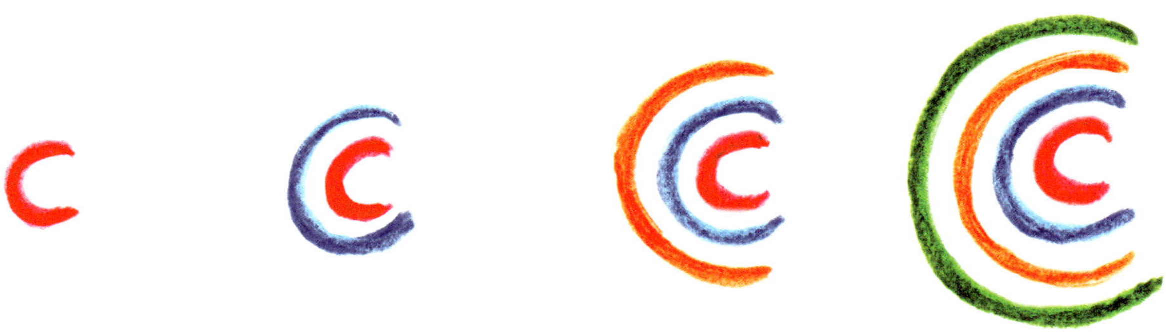

Then we turn the curves around:

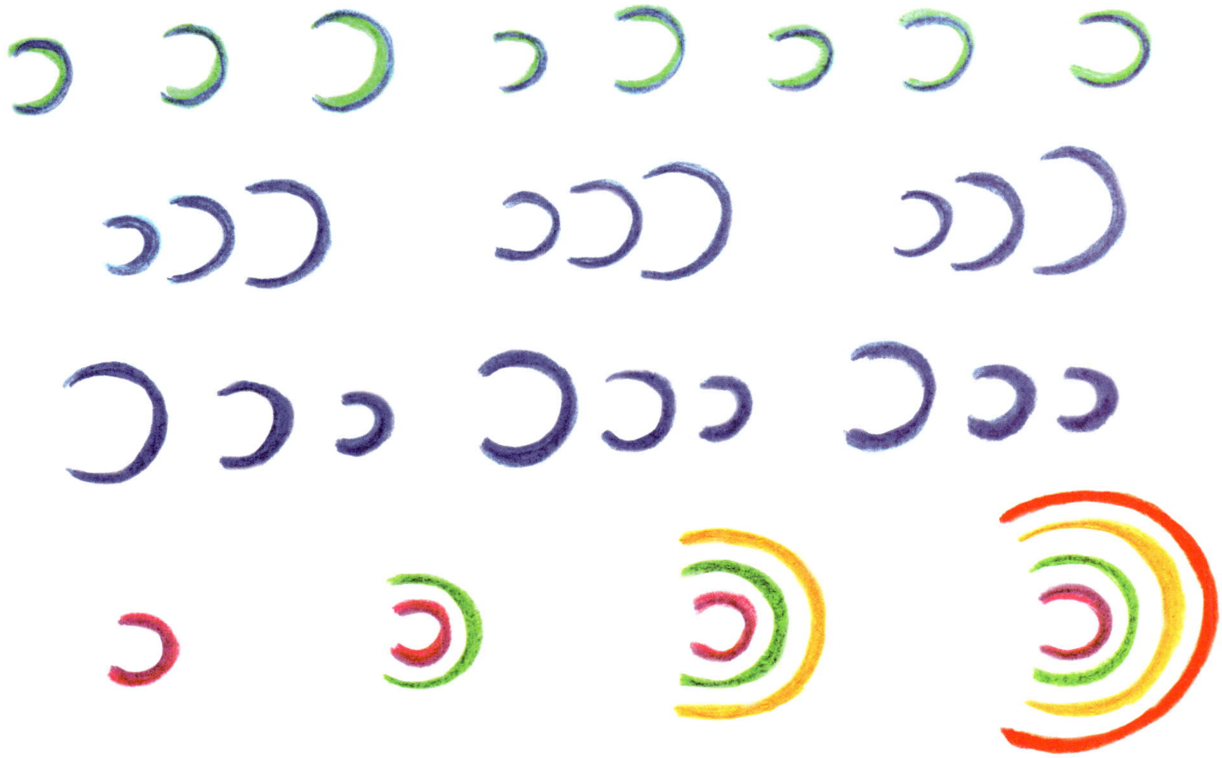

The children can draw over the forms in these sequences several times from above to below, and from below to above. This develops fine-motor skills, co-ordination and focus as well as giving a flowing movement experience.

Curves and straight lines can be combined using different colours and drawing in both directions. The children need to experience the movements and contrasts in the lines, but they will enjoy colouring in some of the forms.

NOTE: the curved lines do not necessarily have to touch the straight line. Leave the children free to sense this relationship for themselves. These forms begin with the straight lines.

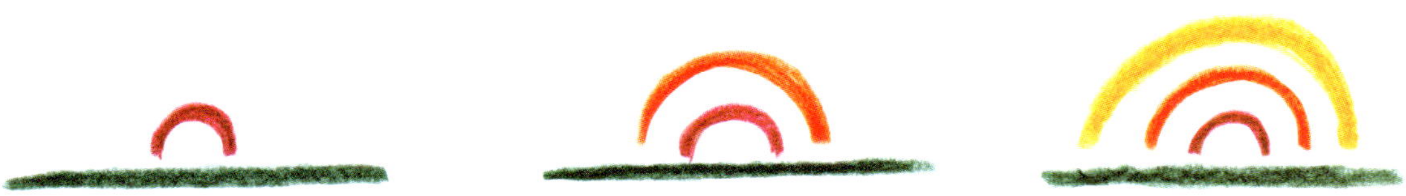

The vocabulary can include:
Straight lines, curves, small, medium, large, above, in the middle, on the inside, sequence, arch, dome, half-moon, bow (as in rainbow), hovering, touching, resting on, brighter, darker, contrasting, curved, curving, arched, arching.

More curves and straight lines

Straight lines and curves can be placed in different positions. These drawings provide:

- Extended spatial orientation.
- Flexible awareness of relationships.
- Experiences of sequences.
- Further co-ordination skills.

These forms begin with the straight lines, drawing in both directions.

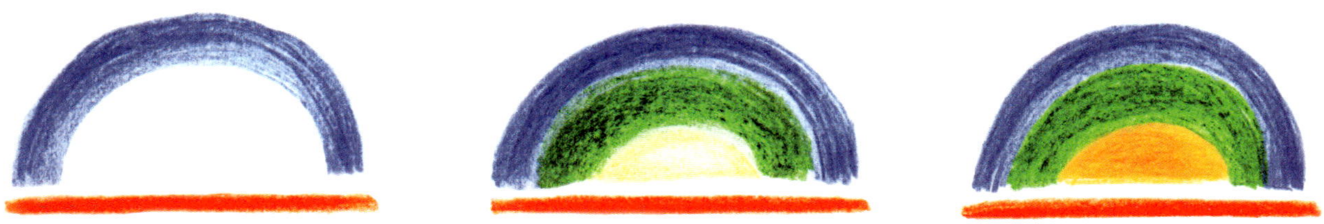

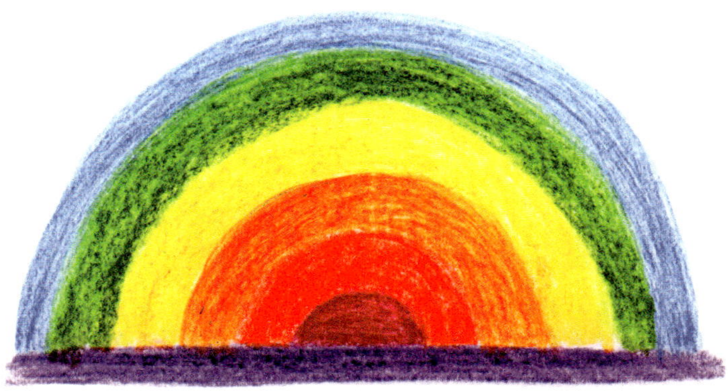

Curved forms are placed below the straight lines. This might feel as though it is a reflection of something which is happening above.

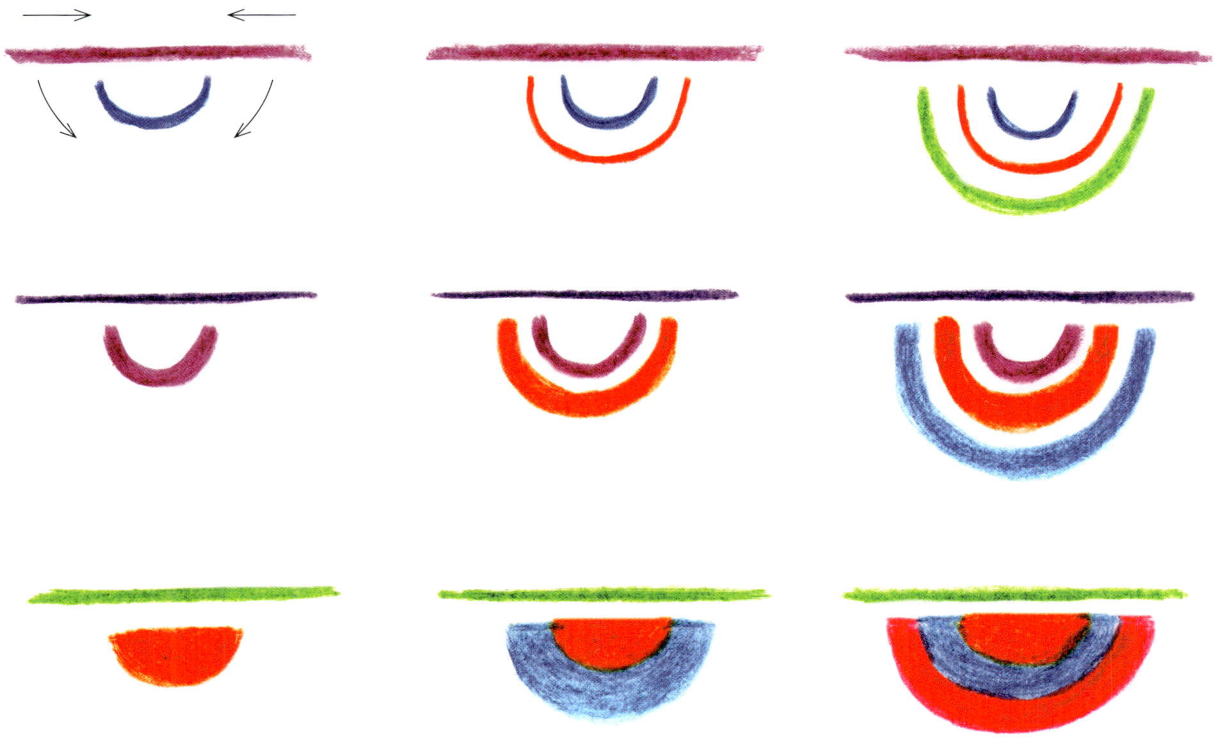

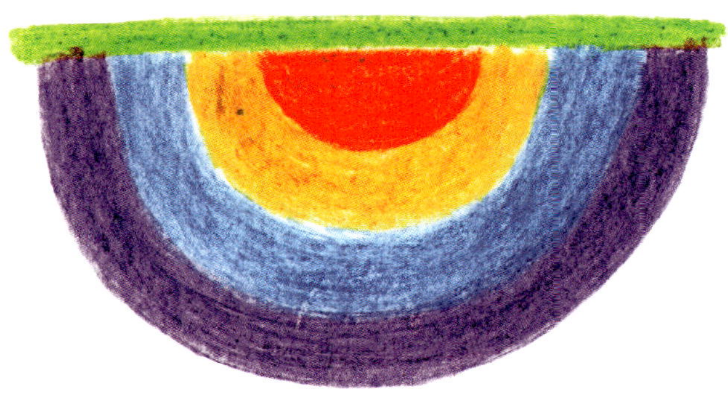

Mirror drawing

The curved arches above and below the straight line have a very special relationship. They can be considered as two-fold, an actual event above and a reflection below. The teacher draws the upper forms on the blackboard, which the children copy into their books and complete by recreating the mirror form below. The forms now have a feeling of wholeness. This exercise provides the children with an essential spatial orientation process (left, right, above, below) as well as enabling them to complete something that is incomplete. This strengthens their life-forces, imagination and independence.

Starting with the large curve on the outside and growing smaller on the inside.

Note: The children draw the same form above and below. The dotted lines are an indication only.

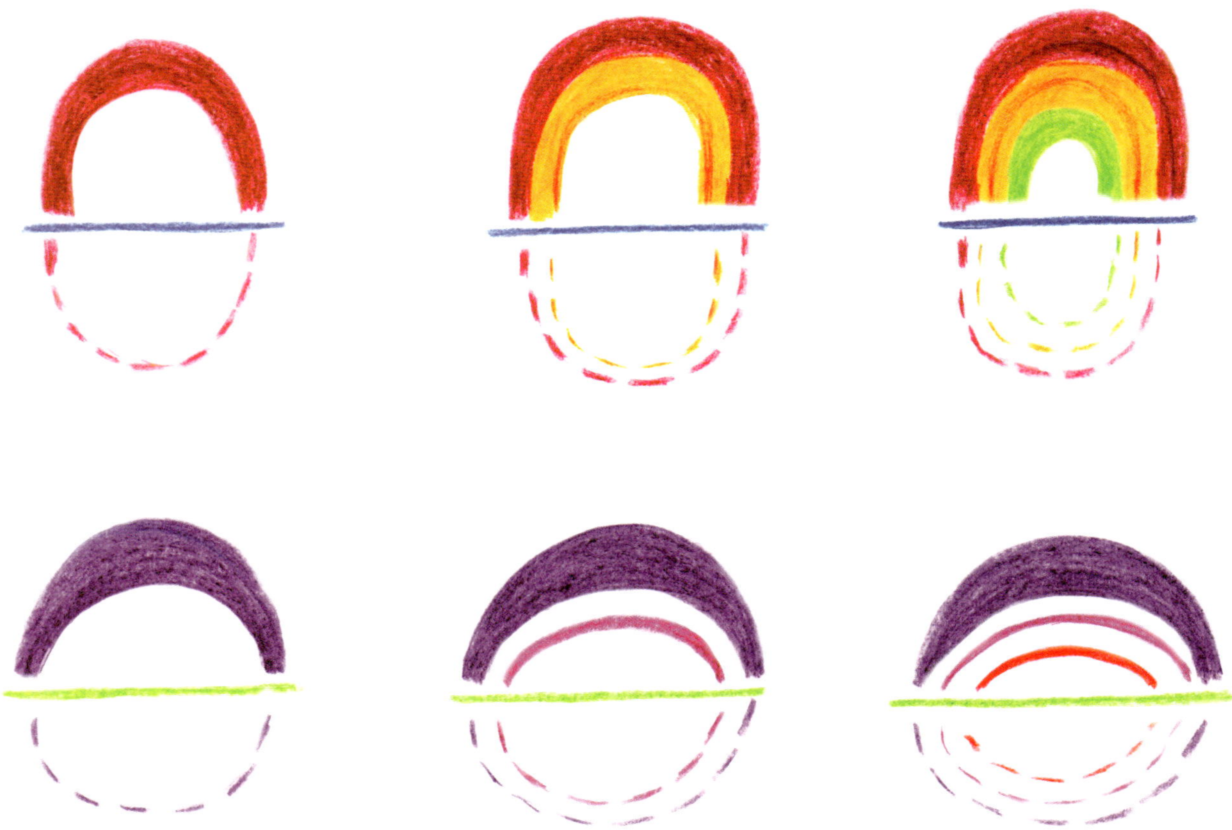

Starting with the small arch, growing larger. The children may copy the teacher's colours or choose their own. The colours above and below need to reflect each other. The children can then create their own mirror drawings.

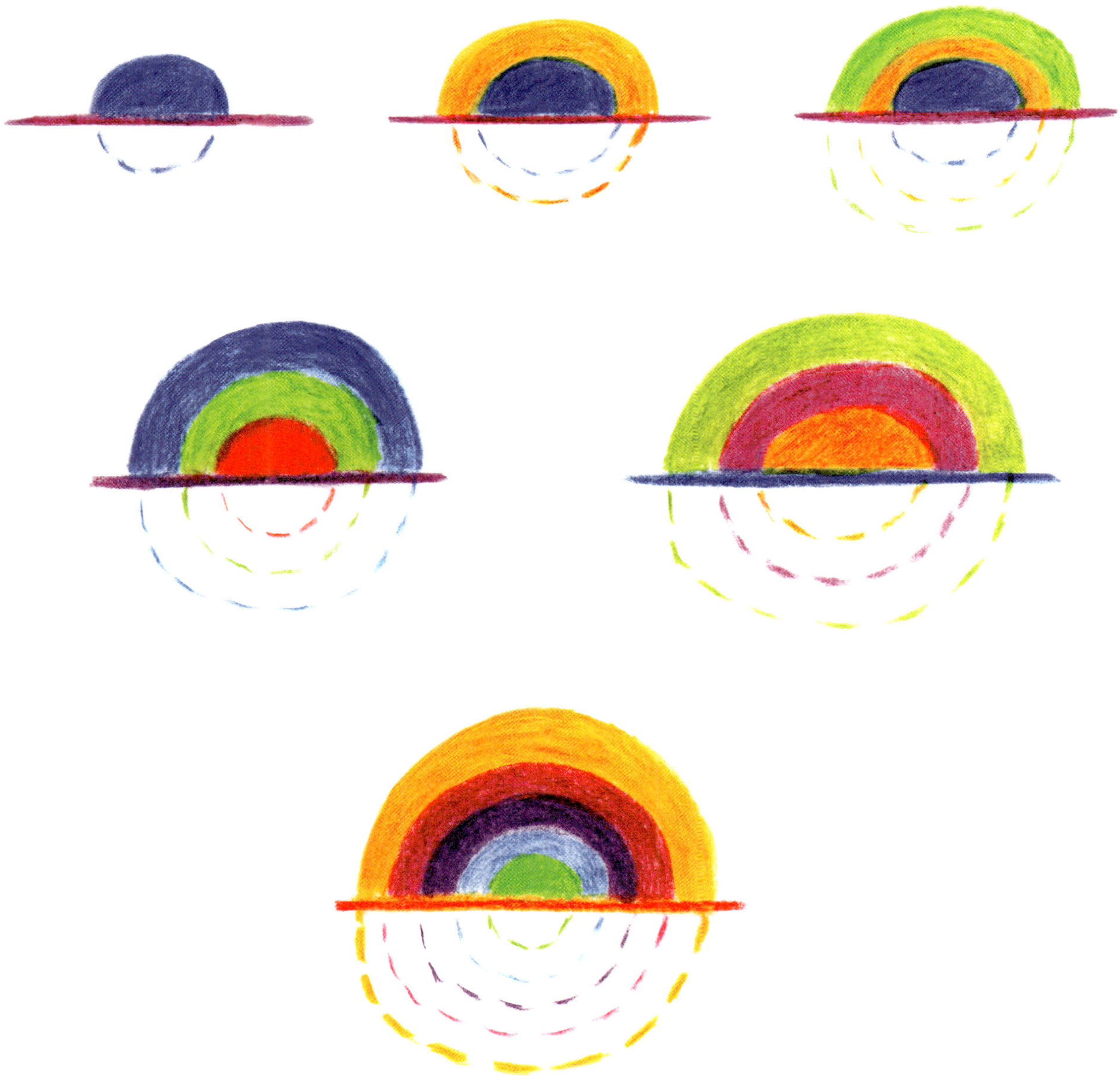

Flowing lines

It is helpful at this stage to introduce a new movement experience – flowing lines. These need to be drawn slowly and carefully across the page in related sequences, from simple to more differentiated.

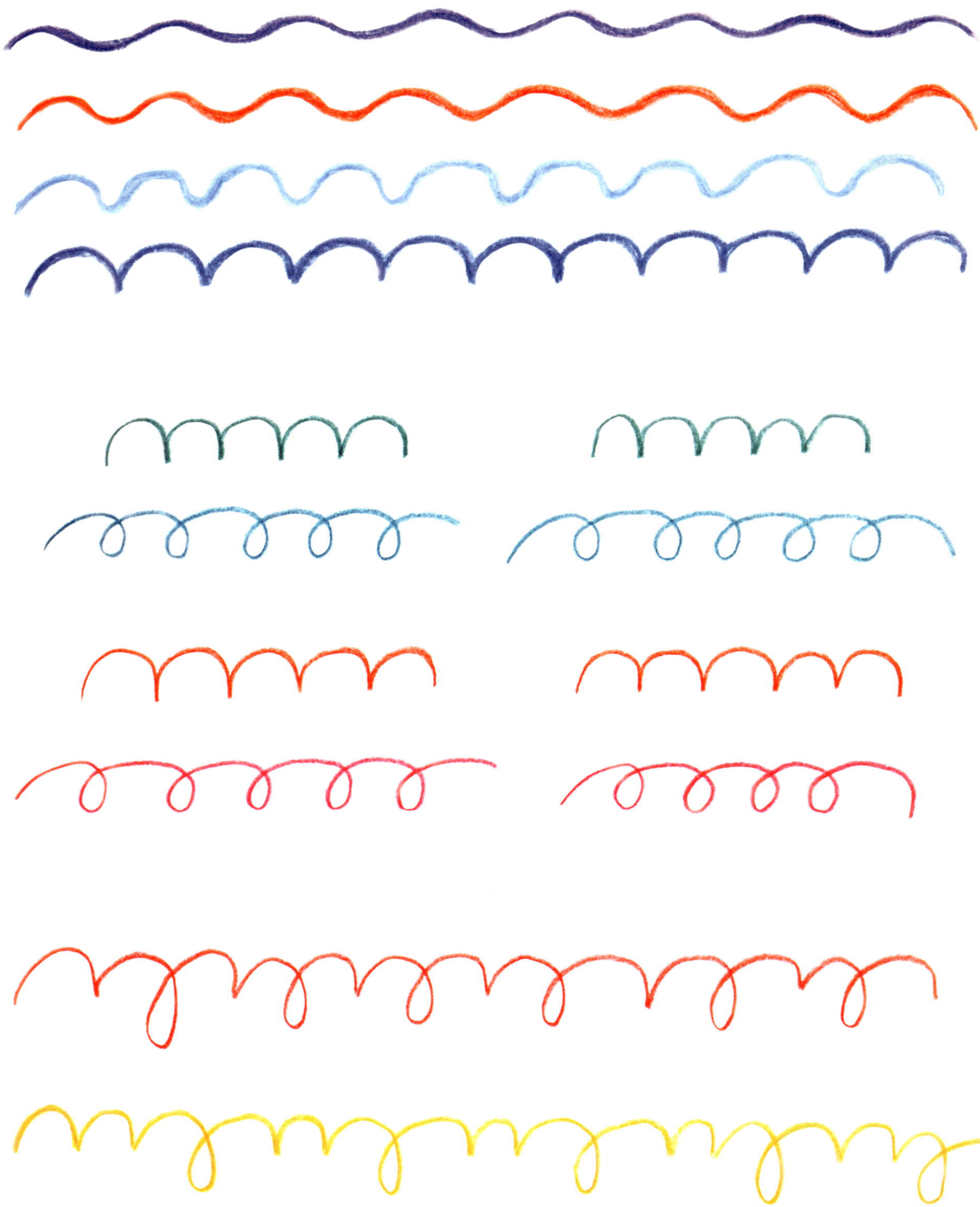

How many different combinations can be made?

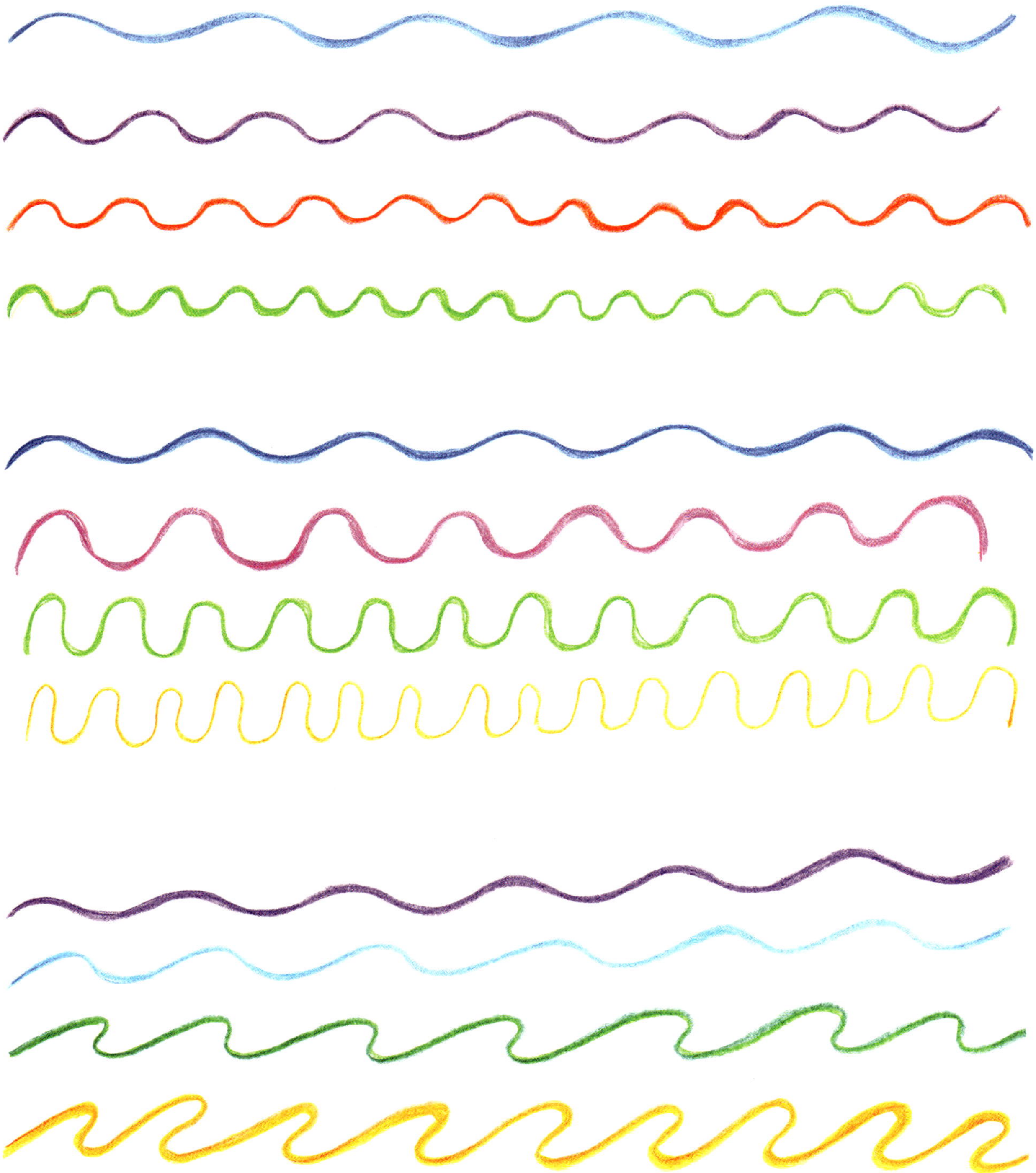

Can we draw larger and smaller loops?
Can we draw them upwards?

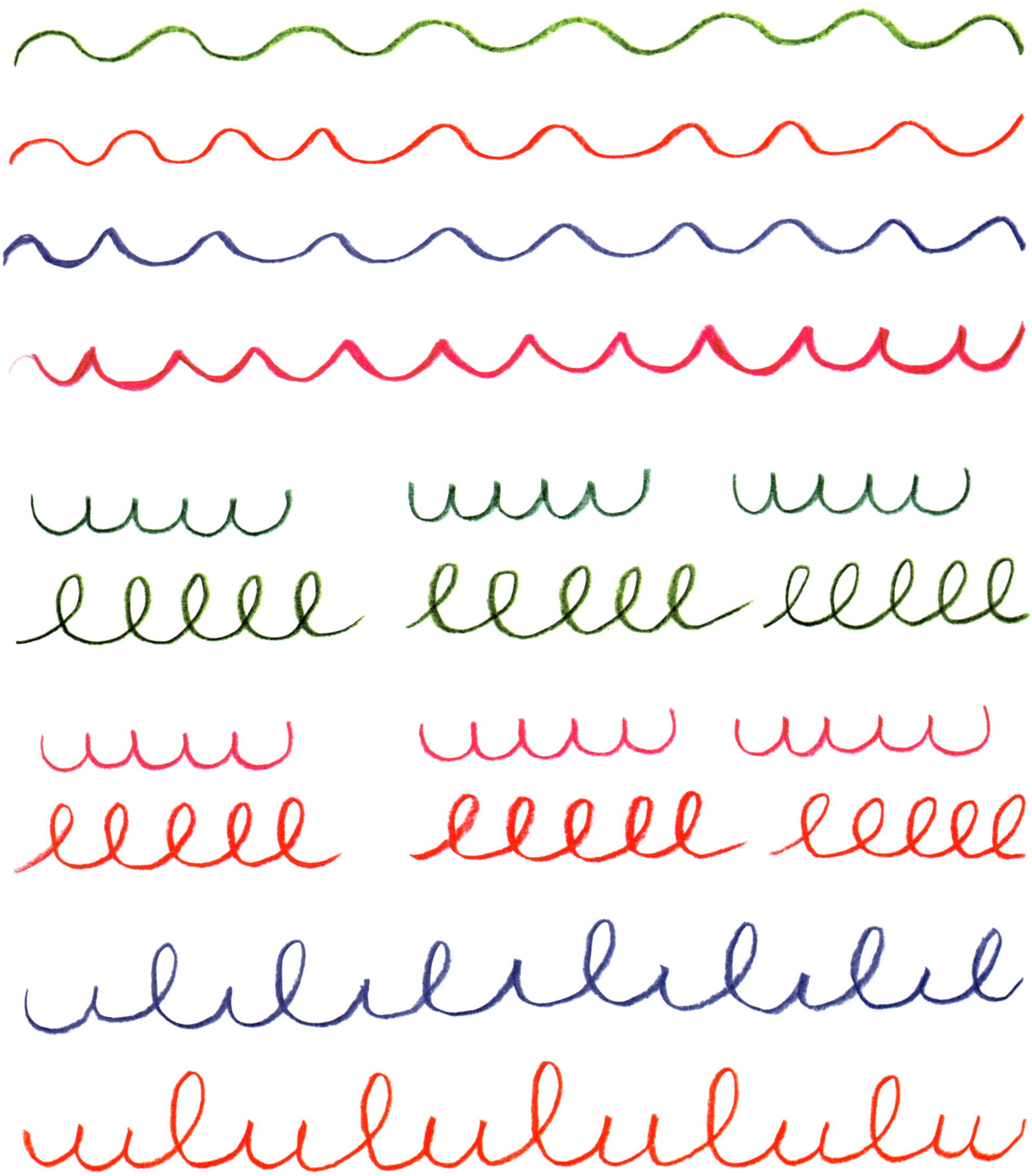

Rhythmical flowing lines

To develop fine-motor skills, the children can vary the firmness of the pressure on their pencils so that the flowing lines become rhythmical. The children can press firmly and then lightly with their pencils by rhythmically pressing and releasing the pencil, as they draw.

If the class is very quiet, they will hear the different sounds which the pencils make when pressing hard and softly. If too many pencils break, try using large crayons or block crayons.

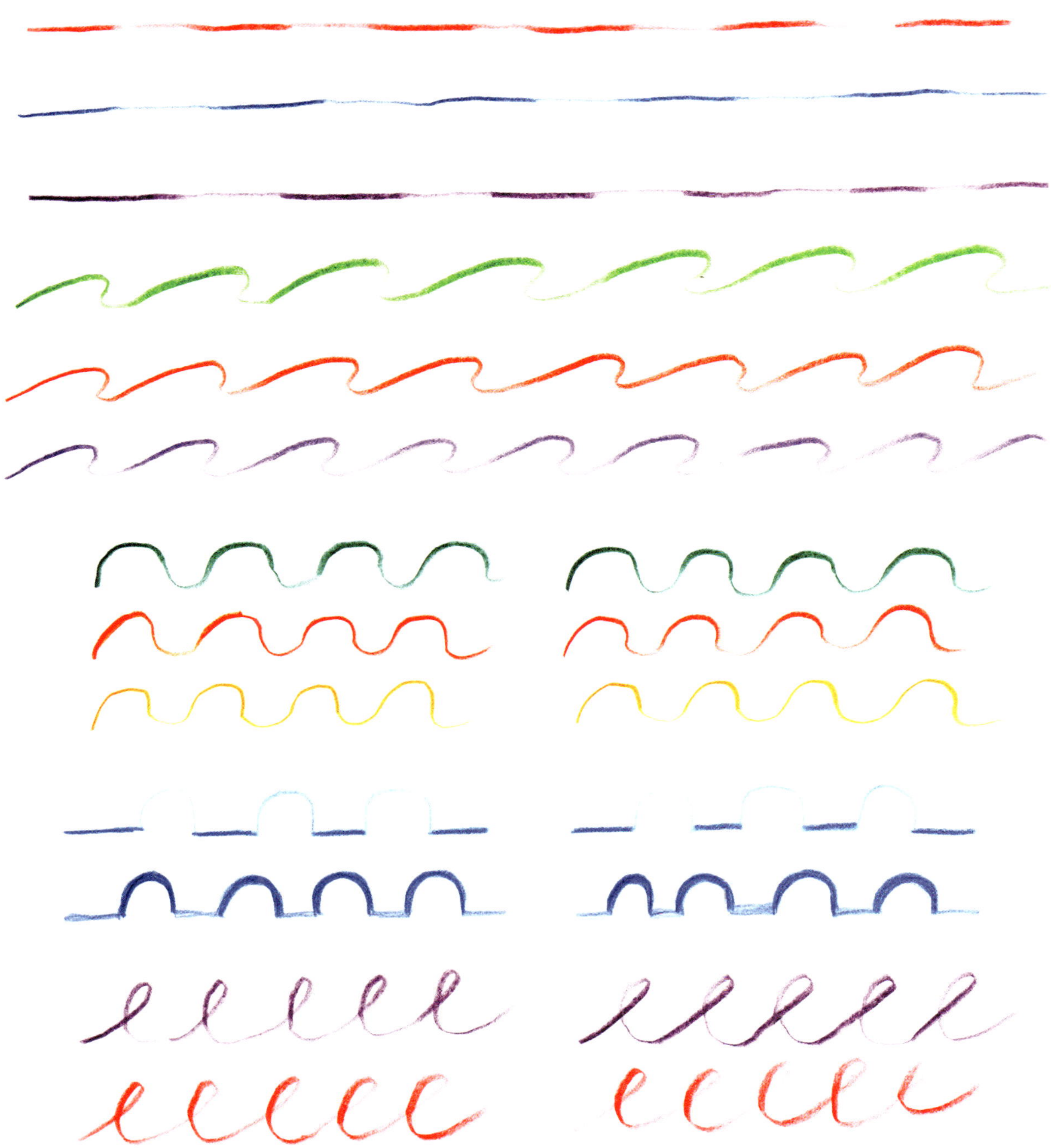

Circles

In contrast with the flowing forms we now come to a contained form, the circle. Remember that the children should:

- walk the form
- draw the form in the air with their hands and arms
- draw the form with their noses
- draw in both directions with both arms at the same time
- draw with their feet (sitting down), one at a time, then both feet together.

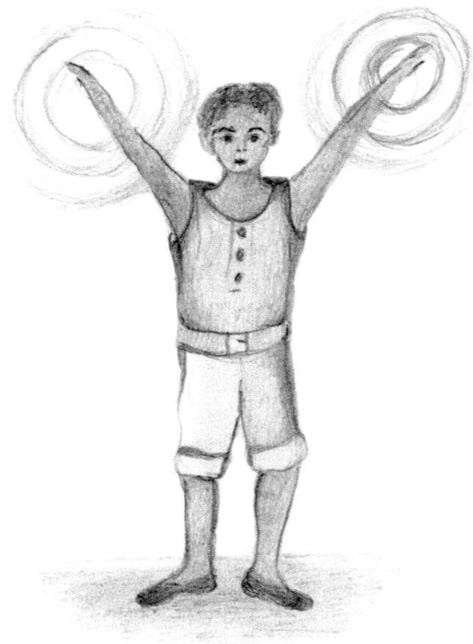

These body movements are essential. The circular gestures bring many health benefits. They ease muscle tension and improve blood circulation. The children can invent ways of moving the circle, for example:

- Hands above their heads
- Arms outstretched
- Sitting down, moving the whole leg
- Drawing circles with each finger separately (and the thumbs)
- Stretching the arms out horizontally and slowly turning around, keeping the arms still. Where is this circle?

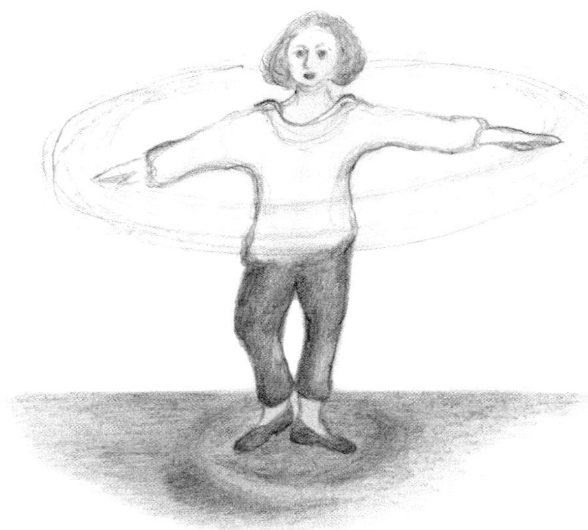

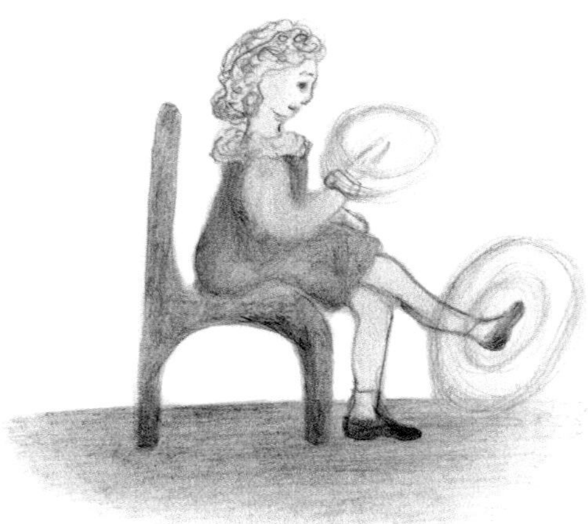

When many different spatial circles have been explored, the children can draw circles in their books.

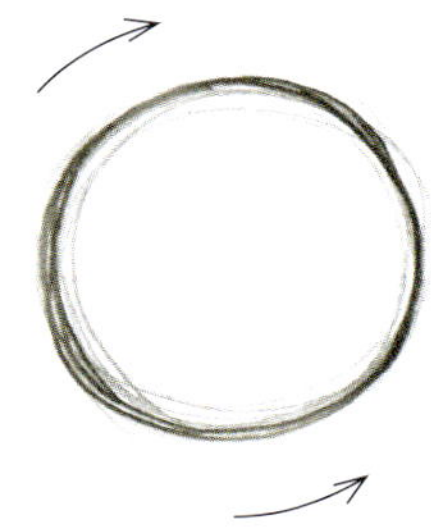

Holding the pencils gently without tension the children draw the circles softly several times over, each one in both directions.

Use the whole arm in a relaxed way and allow the movement to be continuous and flowing. They can draw a variety of sizes, either freely on the page or arranged in sequences.

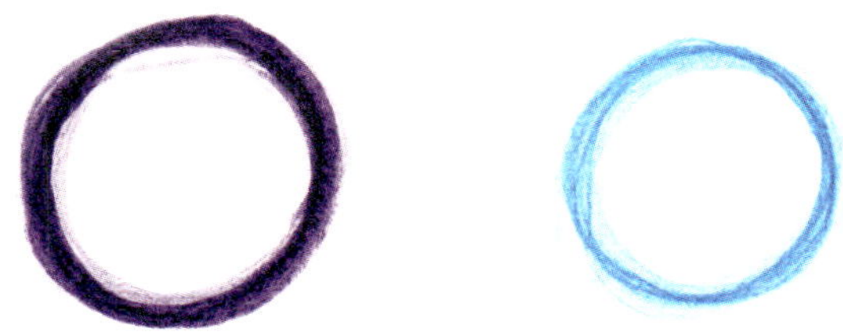

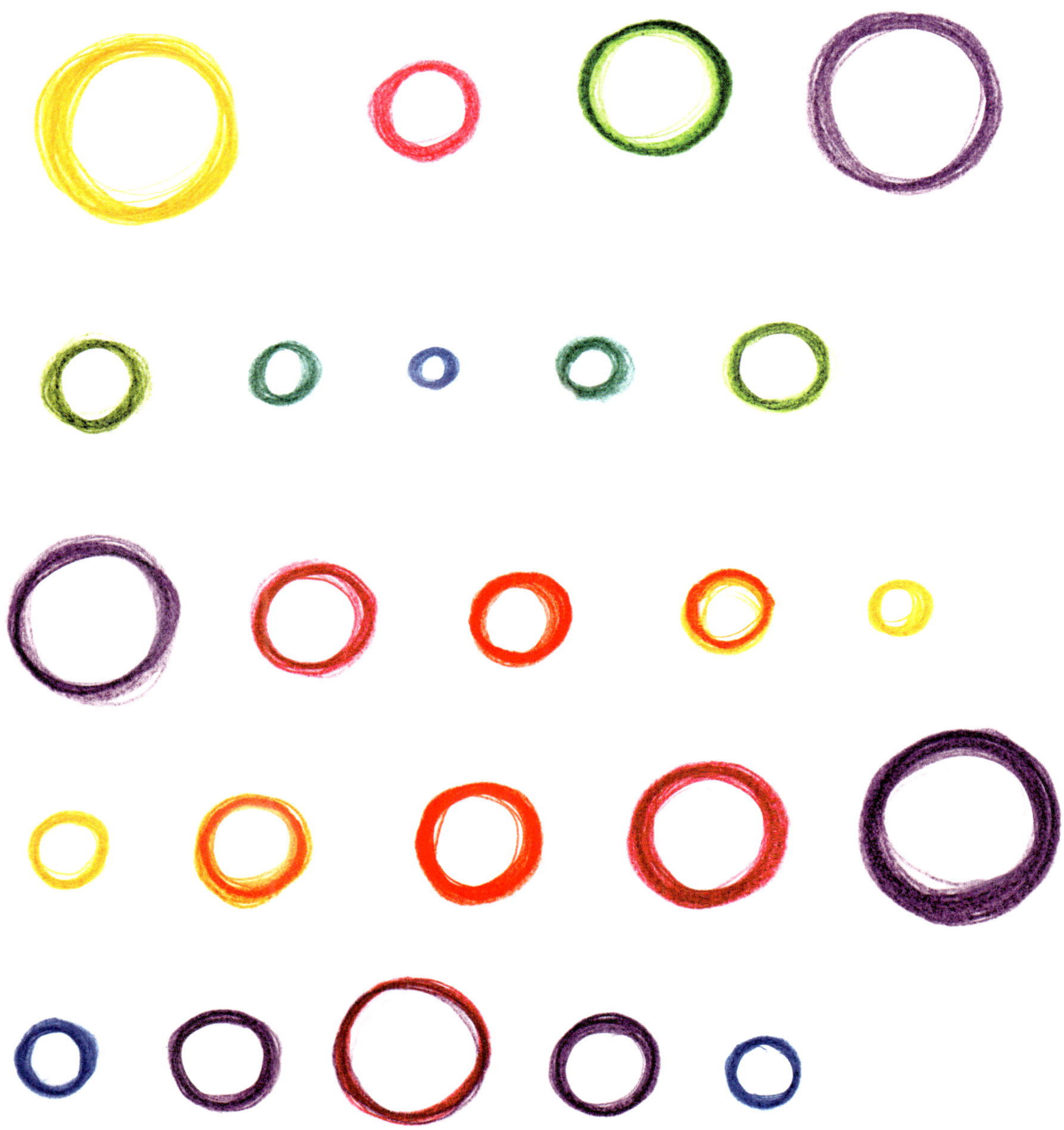

Further circles can be drawn with the addition of straight lines, wavy lines and curved forms.

Vocabulary:
Larger, smaller, increasing, decreasing, circular, round, flowing, continuous.

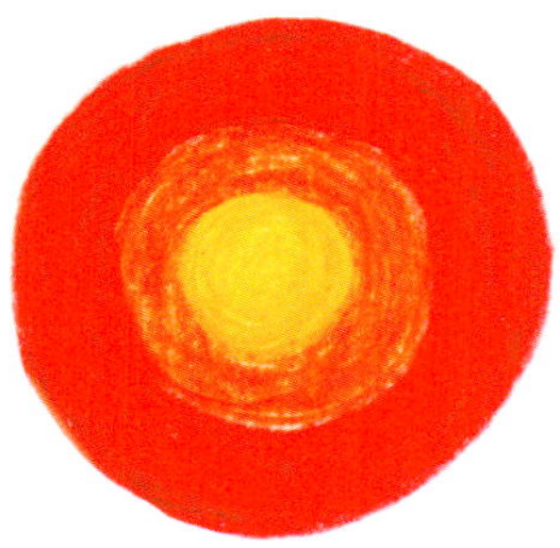

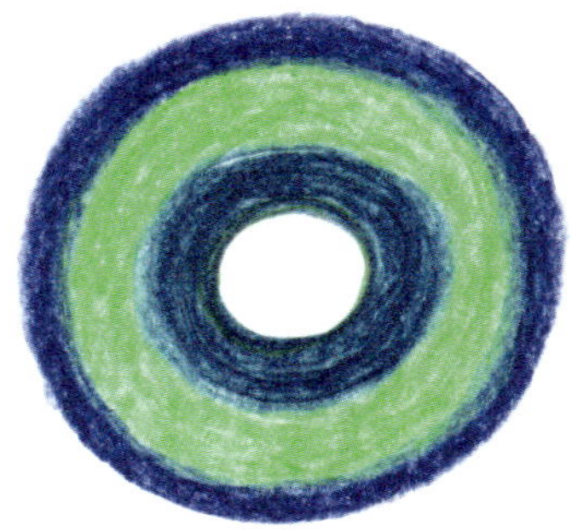

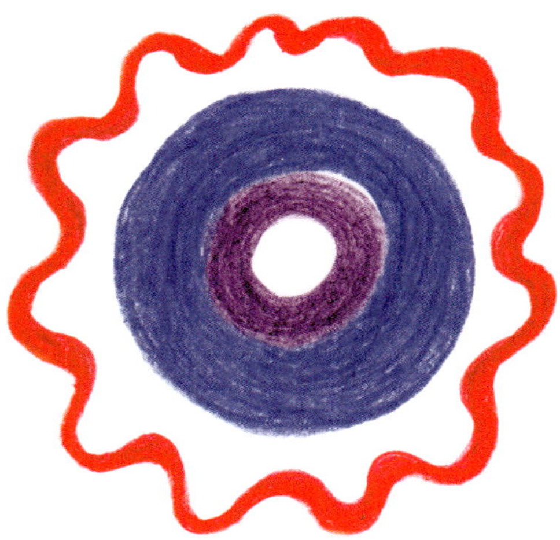

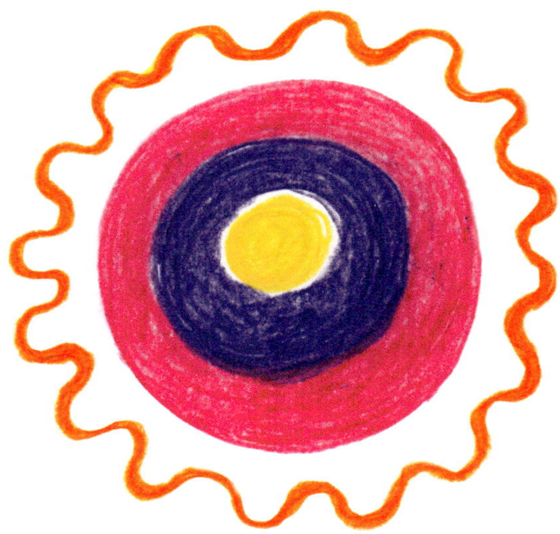

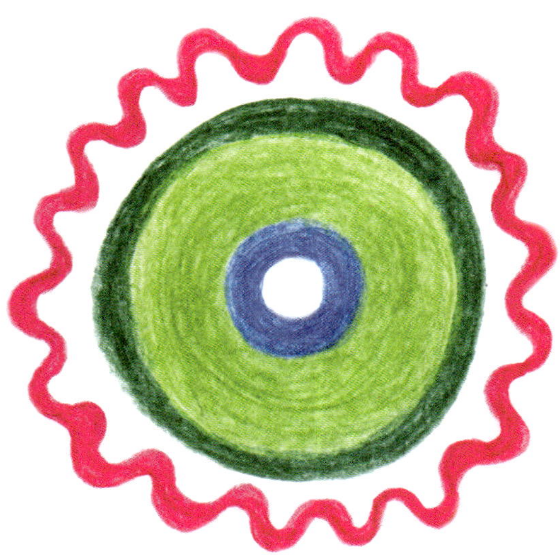

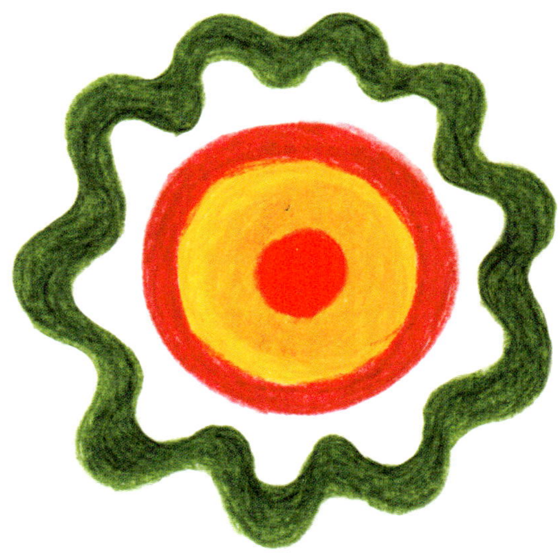

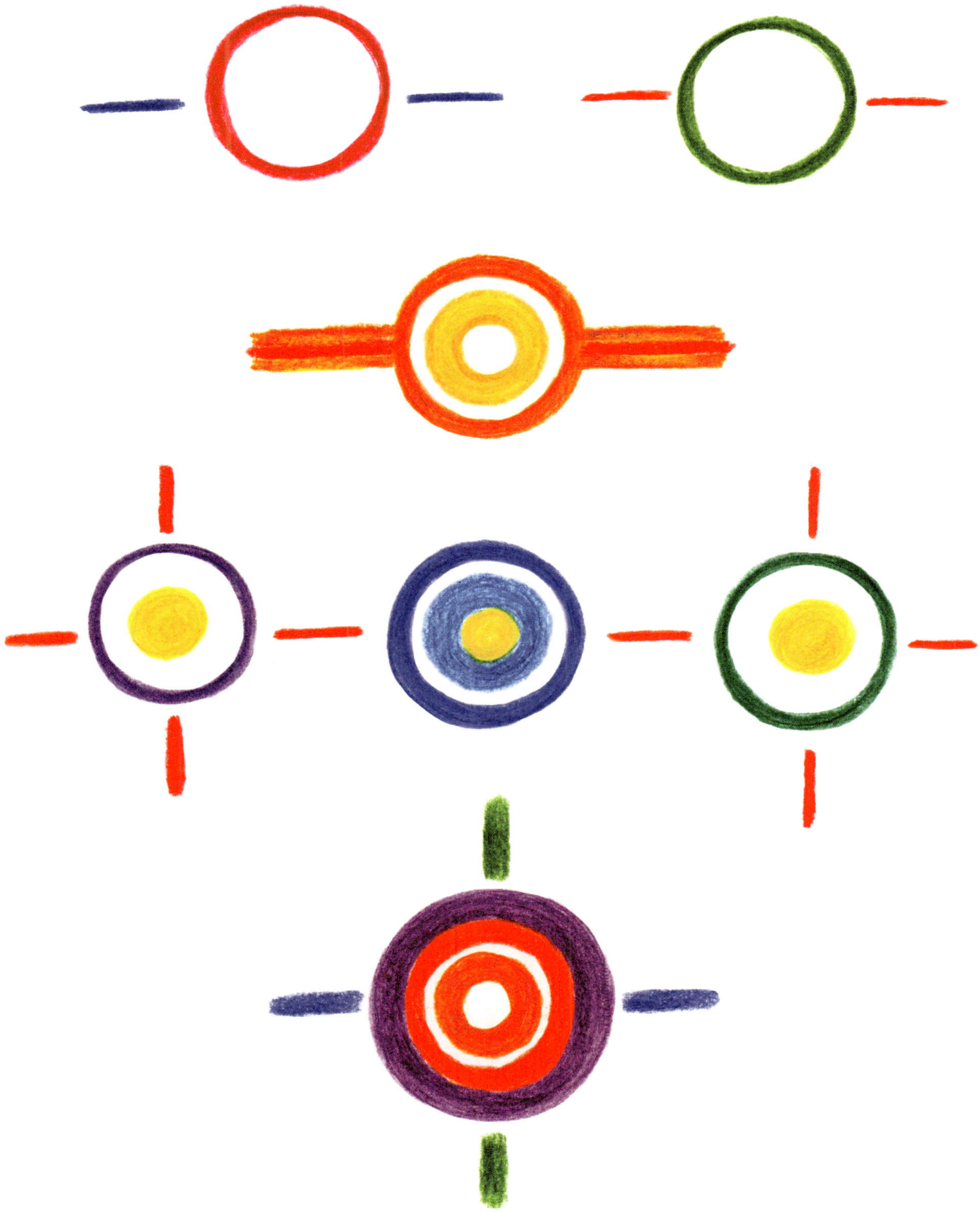

Variations

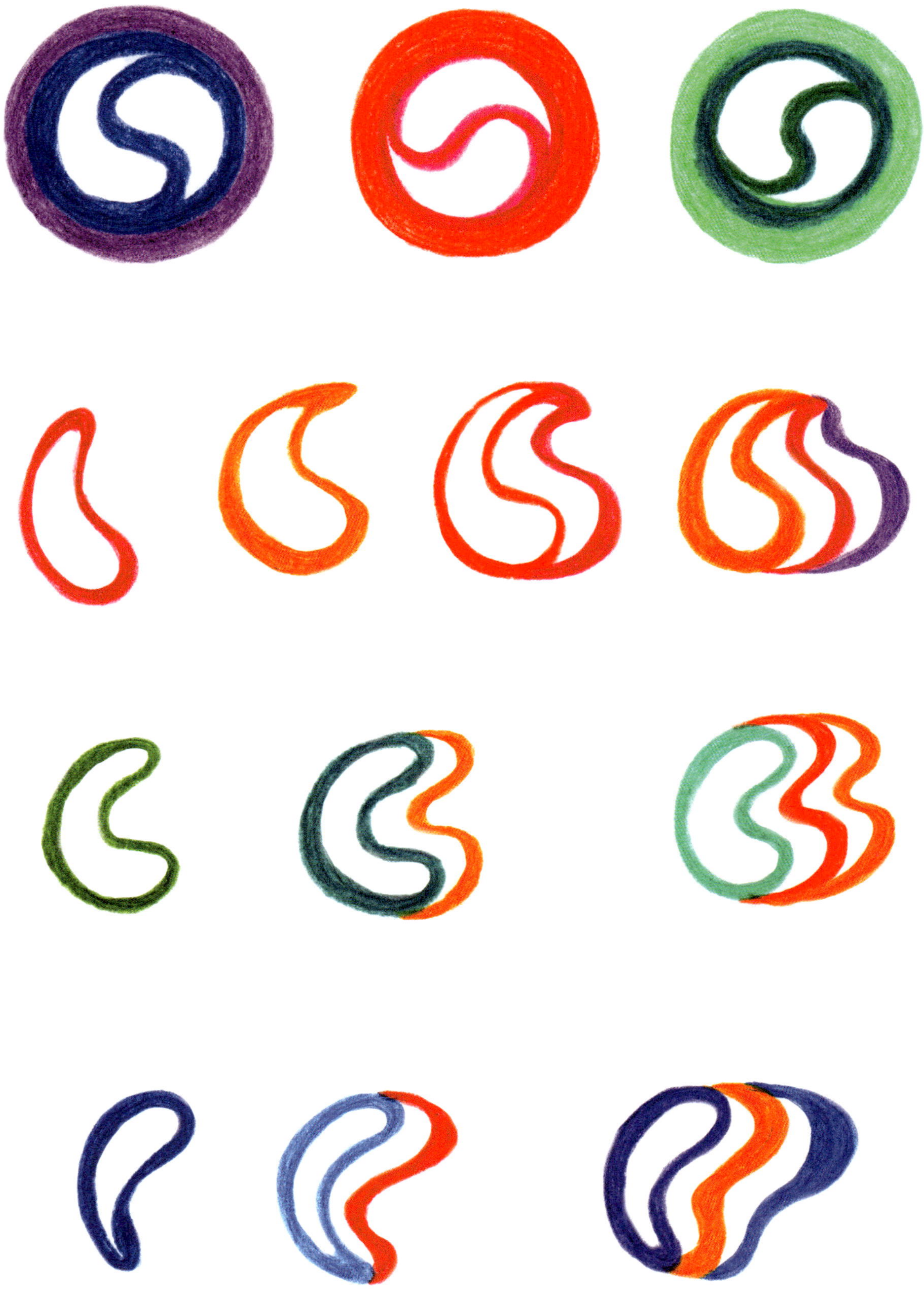

The lemniscate or 'figure of eight'

The closed circular movements open and extend into flowing 'figures of eight' forms. As with the circles, these forms are drawn in large body movements first.

Lemniscates are drawn rhythmically in a continuous flowing movement. The children can draw over each form several times. It may take some practice for the crossing point to be in the centre – this will come!

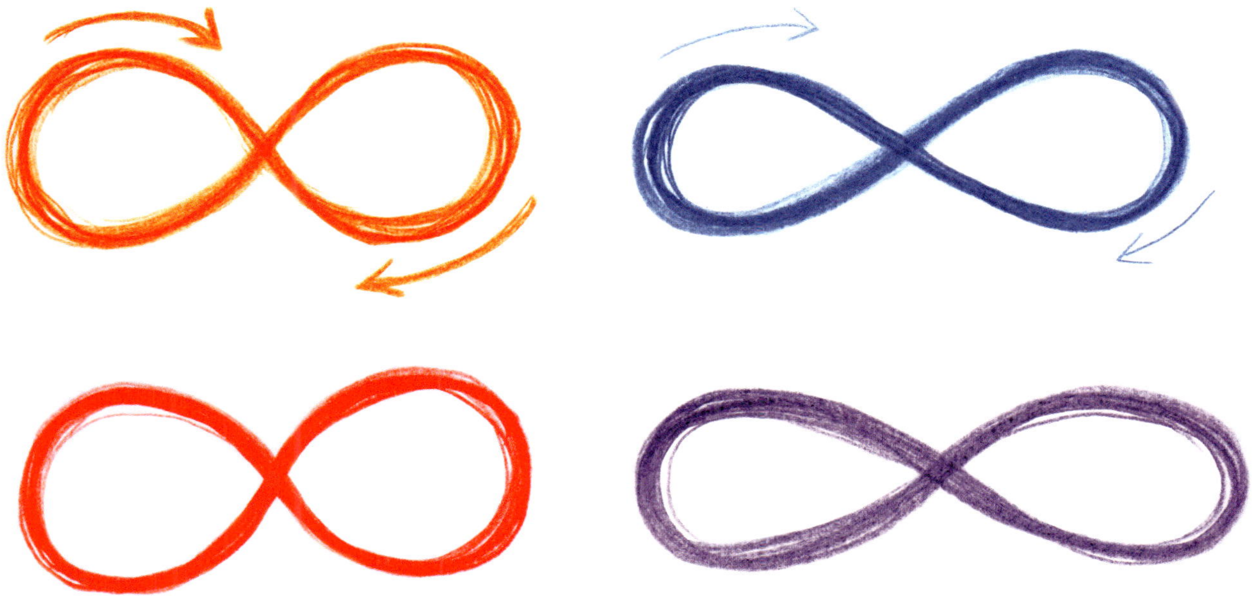

The children can listen to the sounds that the pencil makes on the paper as they are drawing. Can they hear the movements? When drawing this form children can experience rhythmical rocking movements from one side to the other.

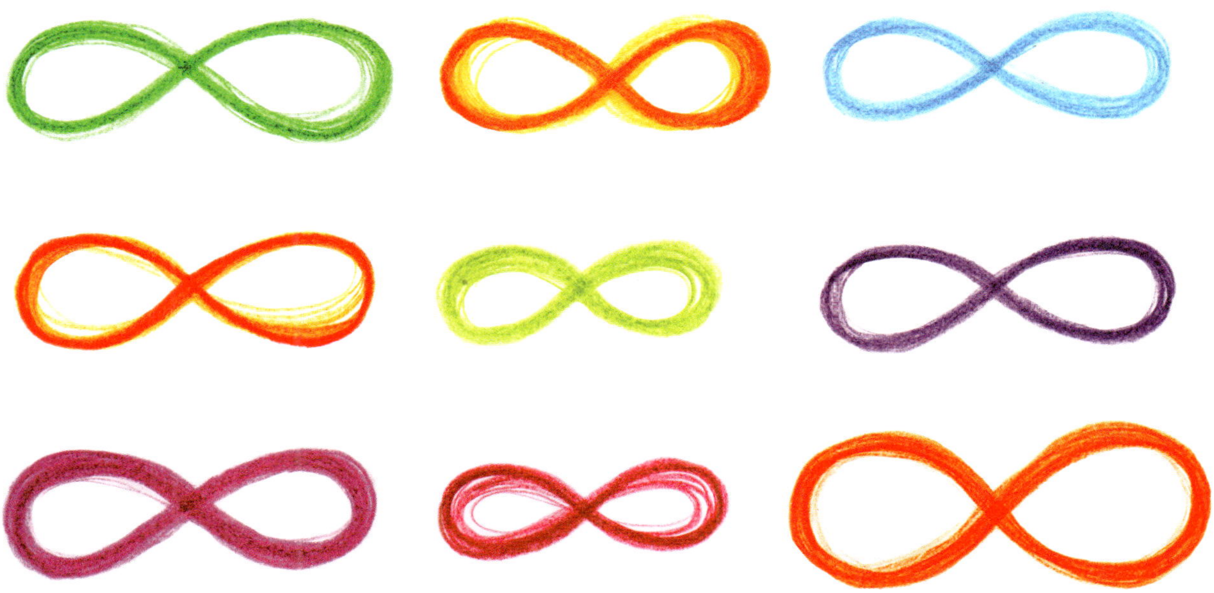

The lemniscates, or figure of eight, can extend into an evenly flowing wavy line, which is crossed over at regular intervals by a second wavy line. Use two different colours for this form and repeat the form several times. Draw each form two or three times over and join them at the ends.

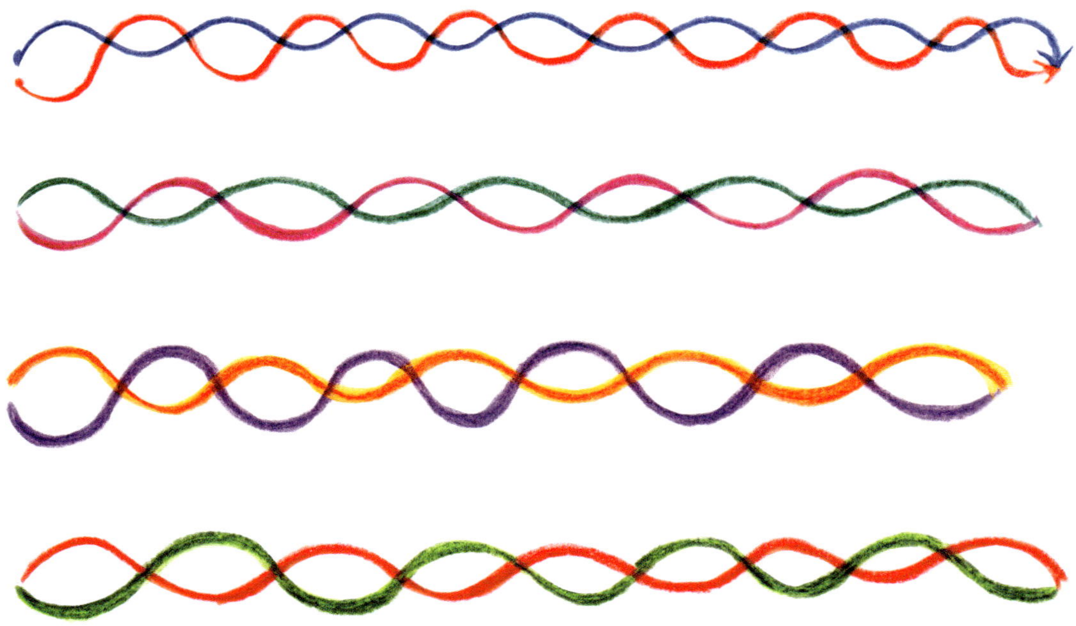

It will be seen that not all forms cross evenly! This takes a lot of practice. Both wavy lines need to be drawn slowly and carefully so that the crossings come in evenly spaced positions.

These forms are drawn in a continuous movement:

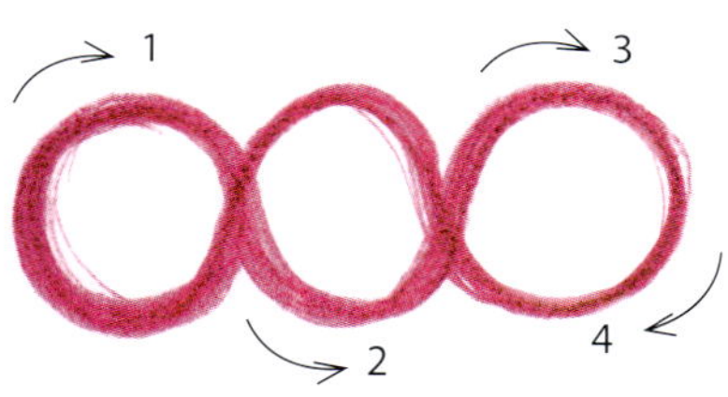

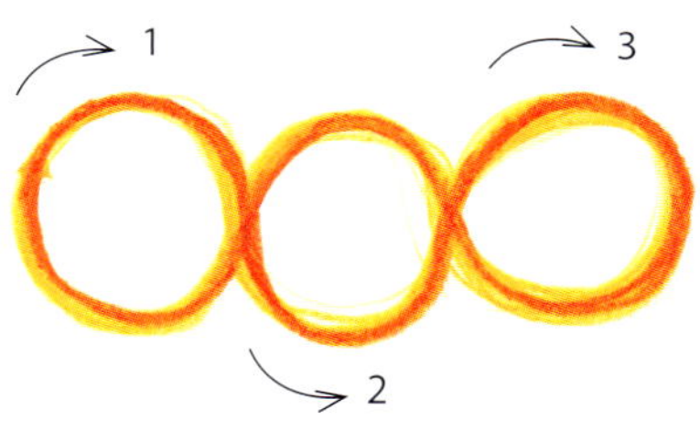

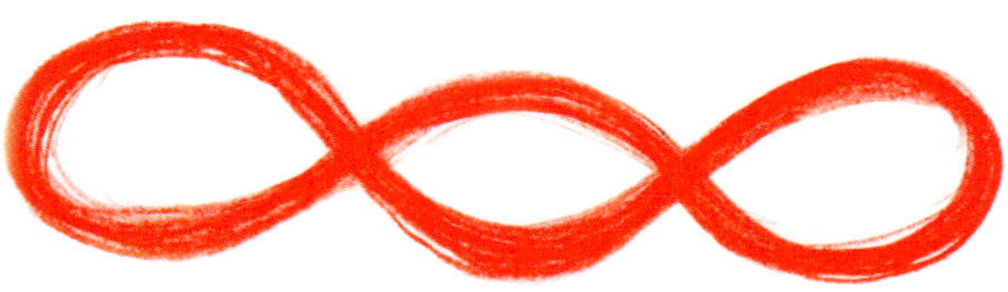

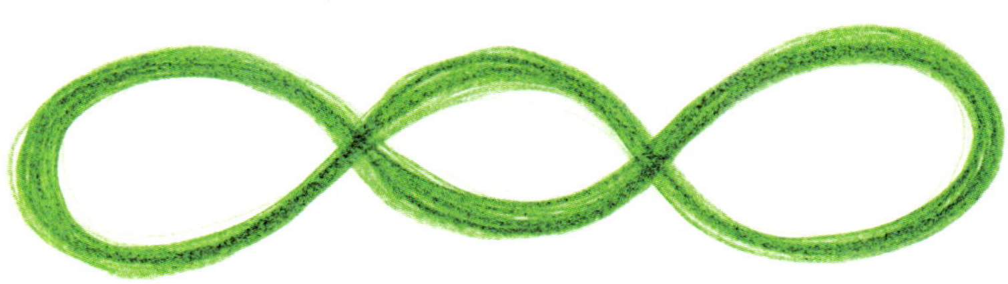

Zig-zag forms

A wavy line can become a zig-zag by 'sharpening' the movements. These need to be drawn carefully so that the spacing is even.

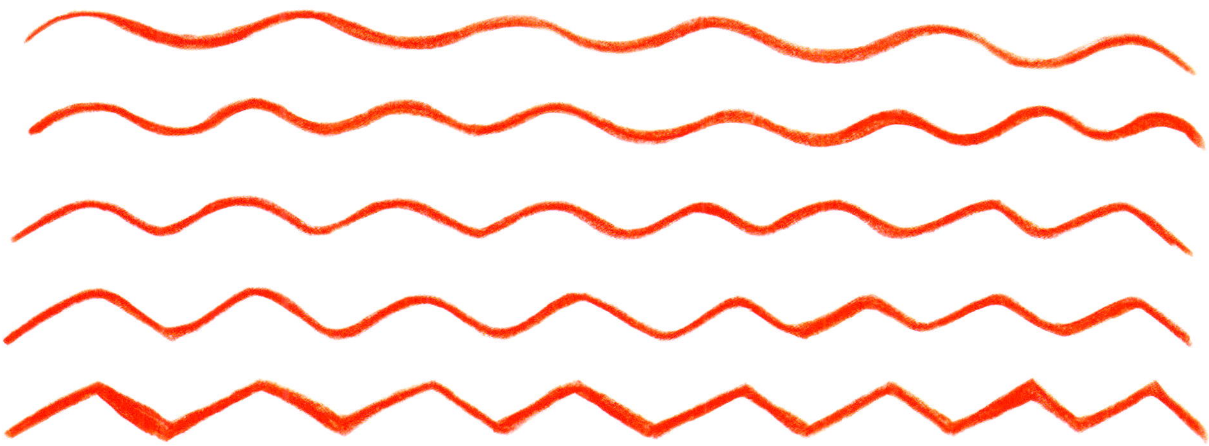

The zig-zags can be drawn starting in a downwards direction.

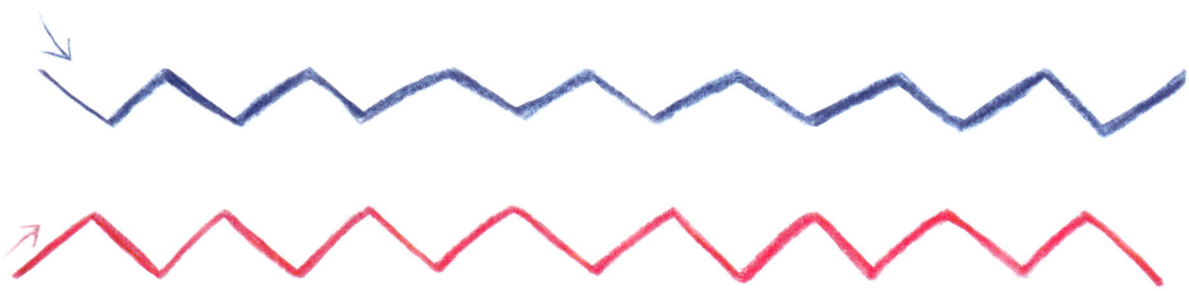

The 'touching' zig-zags can be drawn over several times in both directions. Two forms cross over each other:

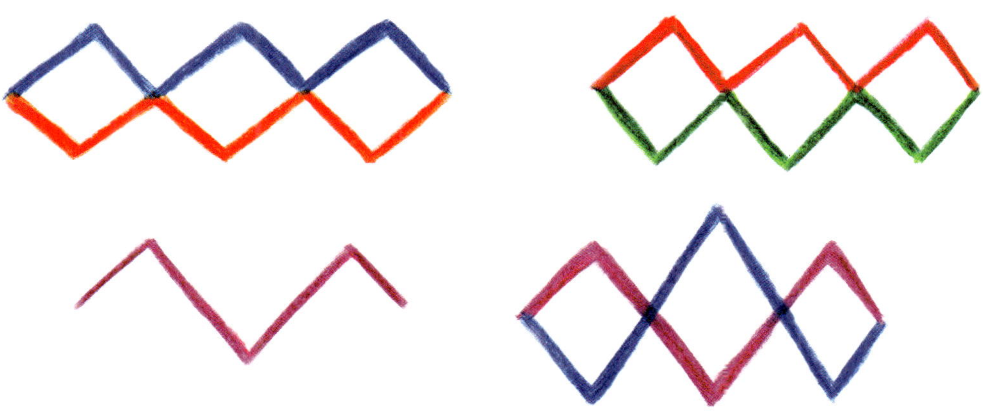

These forms are drawn in one continuous line.

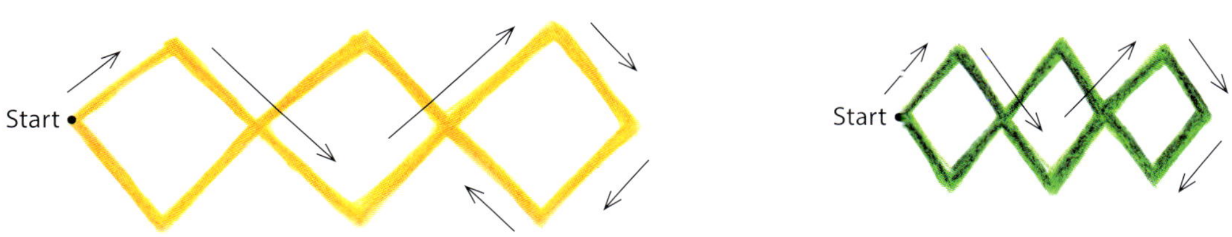

Diamond forms

The zig-zag lines have now become diamond forms. These can be drawn in different sizes, using different colours, with colouring-in to accent the diamond shapes. The children will see that when they are colouring these forms there is always another diamond inside!

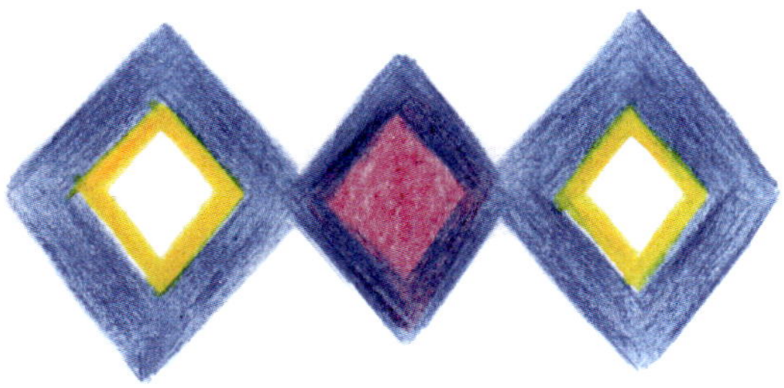

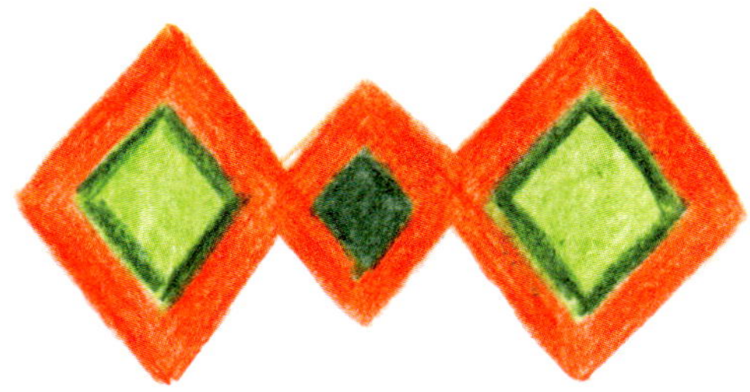

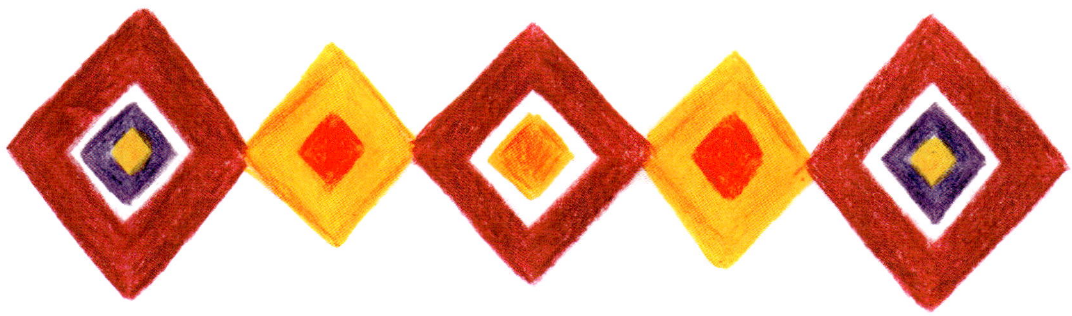

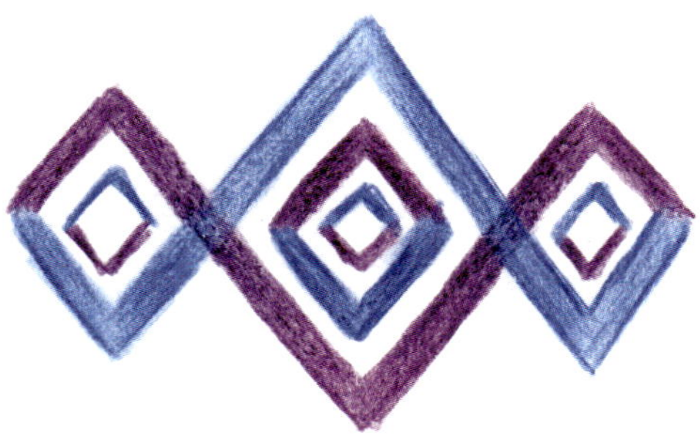

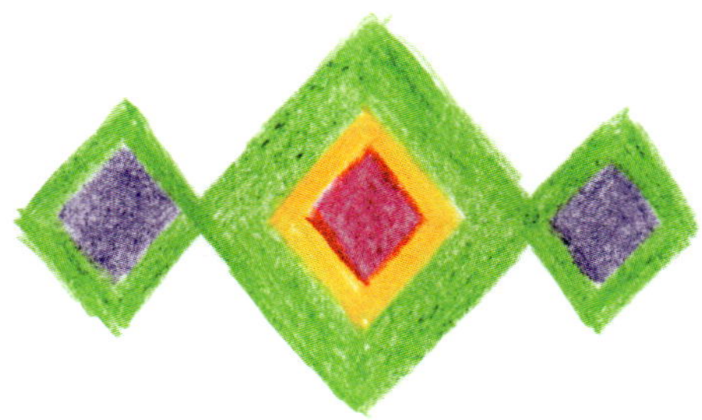

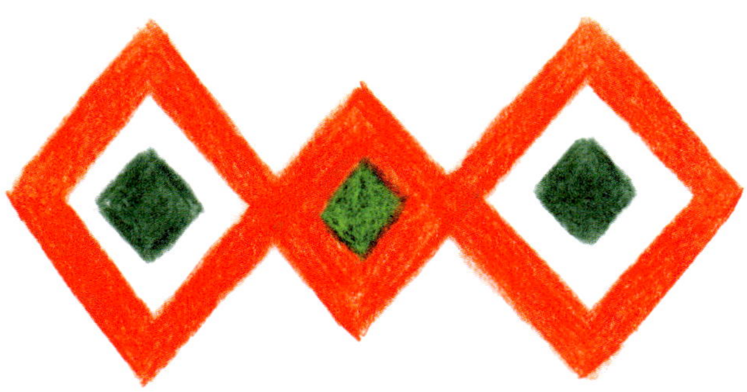

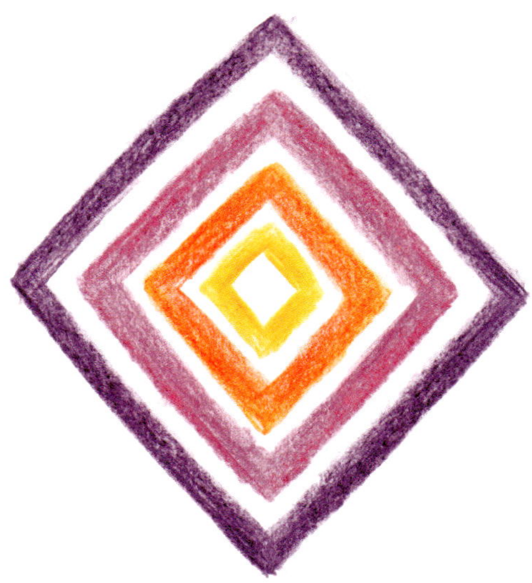

Diamonds into stars

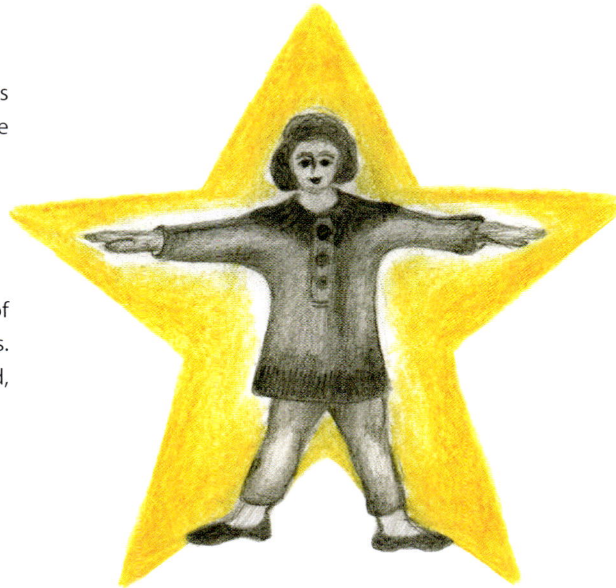

In a following lesson the children can stand with arms outstretched and legs apart. They make angles like the diamonds, but now they make a very special form – a star!

The children can 'walk' the star, individually and in groups of five together, with each child standing on one of the points. They all move to the next place together: head, foot, hand, hand, foot, head.

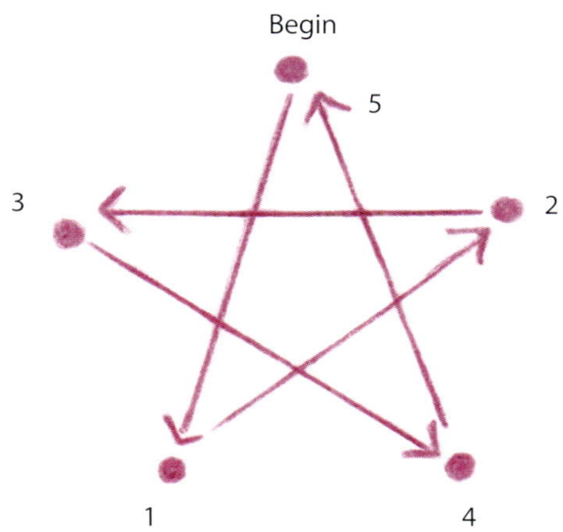

Next they return to their seats and one by one come to the blackboard, then two or three children can come at the same time, to draw their own star, in just the same sequence. The blackboard is full of dancing stars! Then they draw many stars in their books.

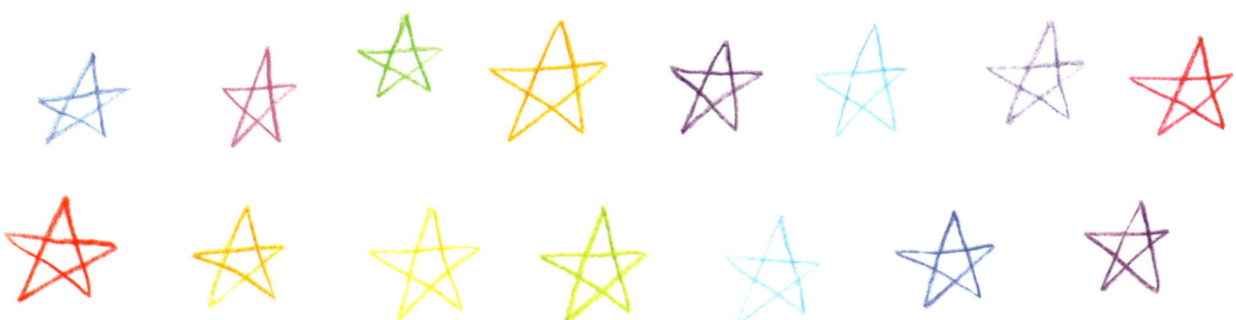

In the next lesson, the children can draw stars of many sizes and colour them in.

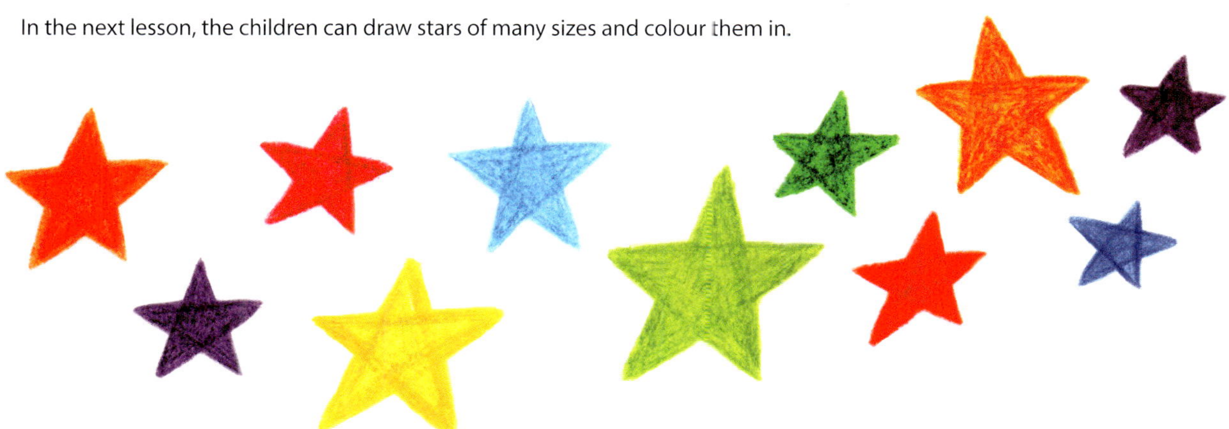

Angles and triangles

Zig-zag forms, diamonds and stars are all made up of angles. The children can explore angles, coming up to the blackboard to draw their own angle. It will appear as though the angles are dancing!

The vocabulary can include words such as:
Wide, narrow, opening out, closing up, direction, upwards, downwards, sideways, sharp, pointy, small, medium, middle-sized, large, big, little, huge, tiny.

Although these forms are geometrical, the experience of angles at this stage is left free: it is a shape in space. We also have them in our bodies. The children can make angles with their thumbs, fingers, hands and wrists; arms, elbows, arms and shoulders; torso and upper legs (when sitting down or bending over); knees, angles and feet. When they have explored creating many angles with their own bodies, they could 'shape a friend into angles.' This will help them see the angles outside of themselves (and have fun!).

Finally they can draw a page of angles in their books, trying to make each angle different.

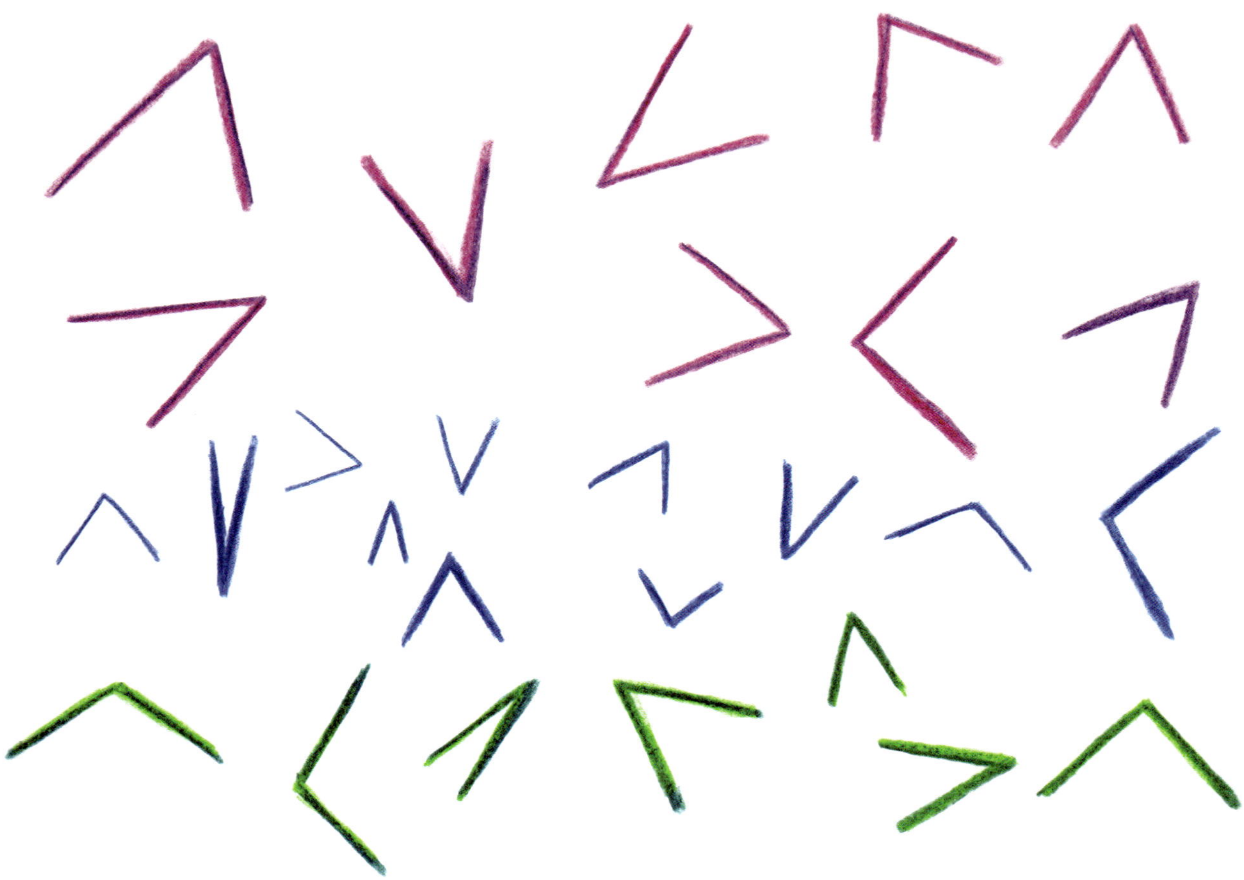

Angle Games

Three children come to the front of the class and turn around with their backs to the class so that they can't see anyone. Everyone else stands or sits and makes as many angles as they can, using their whole body, arms, hands, legs and feet. They may use a desk or a chair to help keep their balance. The teacher calls out, 'Angle Time!' when everyone is ready. The three children move around the room and with the help of the teacher, choose three children who have the most angles to take their place at the front. This can be repeated four or five times.

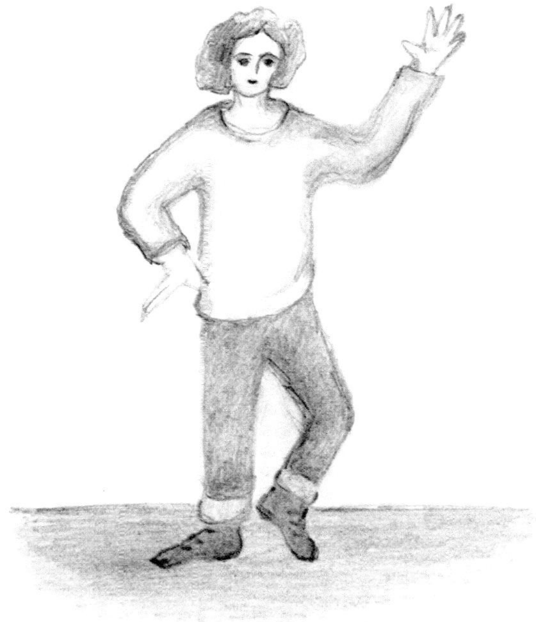

Variations

- Choose the person (or people) with the most unusual angles.
- Choose the person (or people) who do not move.
- The class is seated, using only hands and arms.
- Groups of three or four children make angles together. Choose one group to come to the front for the next turn.

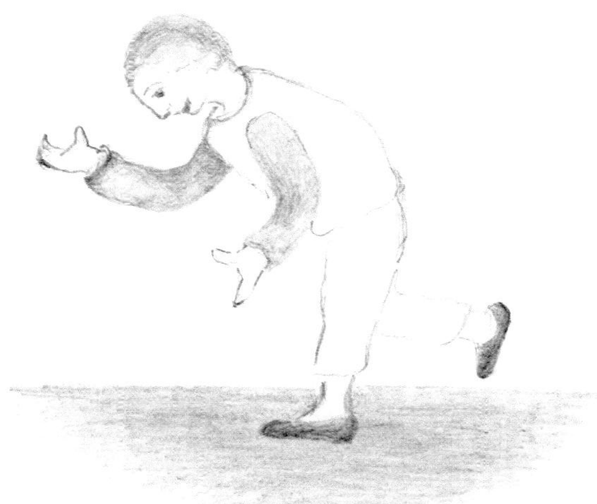

Mirror angles

The class divide into groups of threes or fours. One group creates angles together. Then the other group mirrors them by creating the same angles. Swap over. This can also be done in pairs with one child making the angles, then the second child copying them. Then swapping over.

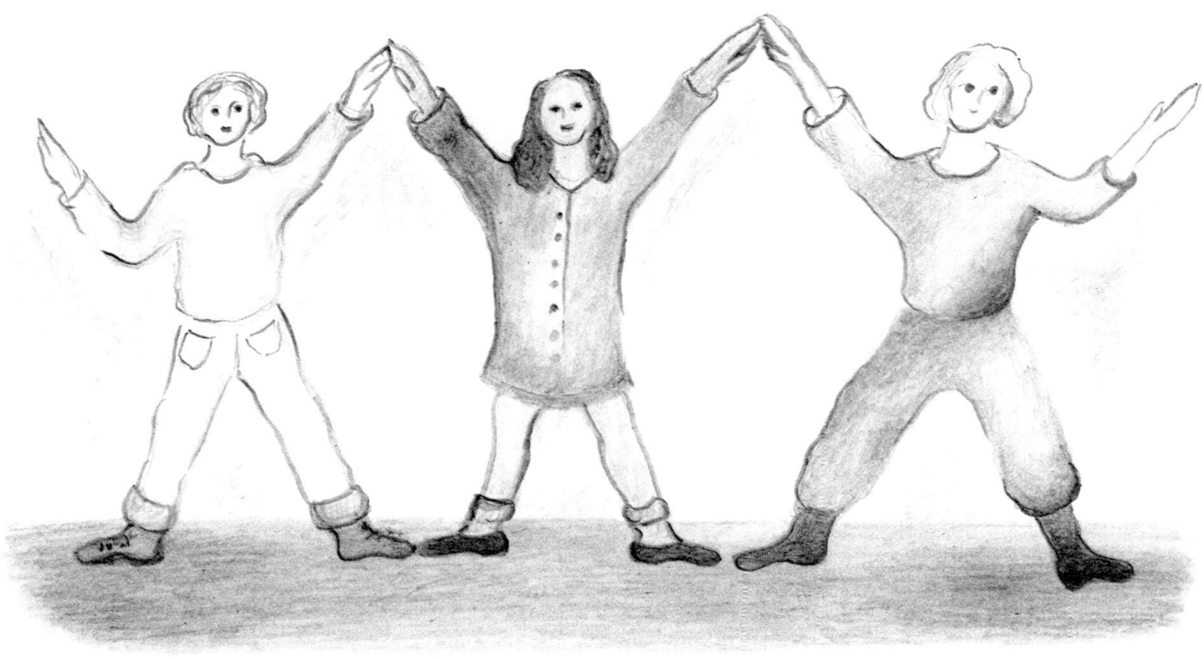

Angles can be arranged in different ways.
In different sizes:

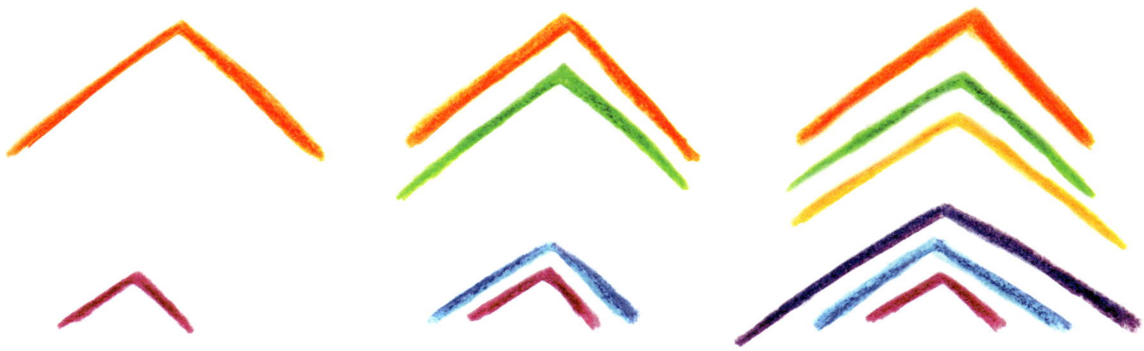

In different directions:

Angles can stand on a straight line. Here the angles become triangles:

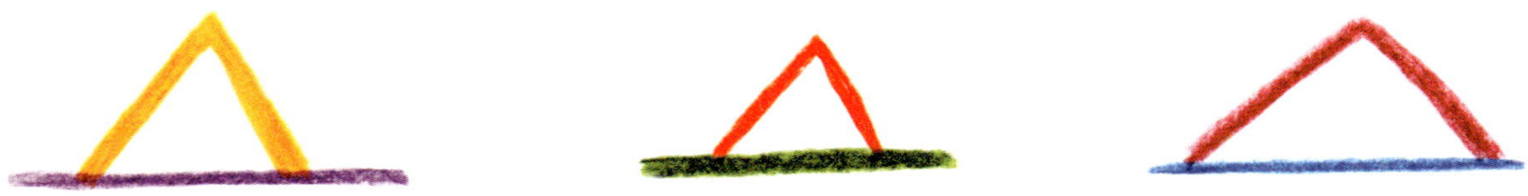

We can draw triangles standing up:

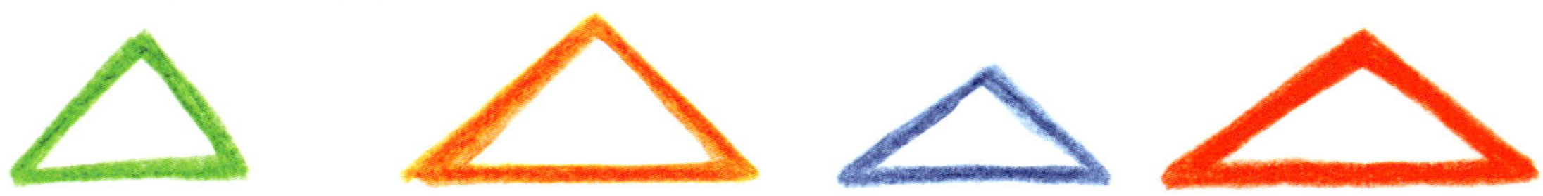

And upside down:

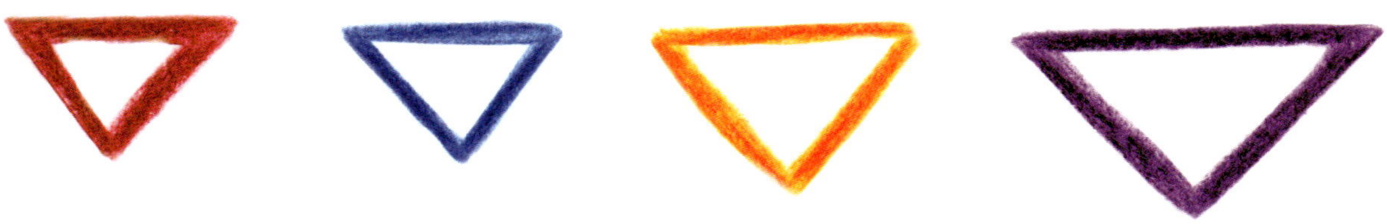

Triangles can touch their points together:

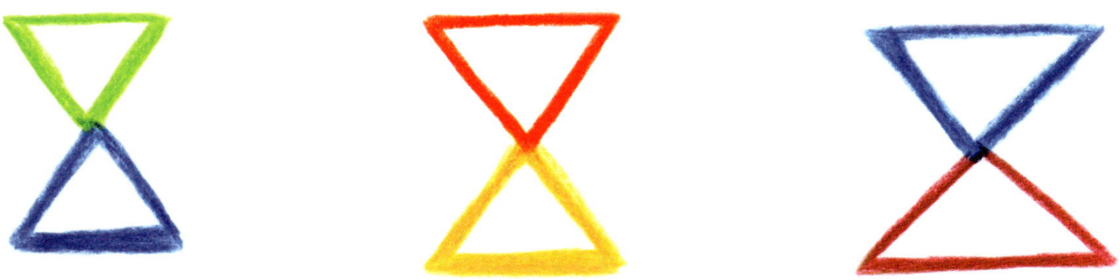

Triangles into six-pointed stars

The touching triangles can overlap.
The blue triangle moves up into the red one.

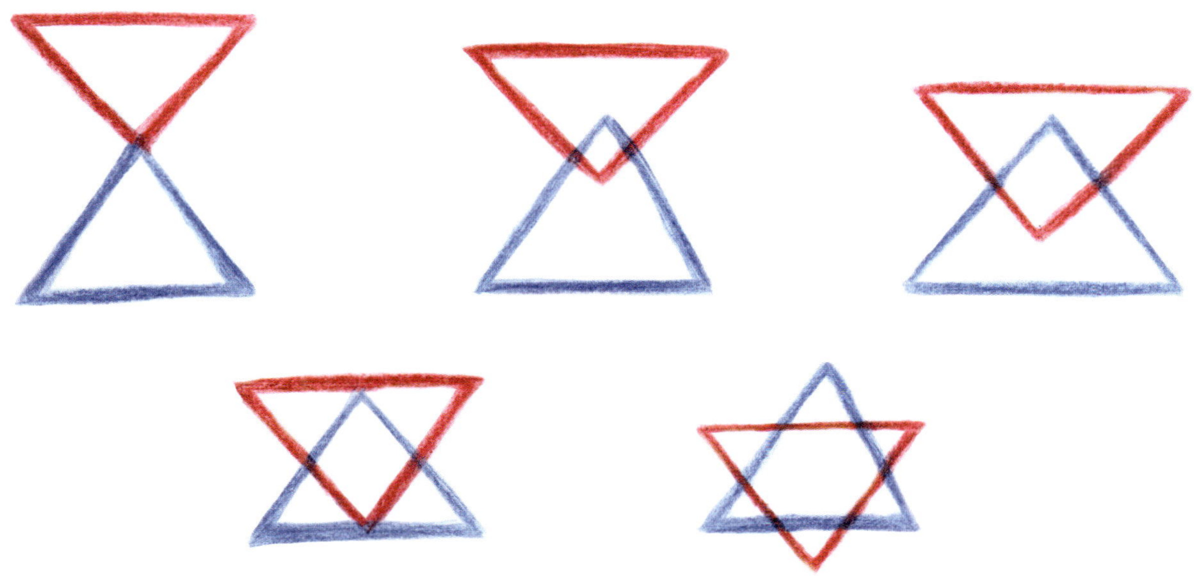

The two triangles touch each other again, and the blue is moved on upwards. The children can watch as the teacher draws this step-by-step on the blackboard. They then draw their own 'touching triangles'. Their stars might not be absolutely even – this does not matter. They can draw many six-pointed stars using different colours, then colour some in.

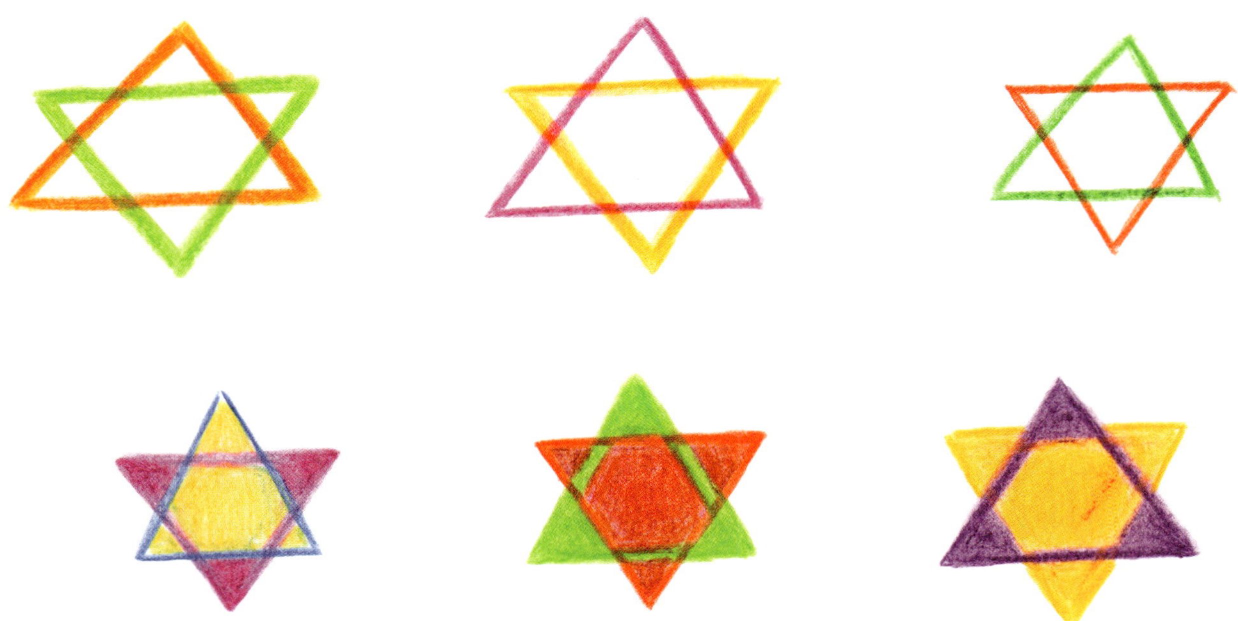

Their stars can be drawn either way (once they have seen and drawn the step-by-step process), with the upper-pointing triangle first, then the down-pointing triangle second.

Spirals

After so many angular forms, a new movement experience can be introduced: the spiral. Follow the same procedure:

- Teacher draws a large spiral on the board.
- Children draw spirals in the air.
- Children walk the spirals, from outside going in, then turning around and walking out again.
- Children draw spirals in their books, drawing from the centre going outwards, and from the periphery to the centre.
- Some children might draw spirals which are related to each other.

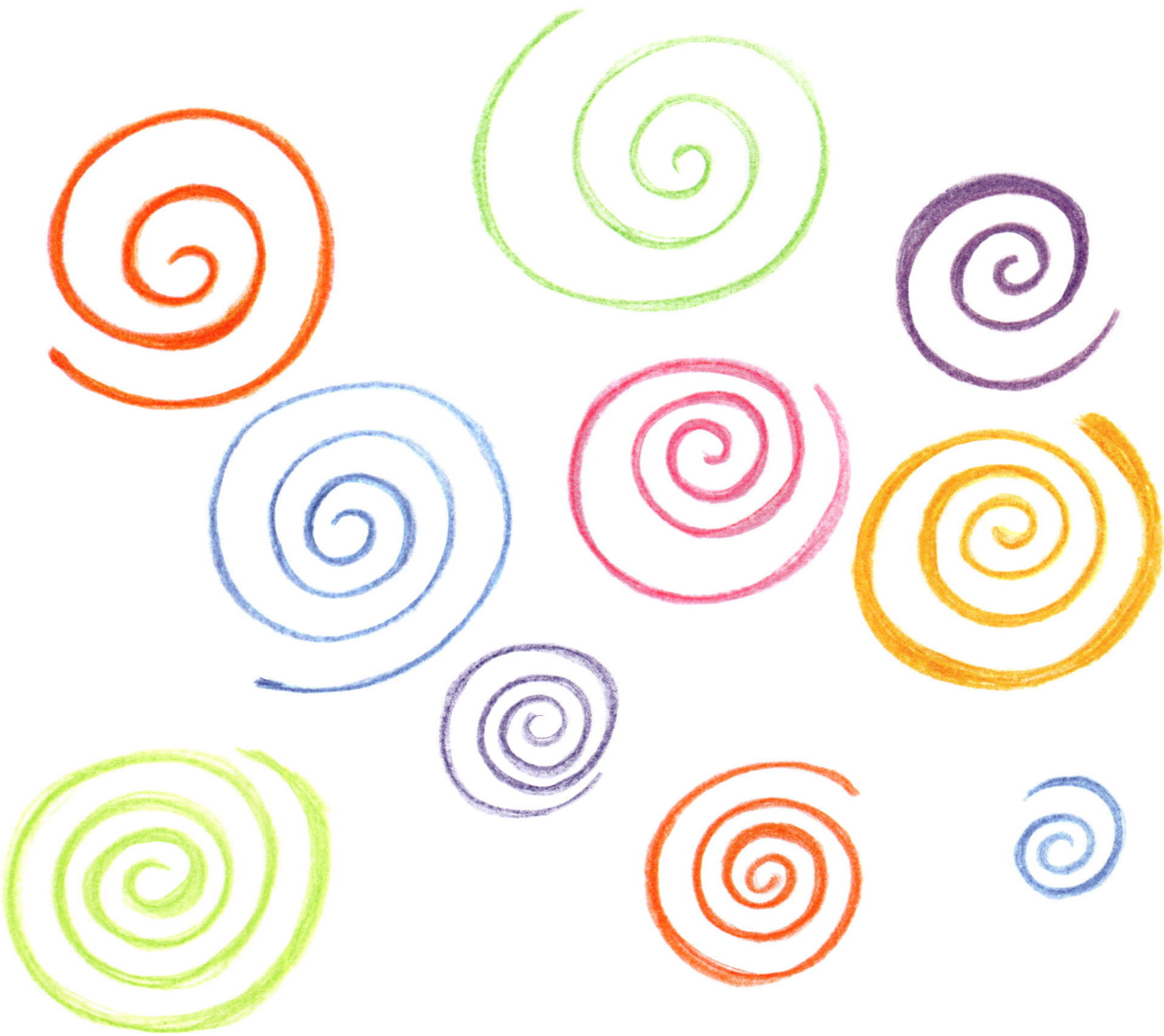

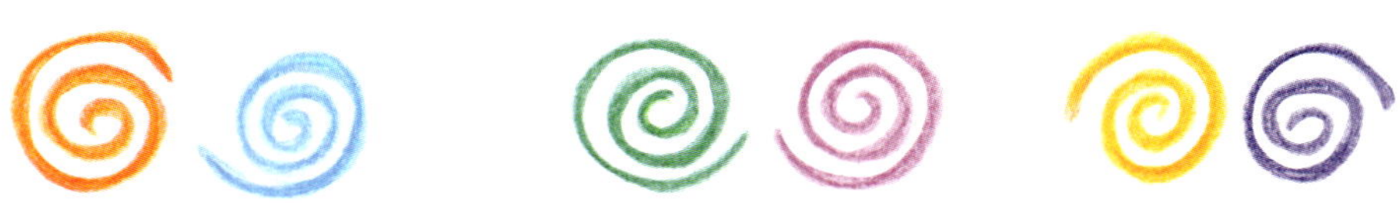

Straight lines, curves and spiral

How does a straight line become a curve?

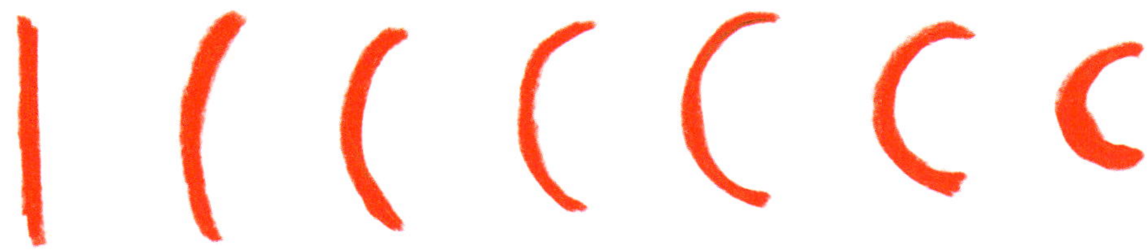

And how does a curve become a straight line?

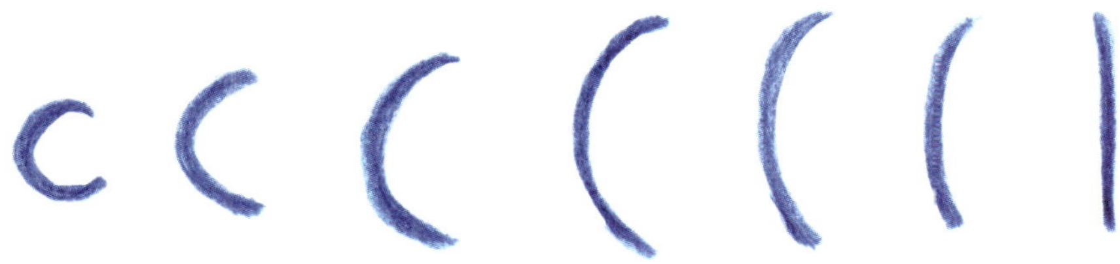

We can draw this with the curve turned in the opposite direction:

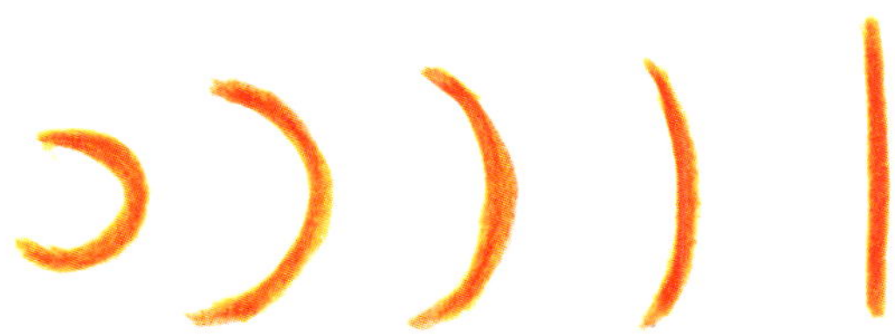

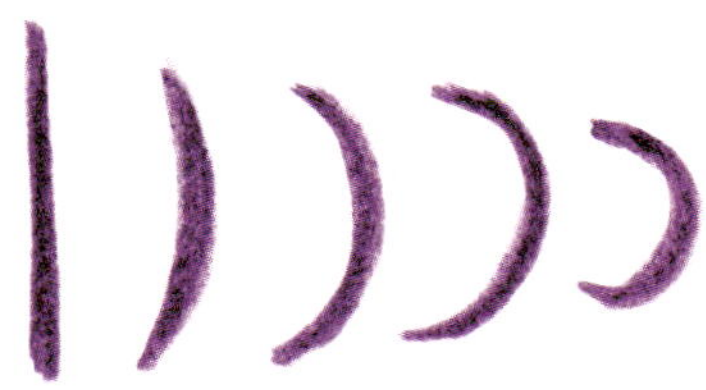

These exercises develop the children's:

- awareness of sequences
- sensitivity to gradually changing forms
- observation skills
- accuracy
- ordering
- experiences of form relatedness
- ability to compare straightness and roundness in a visible sequence.

Can the straight line become a spiral?
And the spiral a straight line?

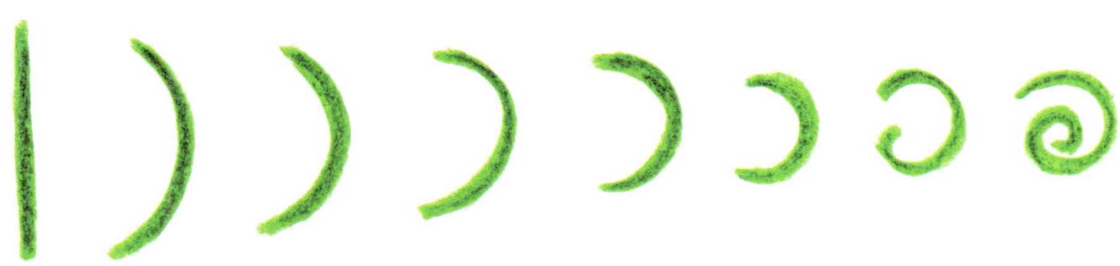

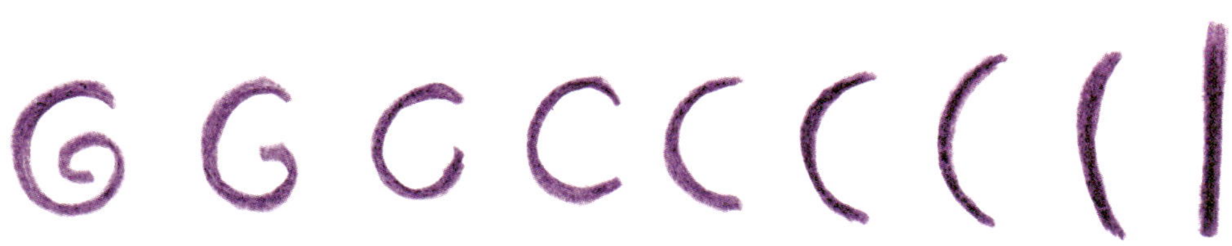

Circle and ellipse (oval)

These forms combine two shapes, the circle and the ellipse (or oval). The children see how one shape relates harmoniously to another.

Using one colour draw the circle several times over in both directions.

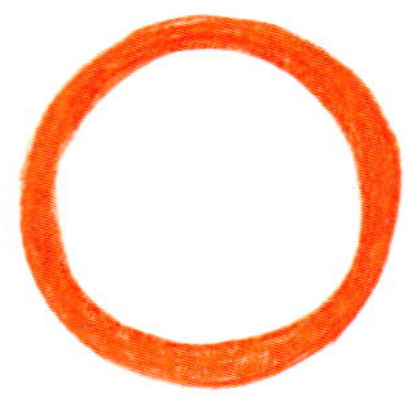

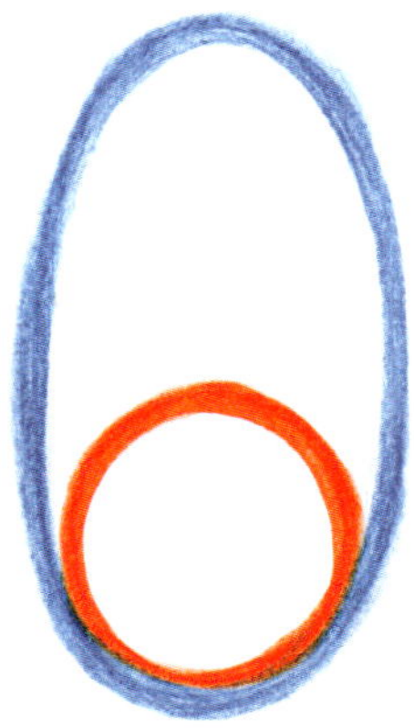

Draw a second circle lower down on the page and draw the ellipse around it in another colour.

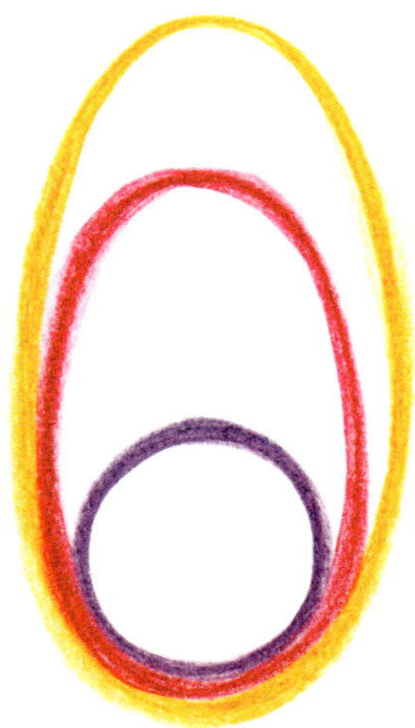

A third circle with two ellipses.

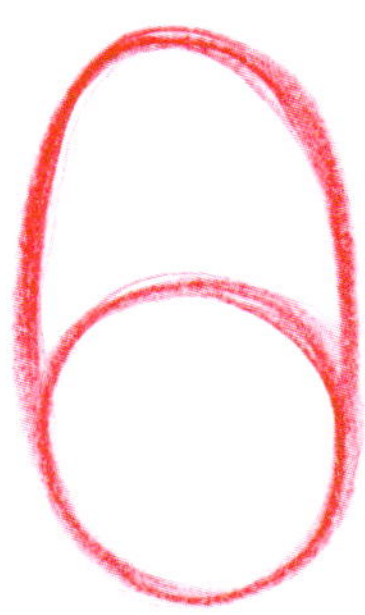

This line moves continously from circle to ellipse without lifting the pencil.

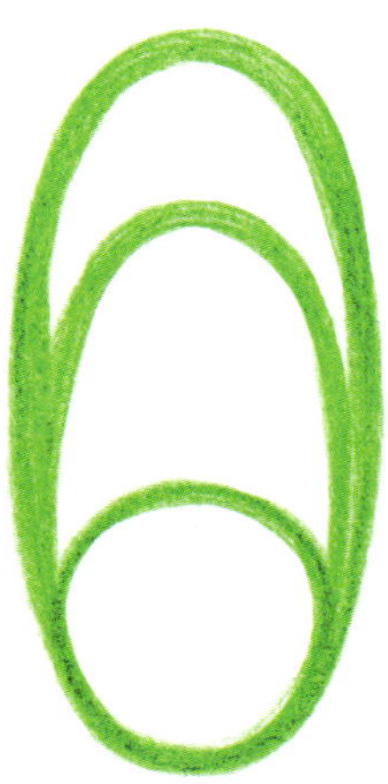

This line moves continuously from circle to the smaller ellipse then to the larger ellipse, without lifting the pencil.

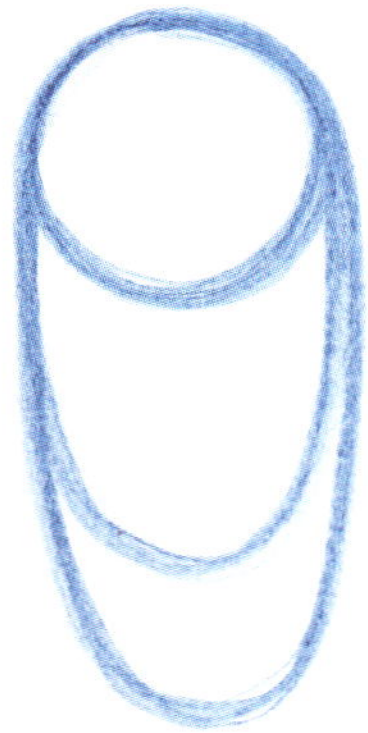

Draw the circle with the ellipses going downwards, in a flowing continuous movement. When the large ellipse is finished draw back inwards to the smaller ellipse and then around the circle. This can be done several times. The whole form feels as though it is growing larger and smaller, then larger again.

This line begins with the larger ellipse, then to the smaller ellipse and to the circle in a continuous movement, without lifting the pencil. It can be coloured in.

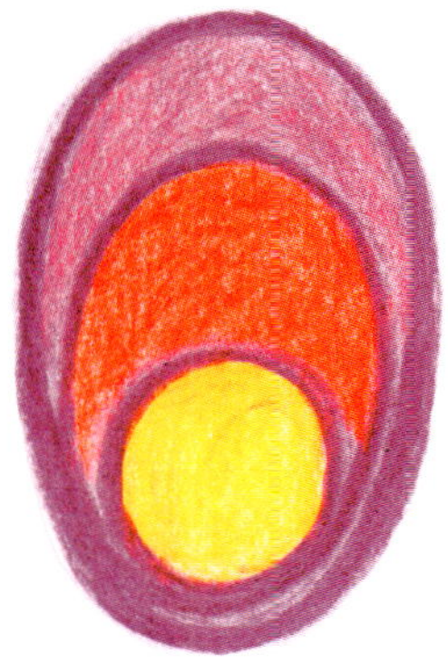

Circles and ellipses can be drawn in pairs. Draw a circle and an ellipse, then a second circle and its ellipse. Draw in both directions. The children can listen to the different sounds which the pencil makes when they are drawing the different forms.

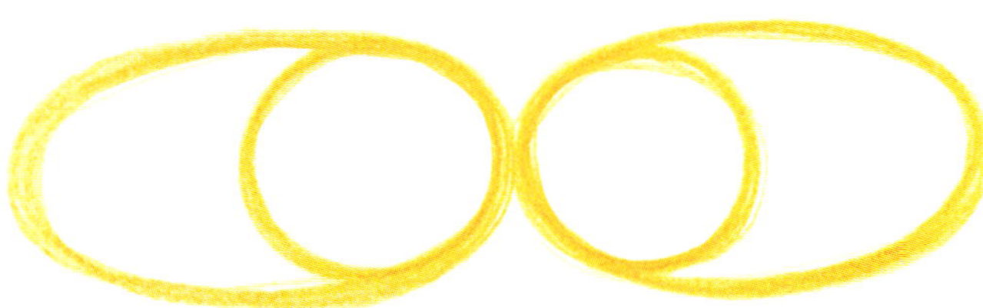

Draw four forms: above and below, left and right. Draw several forms like this and colour them in.

Vocabulary:
Ellipse, oval, inside, outside, surrounding, encompassing, inner, outer, smaller, larger, continuous.

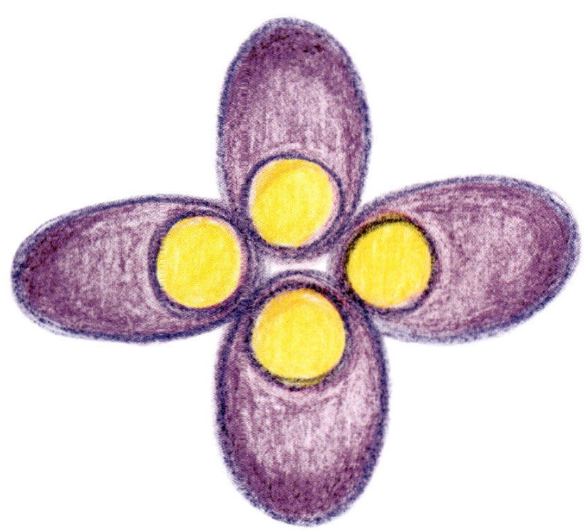

Giving and receiving

Use two different colours, one above and one below.
Draw over the forms several times in both directions, beginning with the upper form.

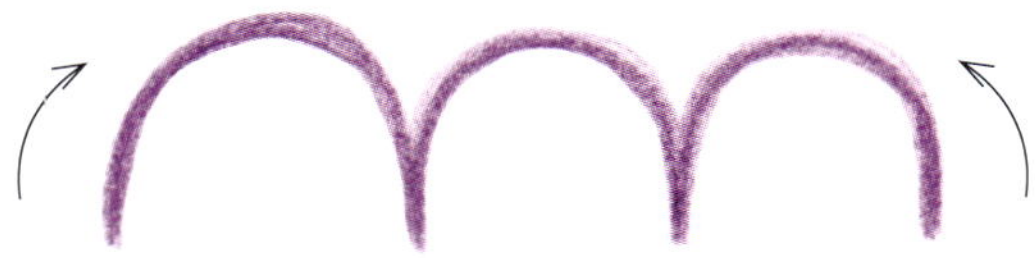
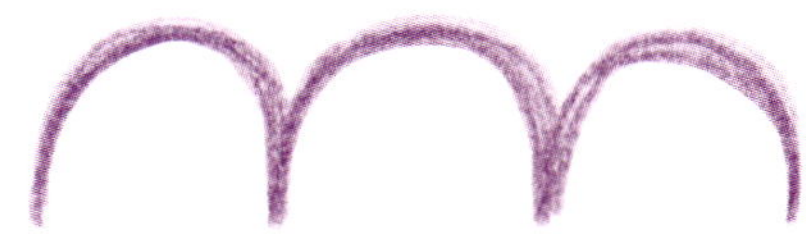
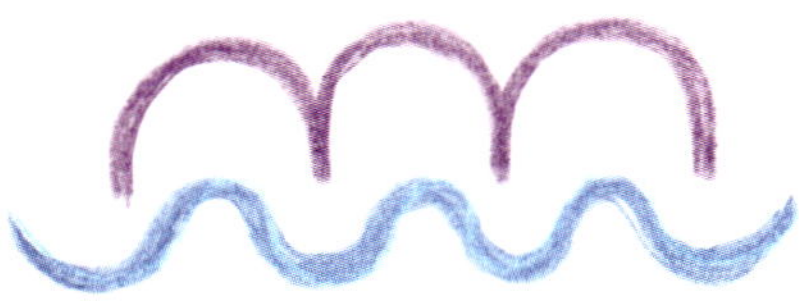
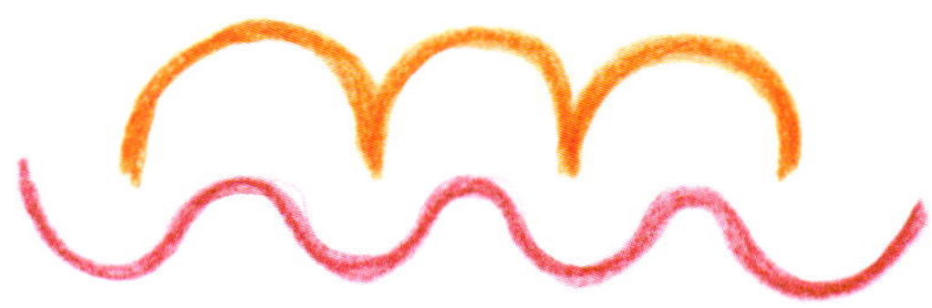

Change the shape of the top form slightly.
How will the lower form need to change?
The children are observing and adapting.

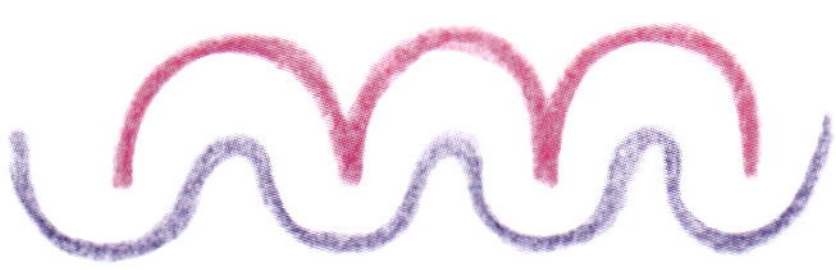
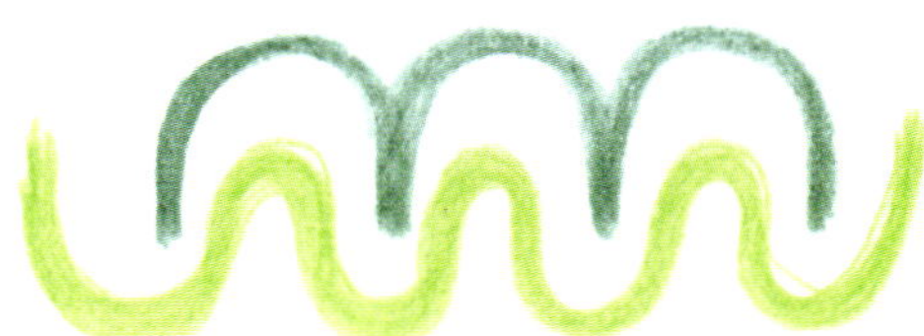

Here, harmonious relationships are drawn.
The forms respond to each other in a natural organic way.

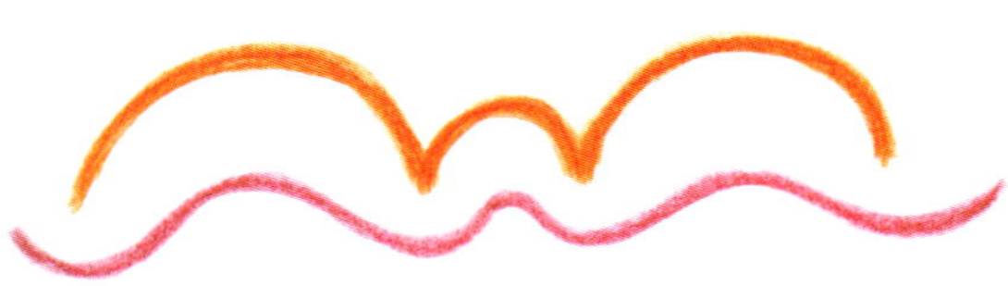
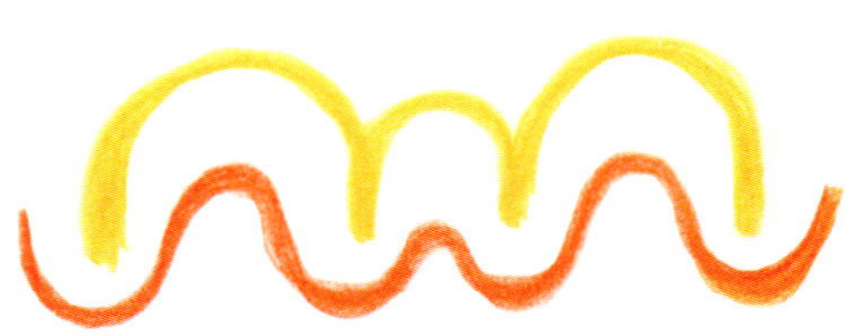

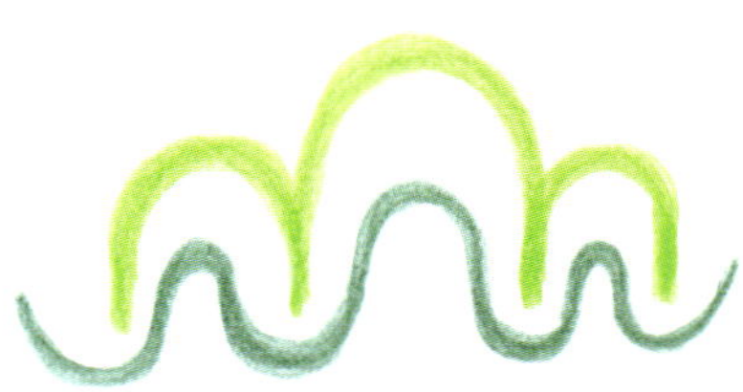

Symmetry and mirroring: Above and below

The teacher draws the upper form, which the children draw with both hands mirroring in the air. Then the completed form is drawn in their books, including the dotted line, drawing several times over in both directions.

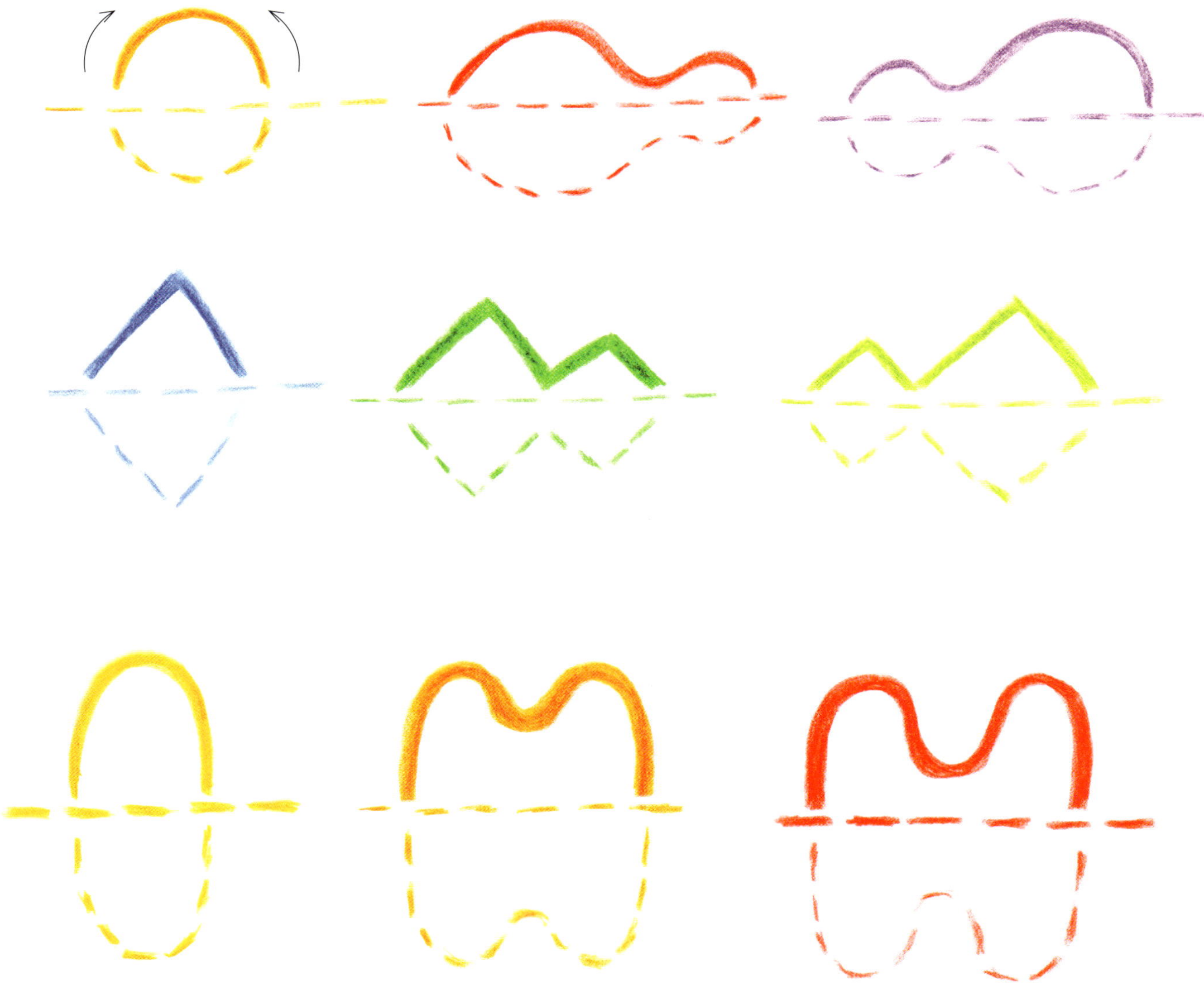

These are important exercises for

- spatial awareness
- spatial orientation
- sense of balance
- observation.

The children use one colour only so that the forms feel complete.

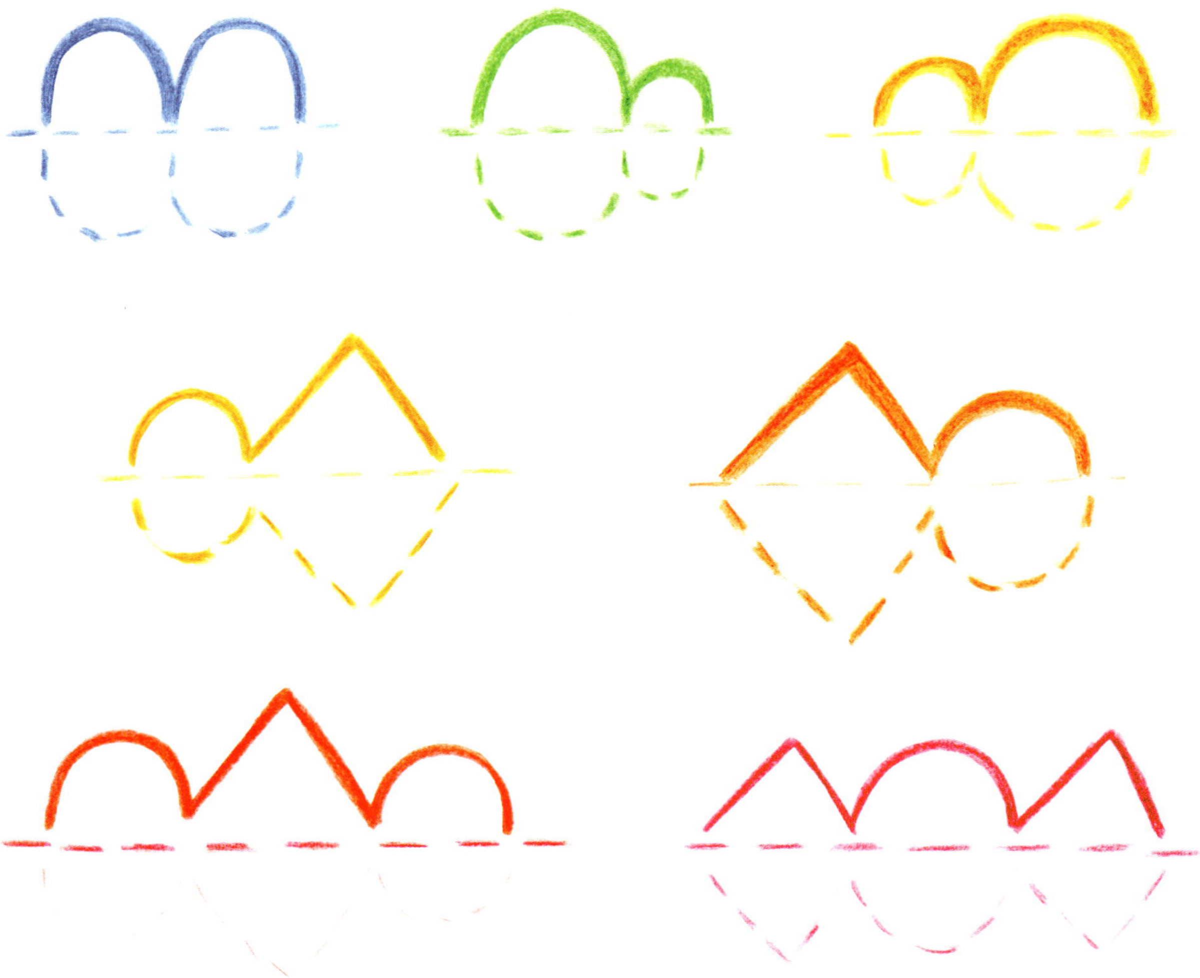

An extra colour may be added both above and below once the children can complete the forms accurately.

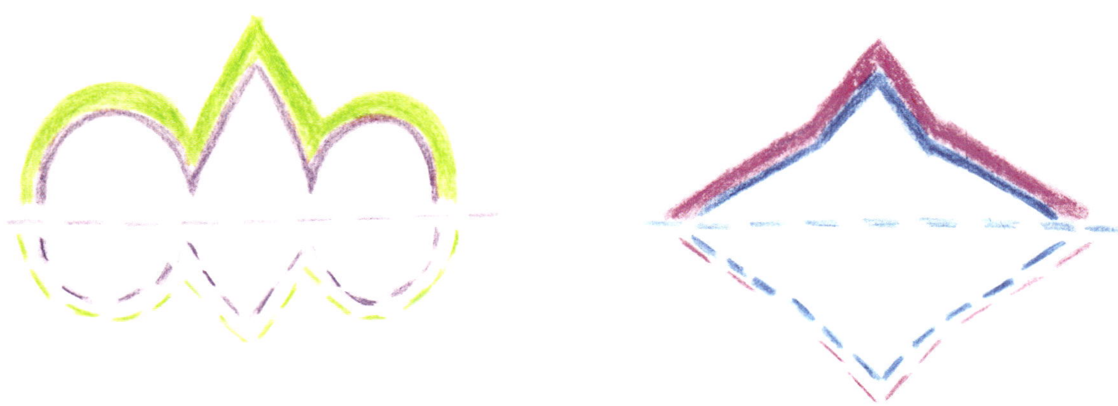

Symmetry and mirroring: Right and left

The teacher draws half the form, which the children draw with both hands mirroring in the air. The whole form, including the dotted line, is drawn into their books, drawing several times over in both directions. One colour is used, and a second colour added after.

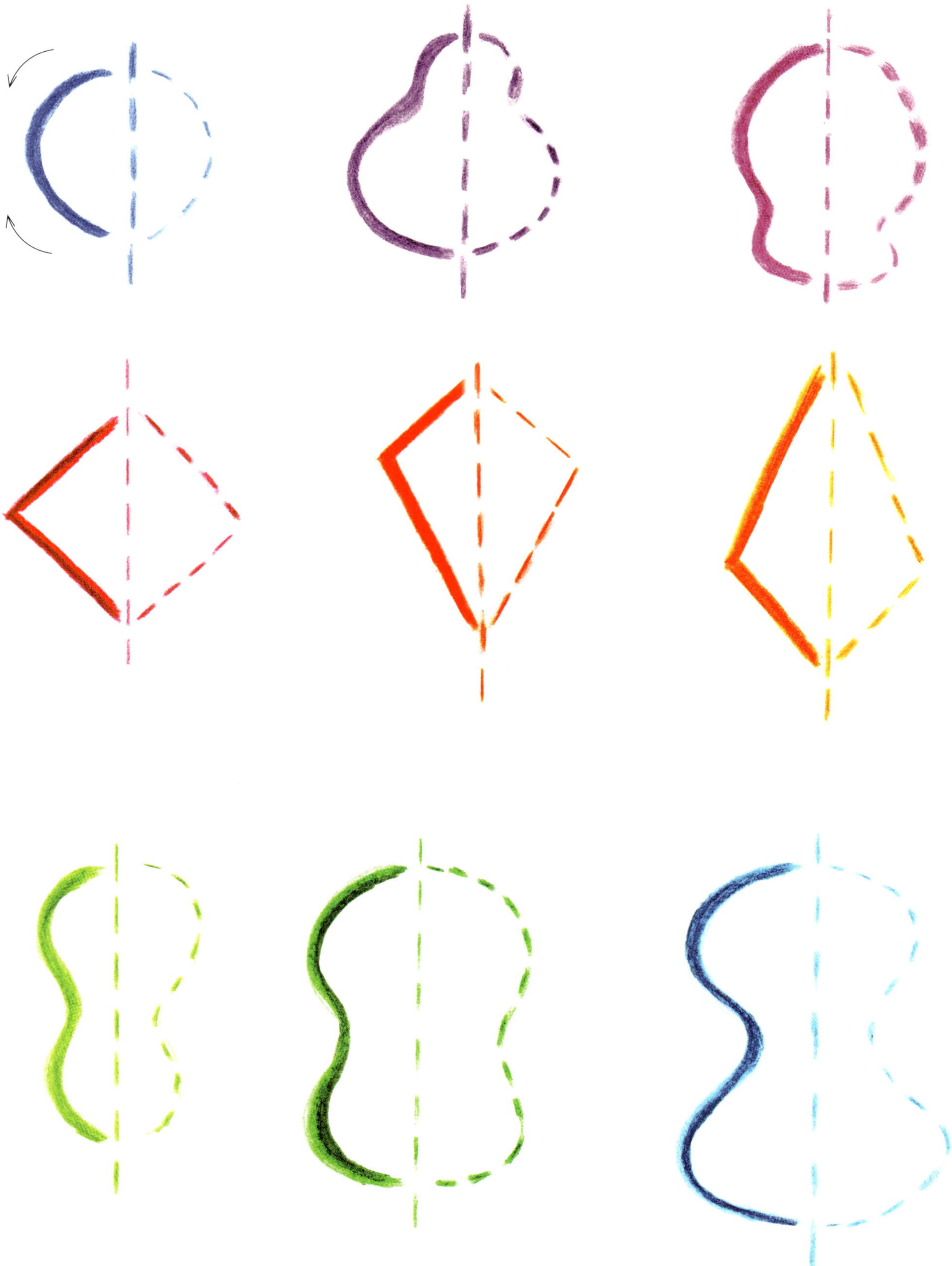

The children will need to look closely at how far and how near these forms are to the dotted line.

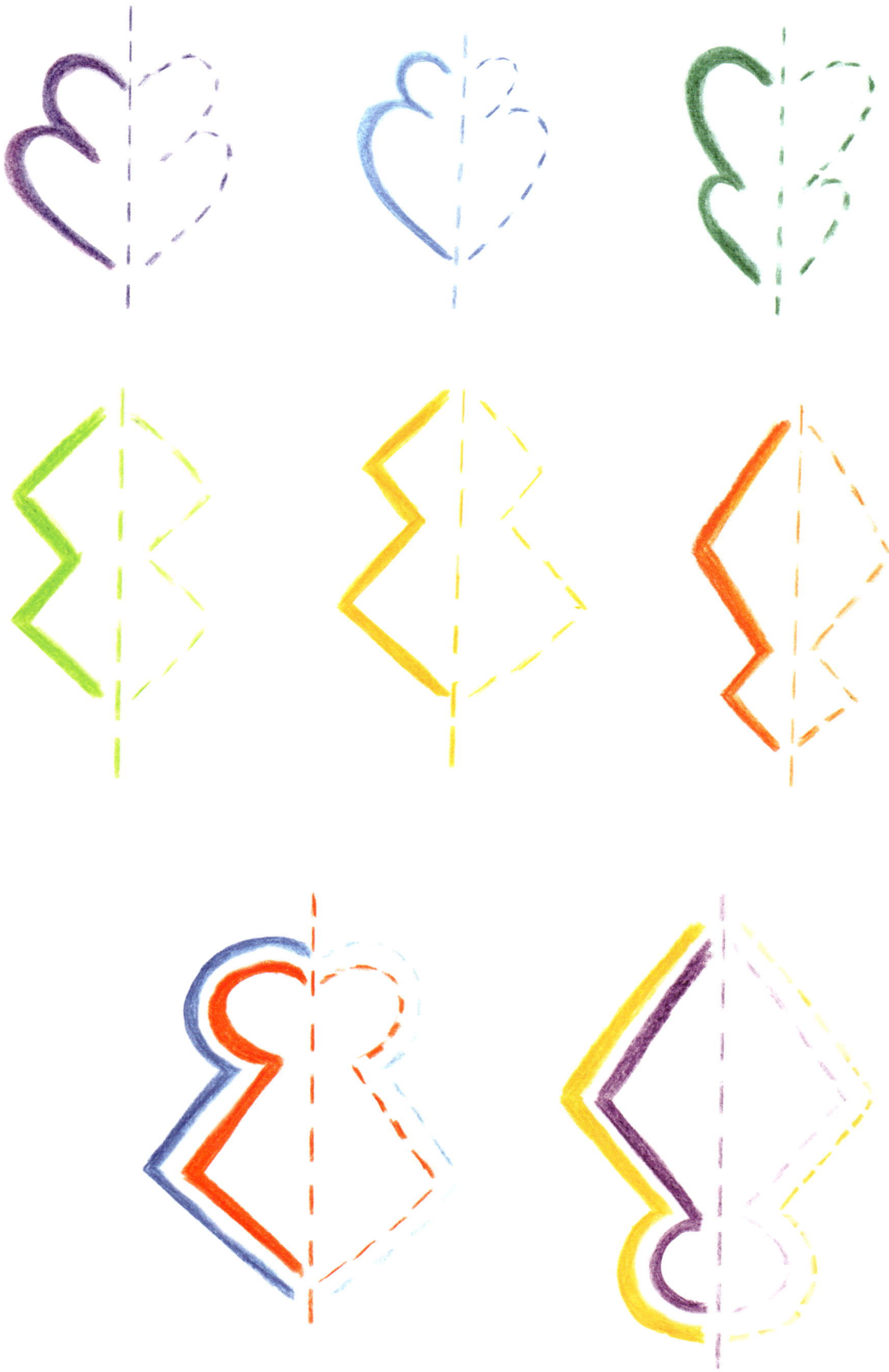

Evaluating the children's drawings

Most children will be able to have completed the drawings in Part One by about 7 to 8 years old. If you notice that a child is having problems, check the following:

- Are they experiencing problems with their eyesight? They may need to have their eyes professionally tested.
- Are they holding their pencils correctly? The thumb is on one side, the first finger on top, with the pencil resting on the second finger. This creates a stable yet flexible little 'triangle' for the pencil.
- Are they sitting correctly? Check their posture.
- Do they need better lighting? They may need to sit by a window.
- Some children are naturally long- or short-sighted. They may need to move nearer to or further from the blackboard.
- Are they having difficulties with all the form drawing experiences? Do they manage drawing in the air? Walking the forms? Are there co-ordination problems? Observe the children when they are playing in the playground to check whether they need extra co-ordinating skills: climbing, running, jumping, ball throwing and catching, skipping and so on. Extra games can be taken with the whole class, especially if children are not having enough exercise.
- Which forms are problematic? There may be a specific left/right or above/below orientation difficulty. If this is serious, check large spatial movements and co-ordination. Games and specific-skills exercises can be given. If the problem lies within the form-drawing process, remember that all children learn at different speeds – they are individuals. Some difficulties will correct themselves in Class Two, as the form drawings repeat (at a new level) many of the fundamental movements from Class One.
- Don't single out children if they are having problems. Try to meet their needs within the context of the class as a whole, so that they don't become nervous or self-conscious.
- Always give positive encouragement. The children should enjoy form drawing and gain great satisfaction from it.
- Some problems may be balanced and corrected in other subjects. If finger dexterity is weak, check their craft and handwork skills. Extra sewing or knitting will strengthen their hands and fingers. Always see the child from many different perspectives, and keep in mind their overall development, co-ordination and well-being.

A note on left-handedness

Children who are predominantly left-handed may possibly experience difficulties. Their forms might not be perfectly symmetrically balanced, and some of the movements might be reversed. See whether they will swap hands, and use their right hands. This can be encouraged but never forced. Allow a left-handed child a longer developmental time if necessary, leaving exercises which are difficult for them until the following year.

Part Two

Class Two

7–8 years old

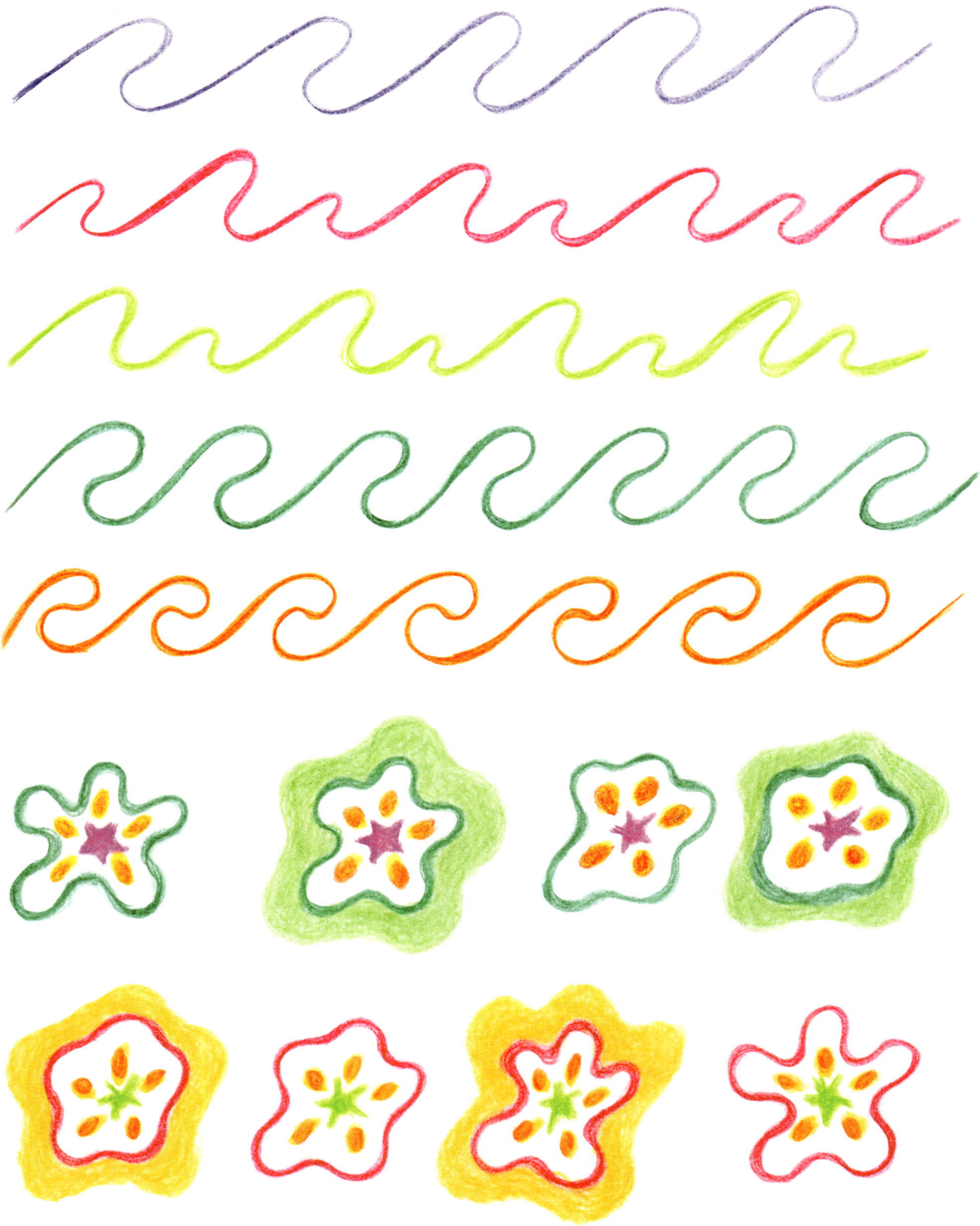

Exercises suitable for Class Two (7–8 years) are developed to strengthen:

- Hand and eye co-ordination
- Dexterity of the hand, by increasing fine-motor and co-ordination skills
- Abilities in handwriting
- Sensitivity and awareness of contrasting forms
- Concentration and focus
- Flexibility in thinking
- Imagination
- Inner senses of balance and movement
- Inner confidence and sense of security.

The examples which are included here bring experiences of:

- Proportion
- Relationships
- Static and dynamic movement
- Contrast
- Polarities
- Transformation
- Inner and outer
- Harmony
- Symmetry
- Principles of balance

Class Two exercises build upon the processes in Class One, extending and elaborating the practised foundations of form drawing. There might be a variety of abilities among the children, but all children should work through all of the forms, regardless of whether they find them easy or hard. If some children are already able to write they will nevertheless enjoy the spatial relationships and processes in the form drawing as an art in itself. It is a subject which has its own place in an educational curriculum. Children who have already developed handwriting will still benefit from the many creative aspects which form drawing brings to them. For children in Class Two who are just mastering the skills of handwriting, the form drawing lessons will support and help to develop their writing skills, and provide the essential spatial orientation experiences which are needed alongside the fine-motor co-ordination and dexterity exercises.

Straight lines and diagonal lines: Star forms

- The forms are all drawn freehand, without rulers.
- Draw each line in a different direction: inwards to outwards and outwards to inwards, whichever directions feel more comfortable.
- Leave a 'breathing space' in the centre. This seems to shine!
- Make some lines longer and others shorter, in a distinct pattern.

Vocabulary:
Vertical, horizontal, diagonal, centre, inner space, longer, shorter, shining, star-like.

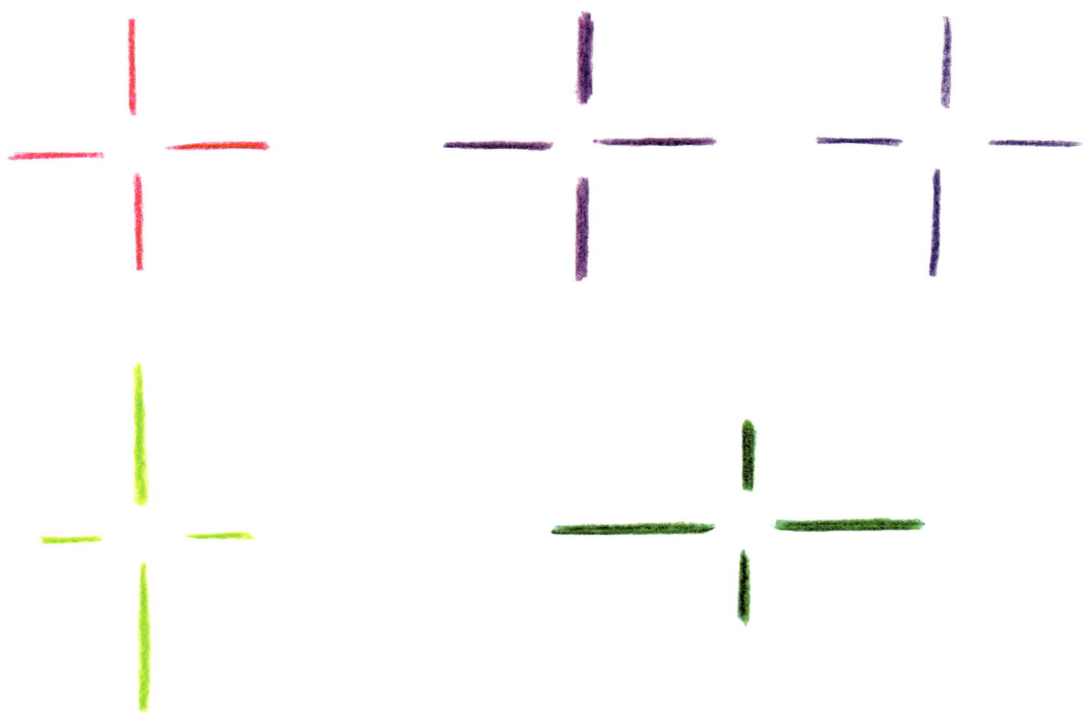

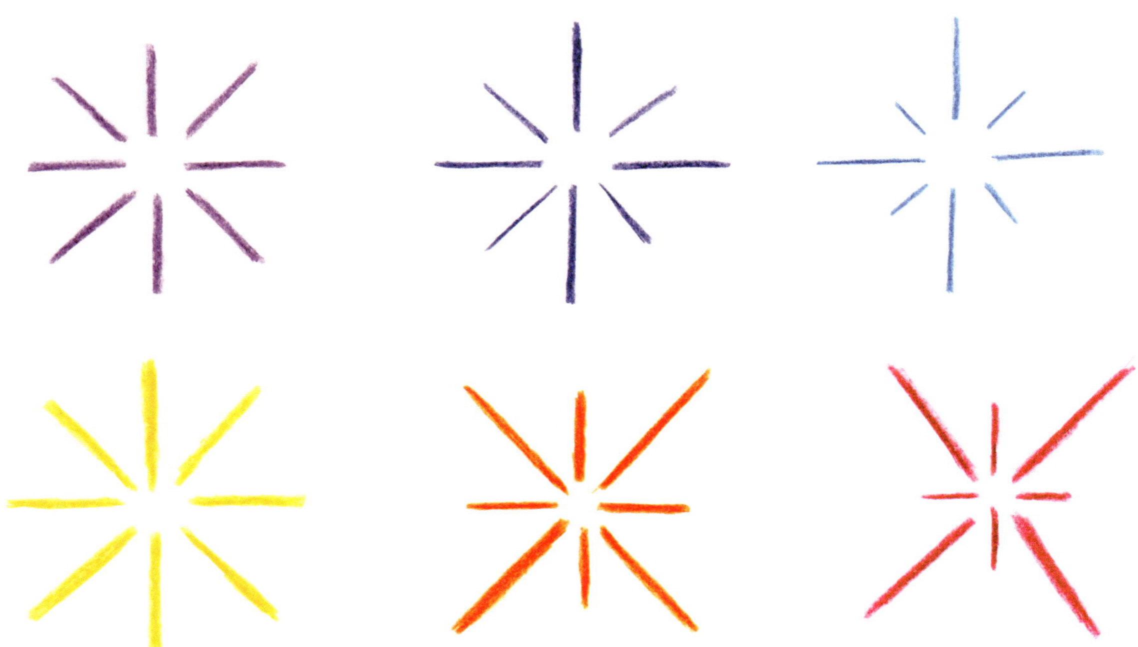

Creating forms with lines: Horizontal lines

- When the children 'draw' with their noses, what do they discover? They are saying 'no'!

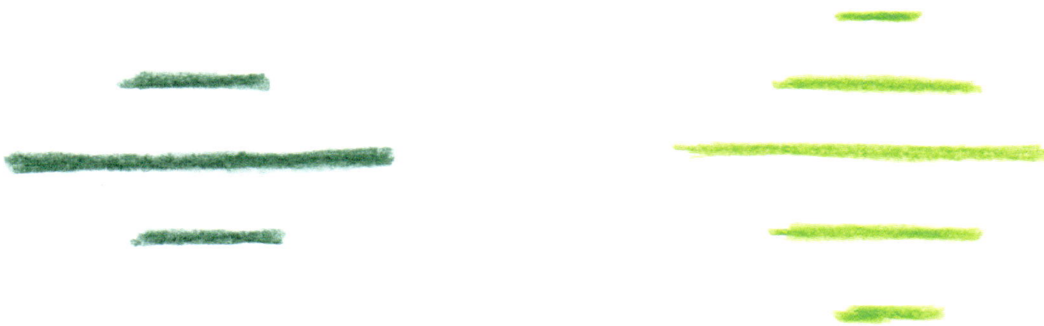

- Move in both directions to draw the lines, from left to right and back again.
- Begin with the central line, going above and below for the shorter lines.
- Turn the books upside down. What do we see?

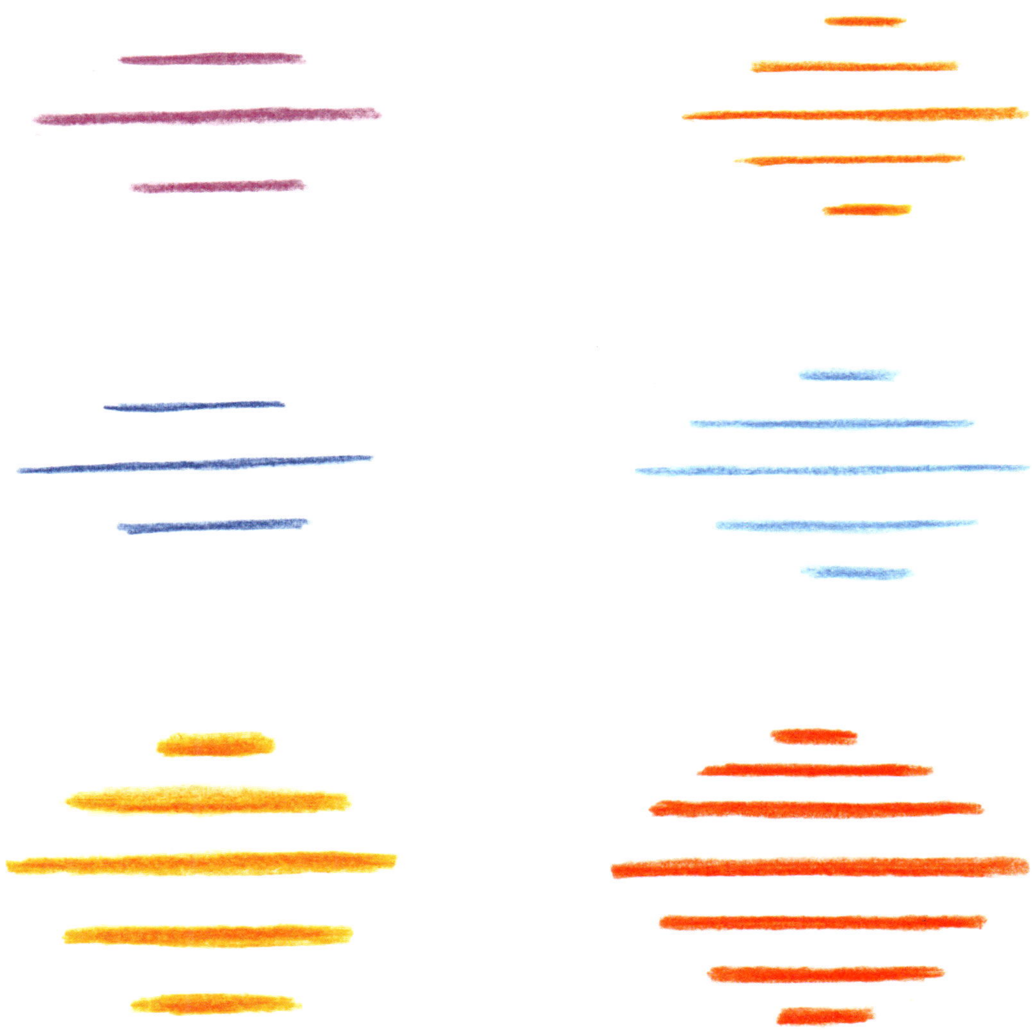

Creating forms with lines: Vertical lines

- When the children 'draw' with their noses, what do they discover? They are saying 'yes'!

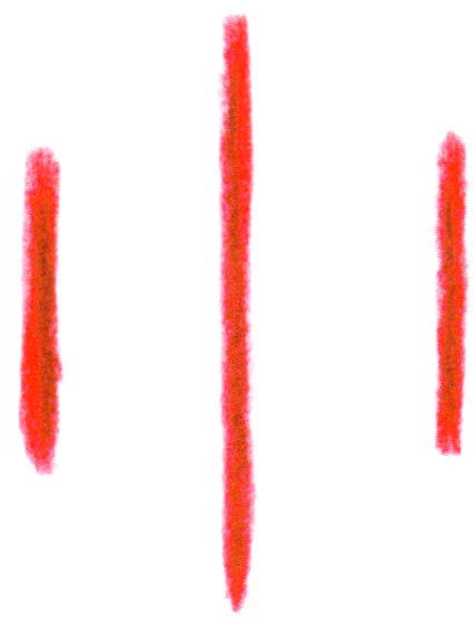

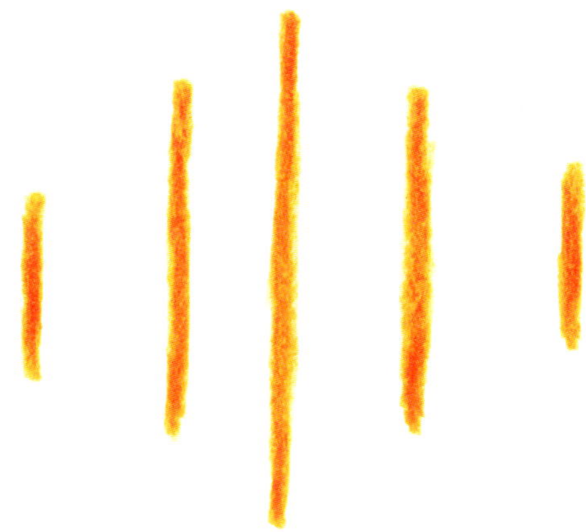

- Draw the forms in both directions, up and down and back again, several times.
- Begin with the central line, moving left and right to each side for the shorter lines.
- Allow plenty of space on the page.
- Turn the books around. What do we see?

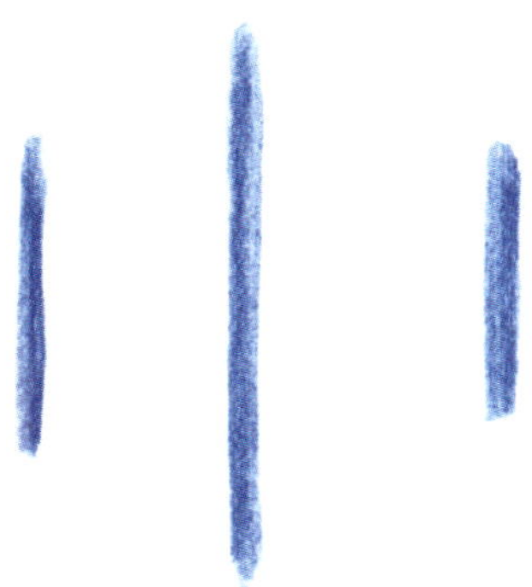

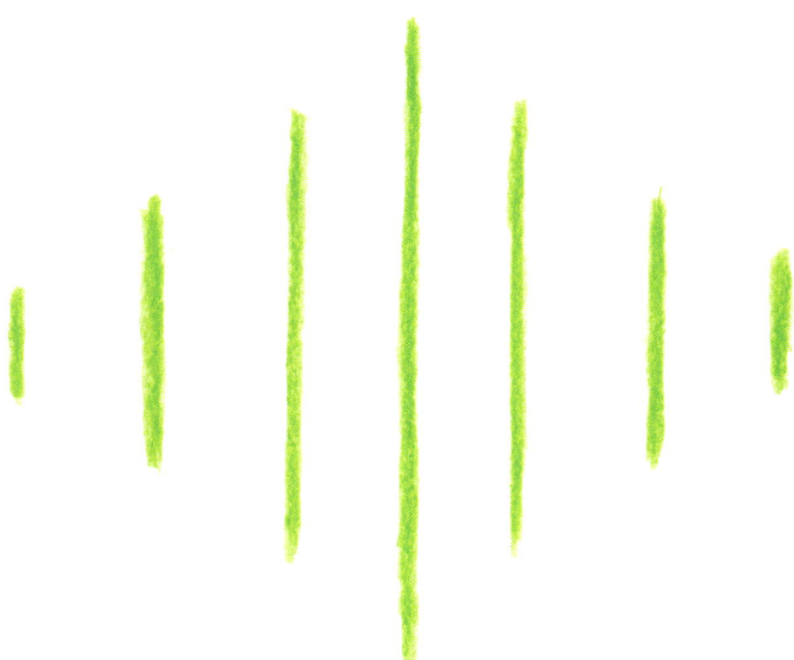

Creating forms with lines: Vertical and horizontal lines

- Draw the longer lines, two upwards and two sideways. They look like the stars which the children drew before.
- Now they make a different form by adding shorter lines beside the long ones.
- Leave plenty of space between the lines.
- Draw several forms using different colours.

Vocabulary:
Vertical, upwards, downwards, horizontal, sideways, left, right, longer, shorter.

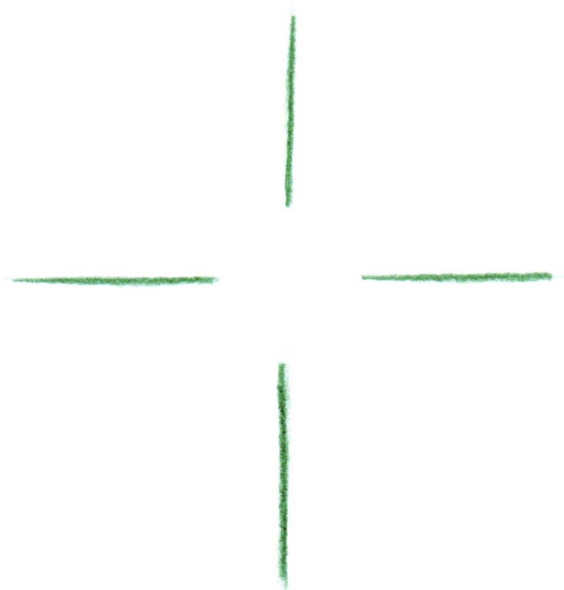

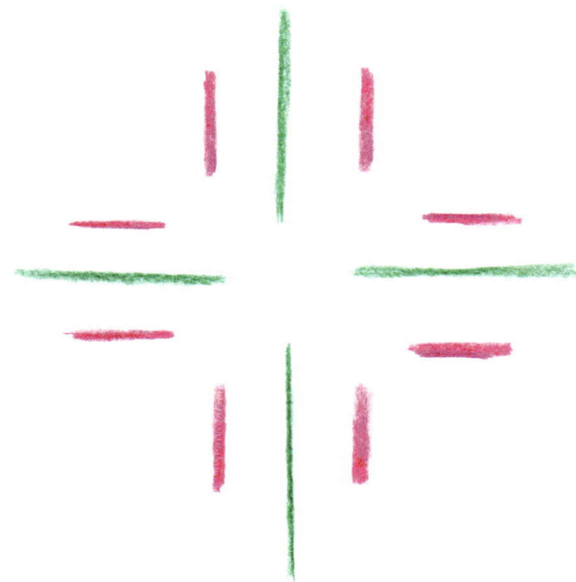

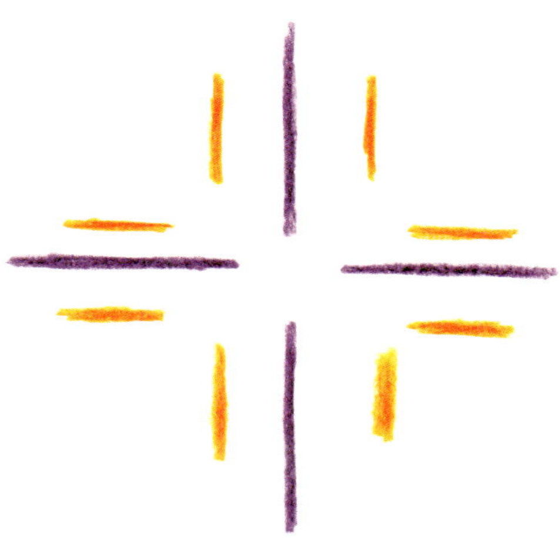

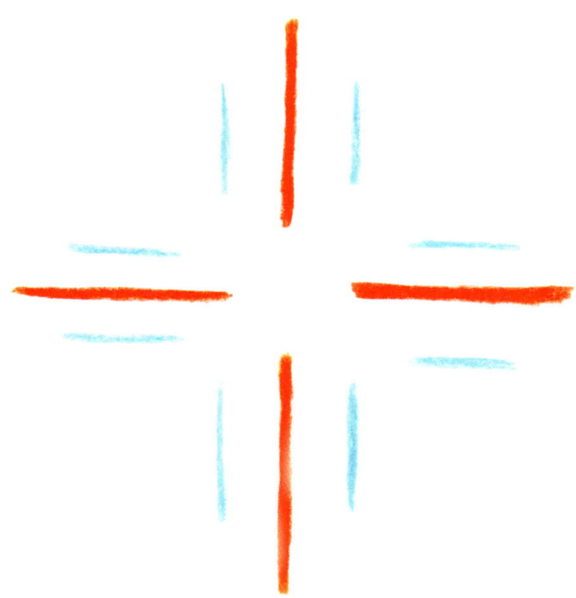

Flowing lines

- Listen to the sound of the pencil. Does it change?
- Draw over the line two or three times.

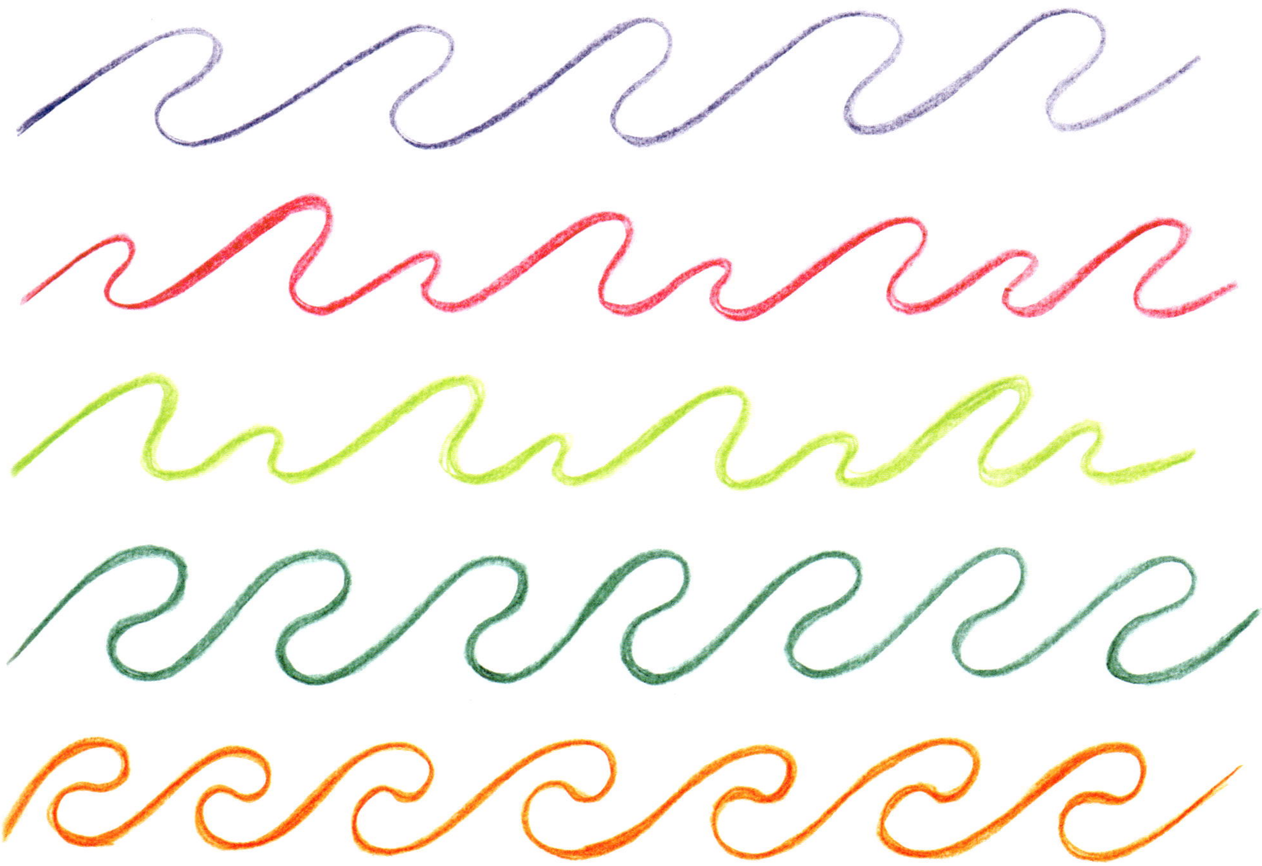

- What do the children see when they turn their books upside down? Do the forms still look the same?

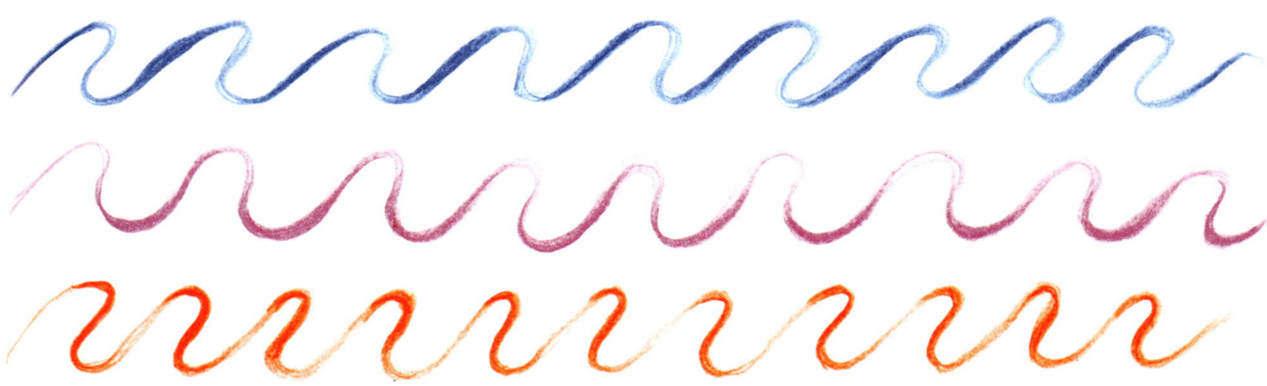

- Pressing firmly and pressing lightly gives these forms rhythm. Don't have the pencils too sharp or they will break!

Flowing lines and loops

- These are drawn in a continuously flowing line.

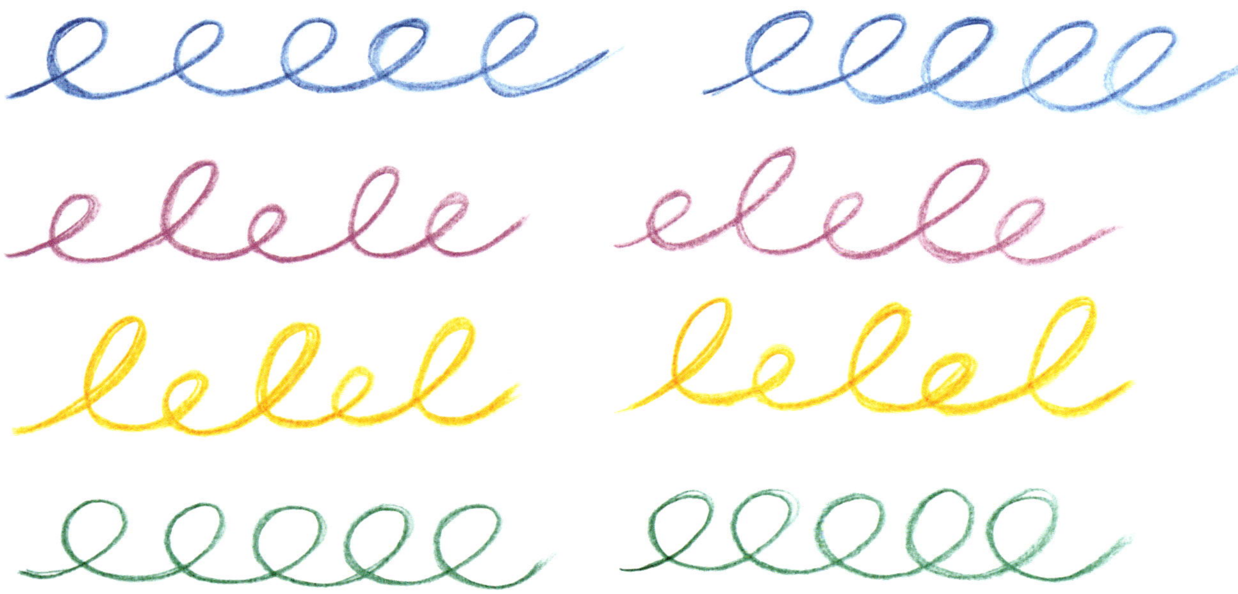

- The children can draw in both directions, from left to right, and from right to left. Each form can be traced over several times (if wished). The lines may not be in exactly the same place but this does not matter.

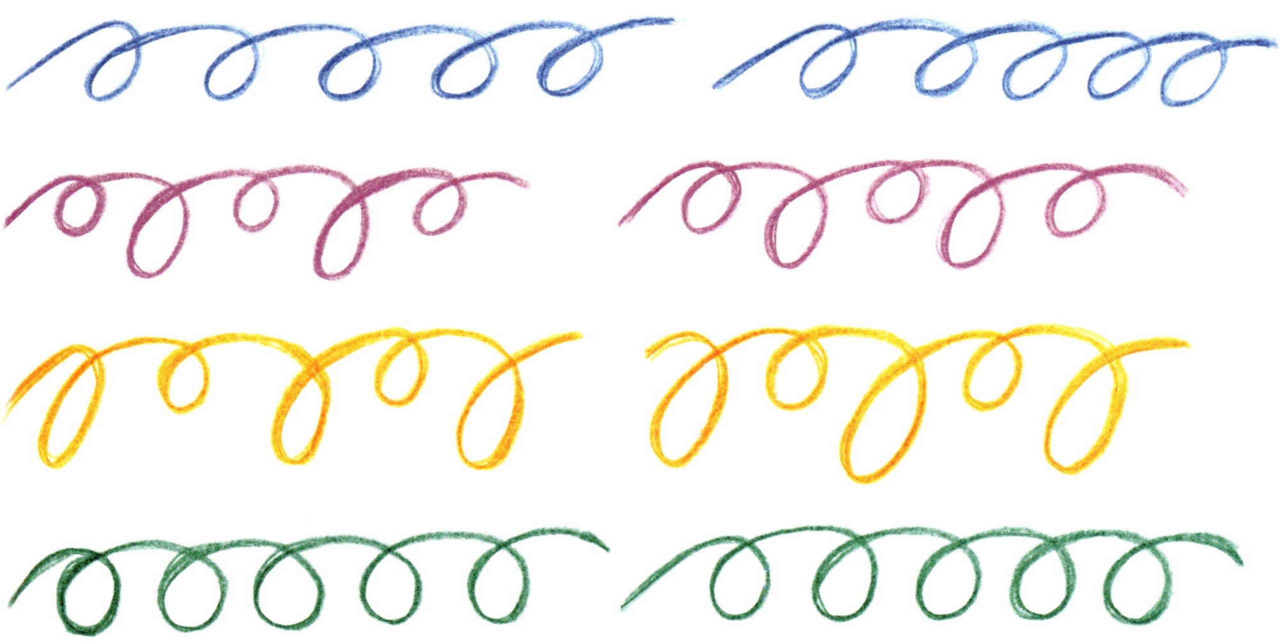

Vocabulary:
Flowing, looping, continuous, larger, smaller.

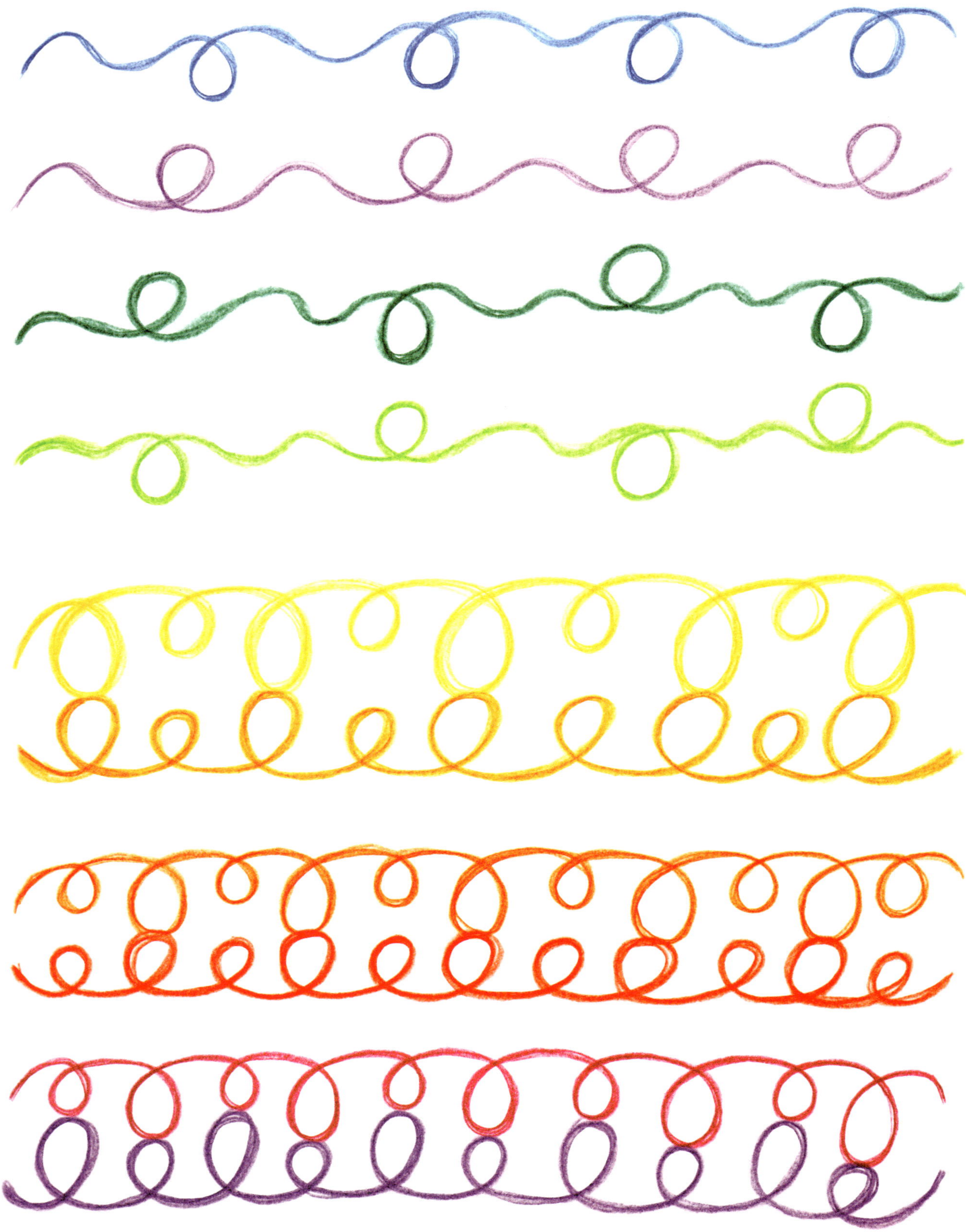

The line transforms

In these exercises the forms gradually change in a step-by-step process. The children can draw three or four times along each form in both directions. They will see and experience the gradual transformation from one line to the next. They may need two or three lessons to complete all the forms, and will enjoy repeating the whole process again. Here they are learning:

- How to compare
- Observation
- How forms are related
- How a process happens
- How a form transforms into a new related form.

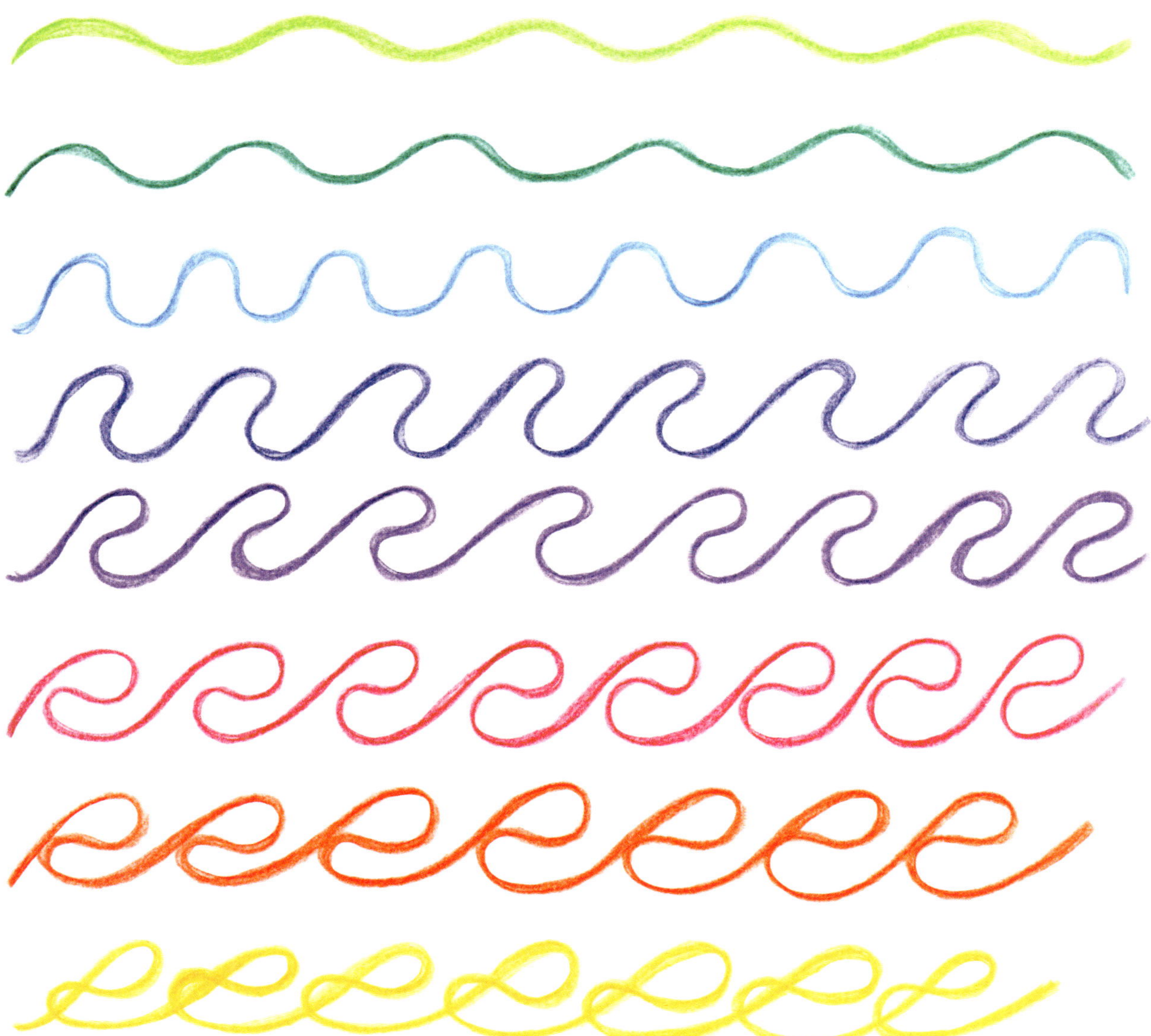

Vocabulary

Transforming, changing, gradually, compare, process, separate, touching, overlapping.

Straight lines and curves

- These forms need plenty of space on the page. Begin with the straight lines.
- Use one colour so that the forms stay integrated. This also allows the children to experience the contrasts in the movement gestures without interruption.
- If the children wish to repeat these forms for homework, then two contrasting colours can be used.

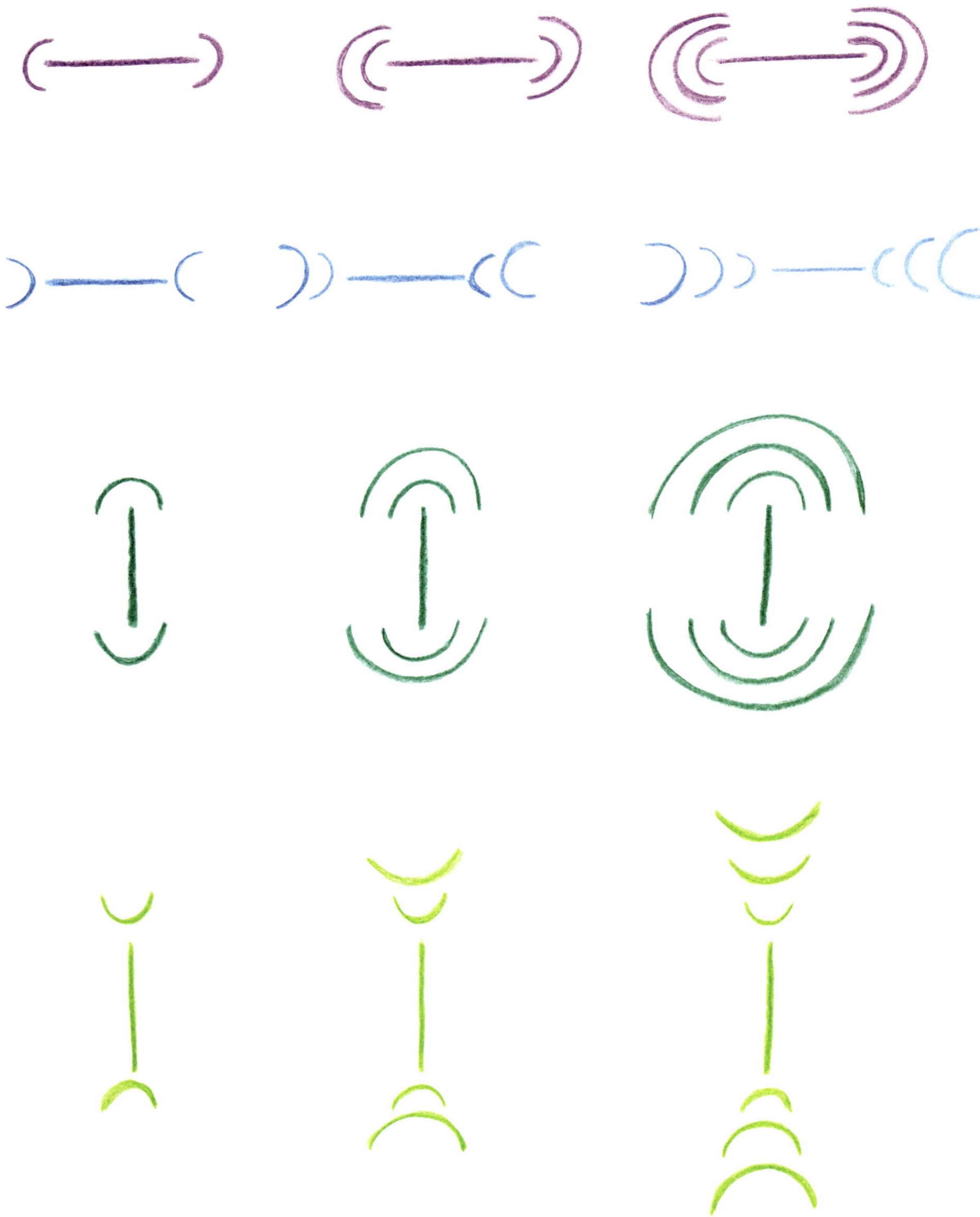

- These forms require considerable skill and concentration. Draw the four straight lines then the curves beginning with the four smallest curves, then the second curves and finally the four larger curves.
- Using one colour integrates these forms. If the children are repeating them for homework, two colours may be used.

Here the children are learning:

- Orientation in four directions in space – above, below, left, right.
- How to draw a balanced form.
- How to create symmetry in a form.
- How to relate varying sizes in the curved forms.
- Comparison of size – small, larger, largest.

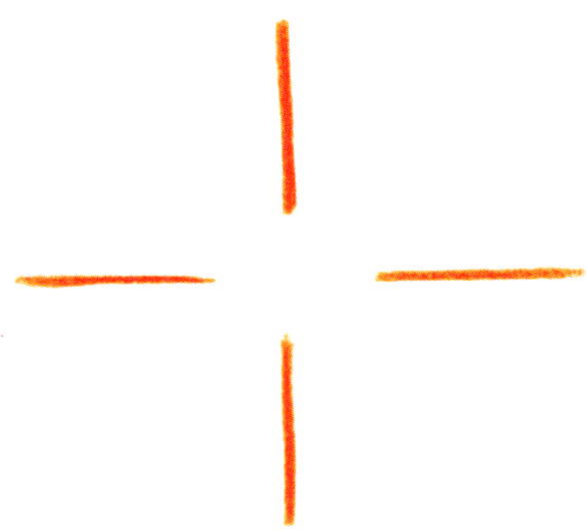

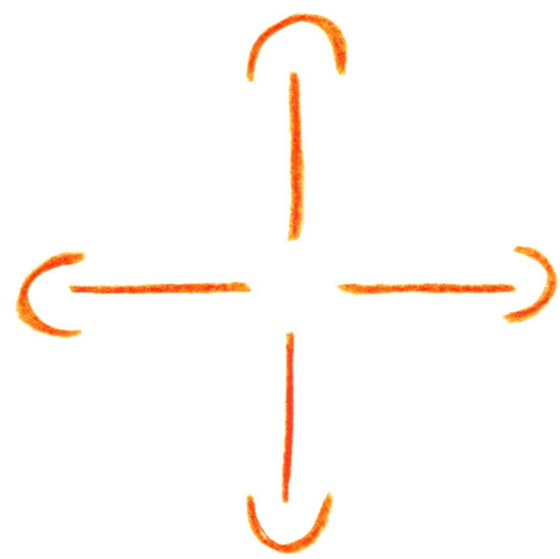

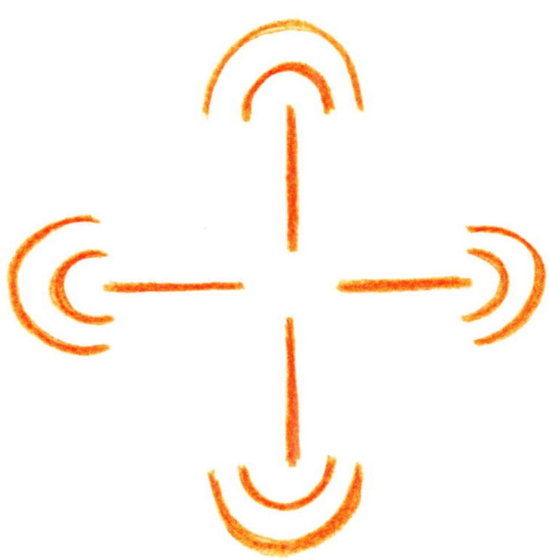

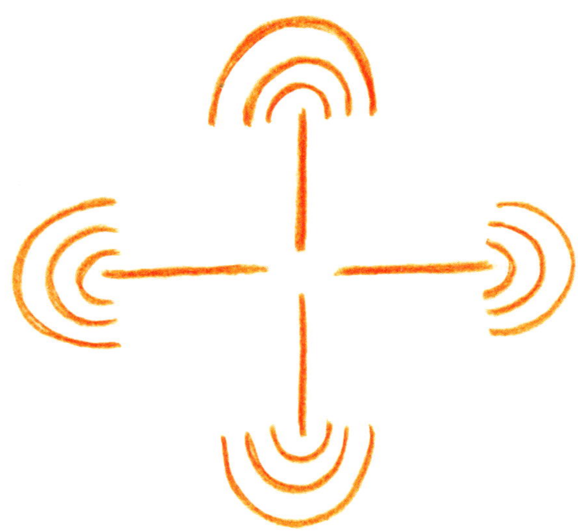

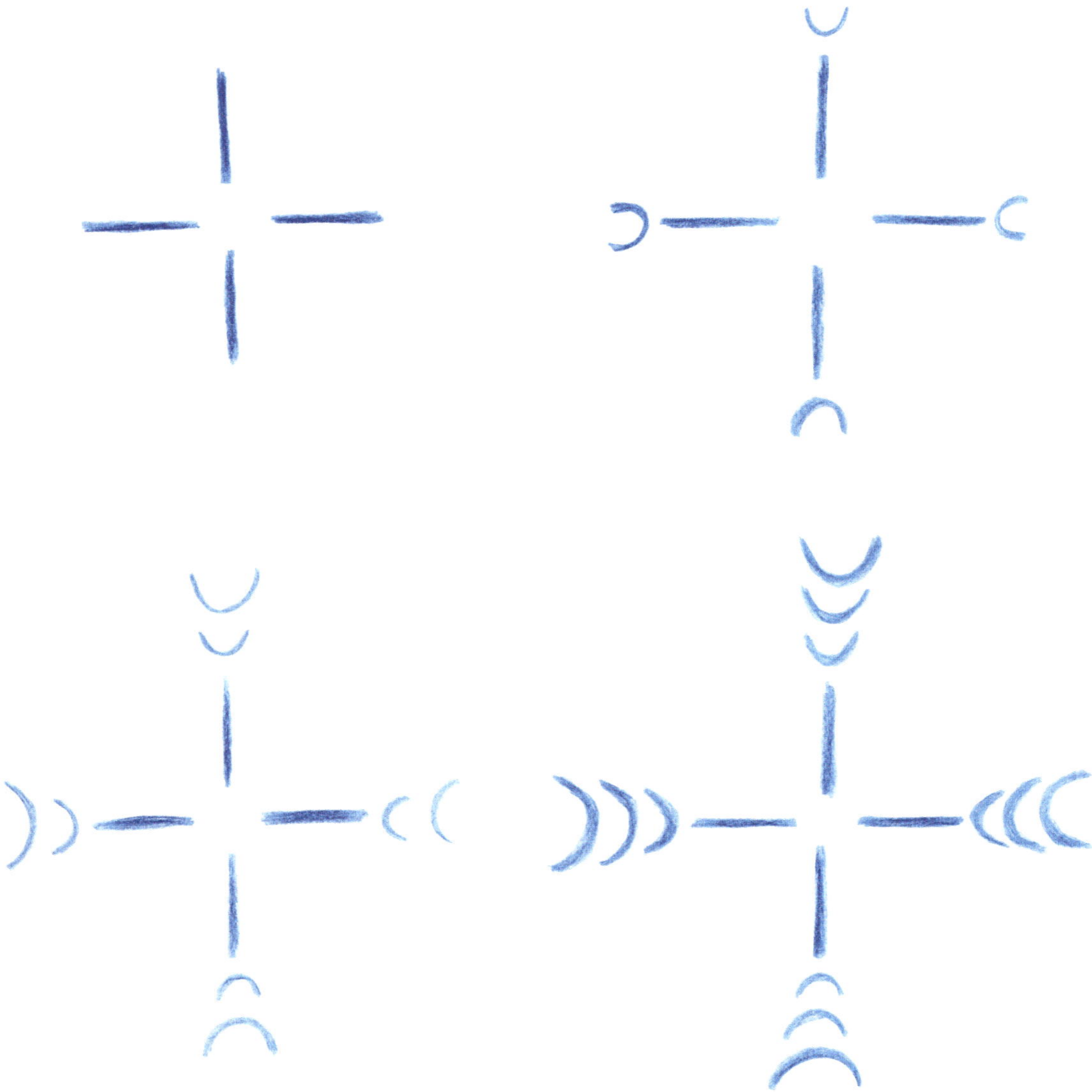

Variations:

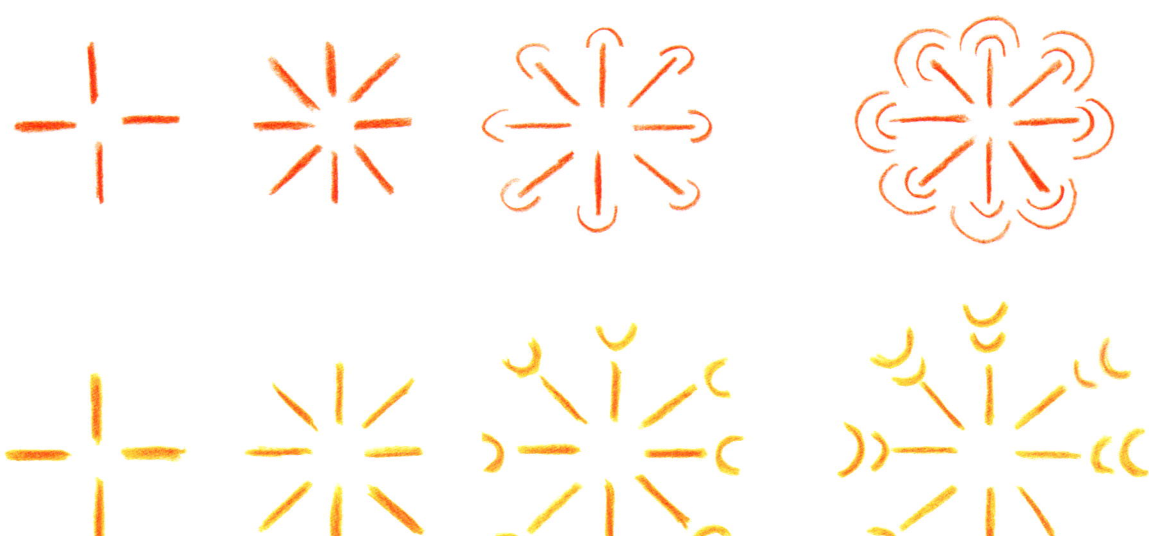

- Draw the straight lines first.
- All the lines can be drawn in both directions.
- Use different colours.
- Remember that these are drawn freehand – they will not be absolutely perfect.

The children are learning:

- Fine-motor skills.
- Observation of details.
- How to draw with greater control and co-ordination.

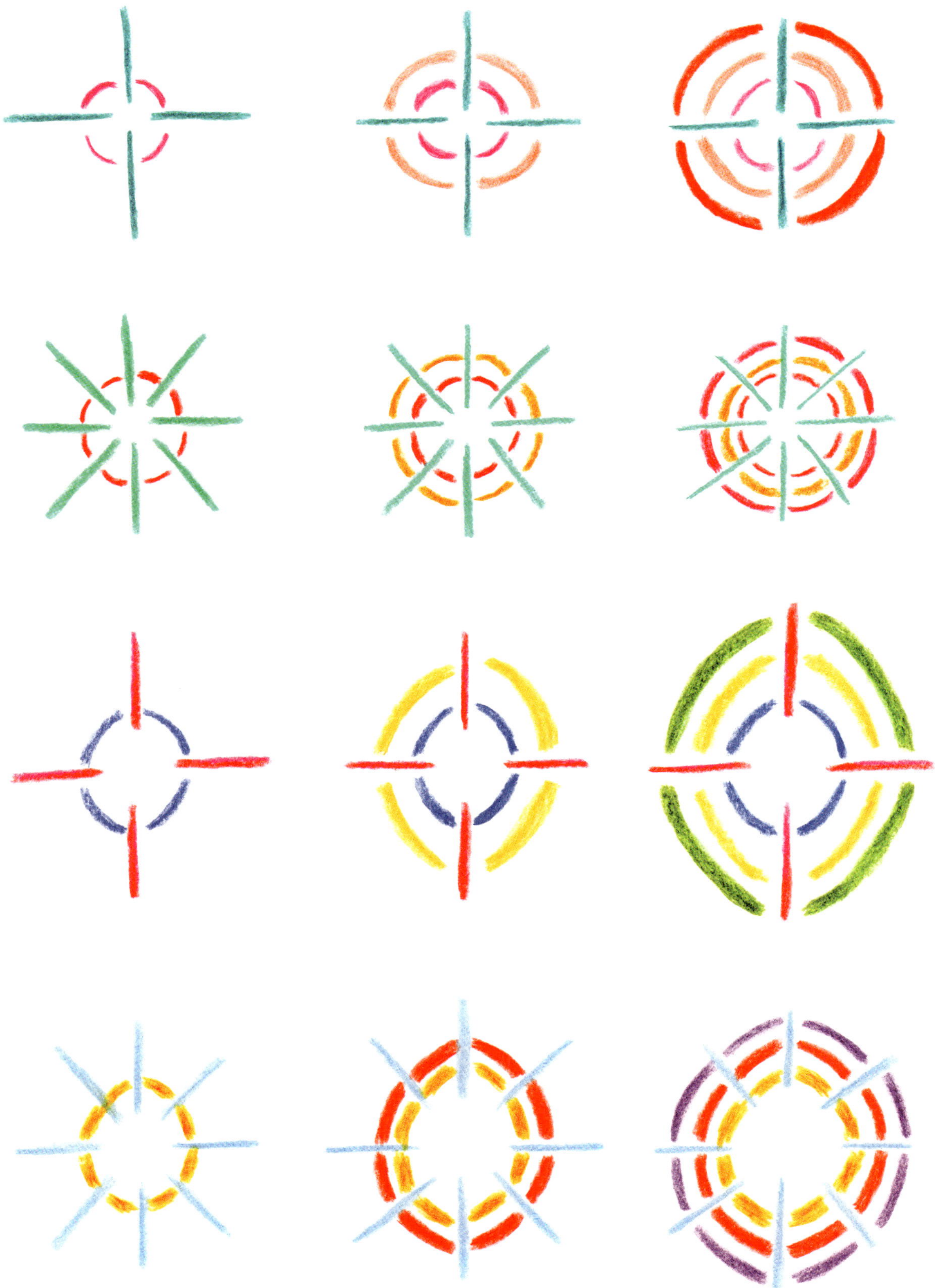

Organic forms

These forms 'loosen up' the more formal structured forms that the children have been drawing. Organic forms have curving lines with movements which are fluid and flexible. It will be seen, however, that they have definite rhythms and patterns with clearly defined centres. They have harmonious relationships between the centre and the periphery. The sequences are also related, with progressive variations in the movements in the outer form. These need to be drawn quite carefully, but each child's work will be individual, as organic forms are not identical, although the children will need to experience the overall relationships and to make these clear in their own drawings. The forms can be drawn over several times to help develop the movements.

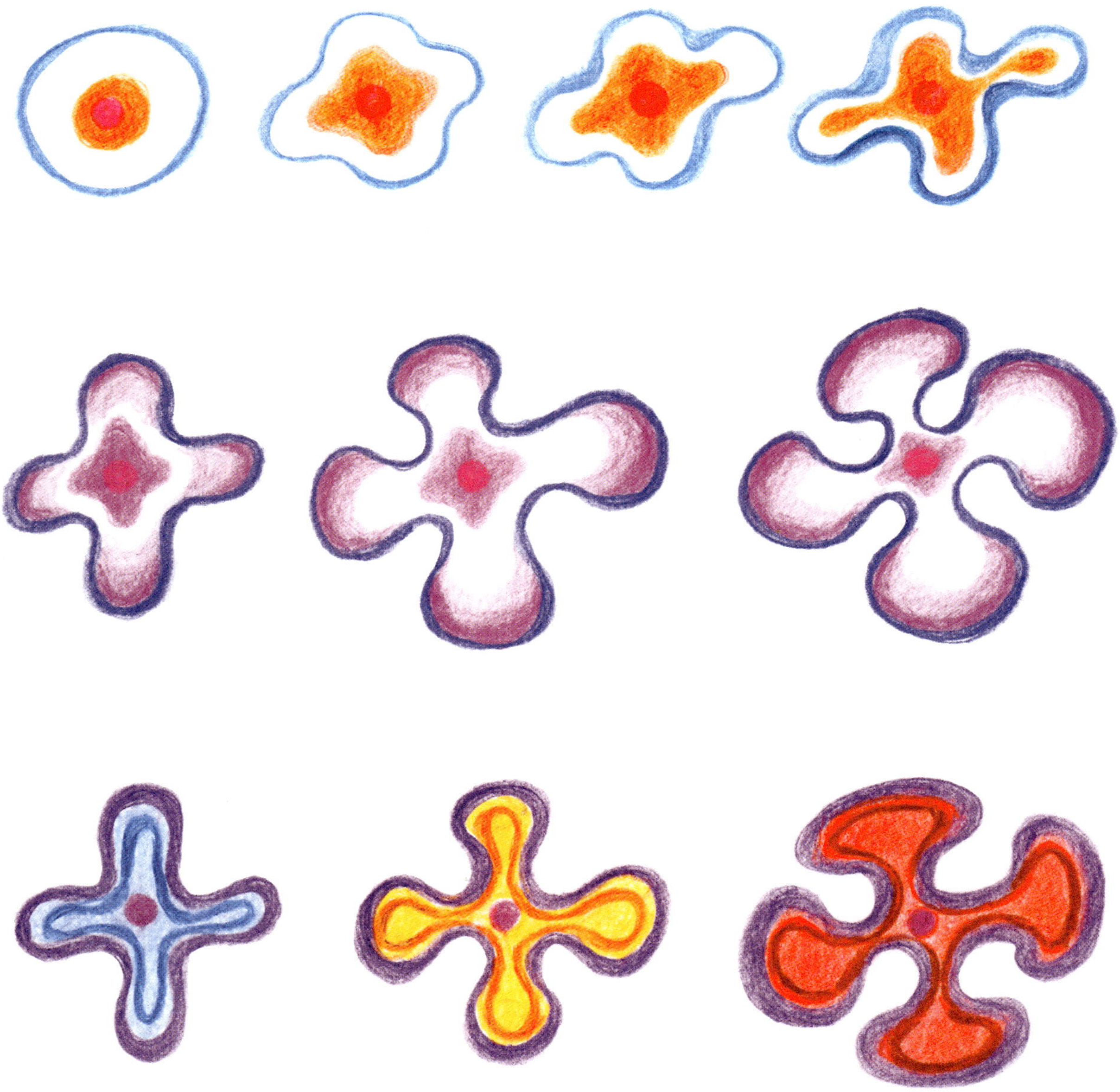

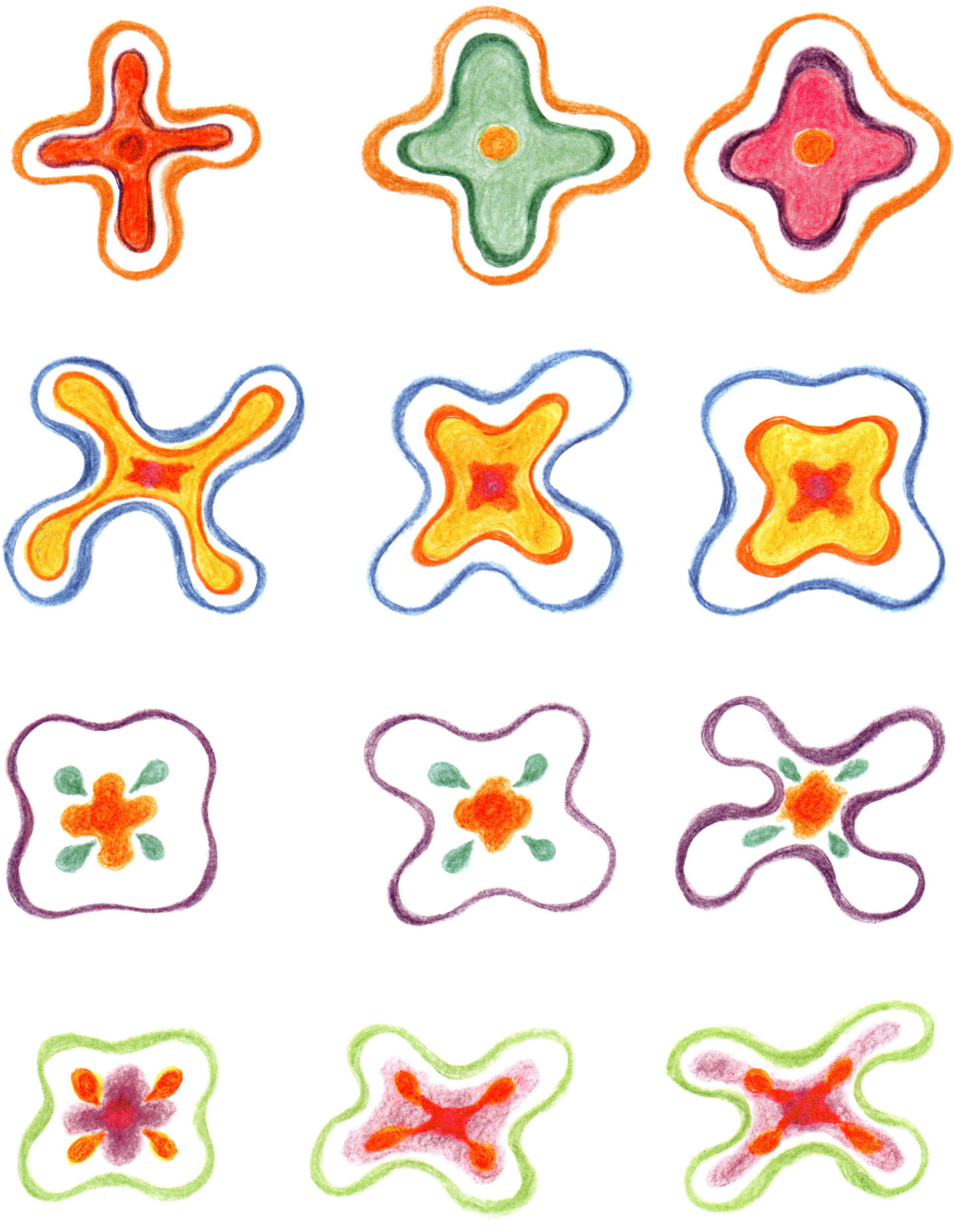

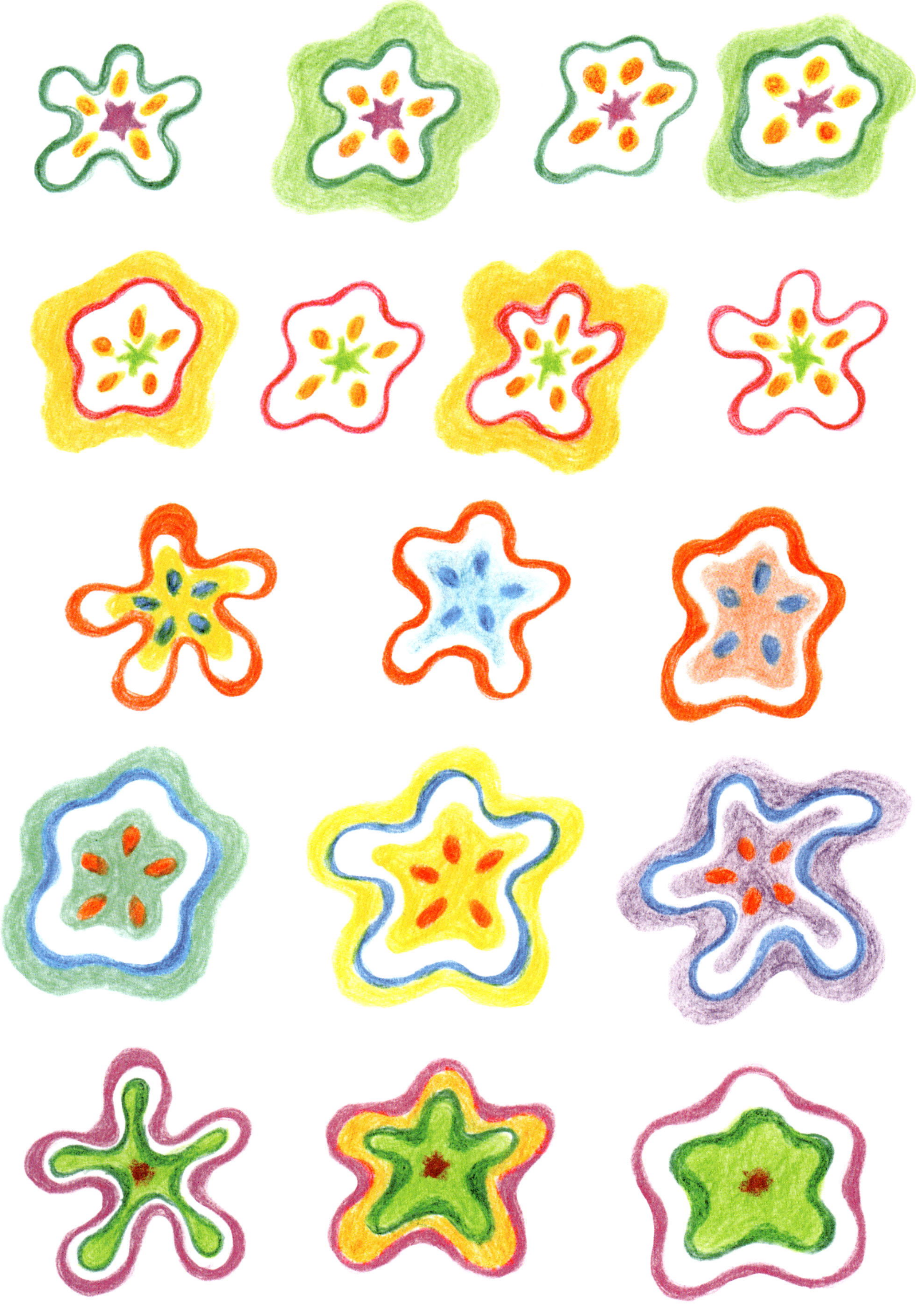

Structured forms: Angles

The children return now to more structured forms, exploring angles and how angles can relate to create interesting designs and patterns. To help with the structures some children might like to draw 'helpful dots' to show them where the points of the angles are. They can do this a few times, and then draw the angles without them. The angles do not need to touch. Patterns can be developed by adding straight lines.

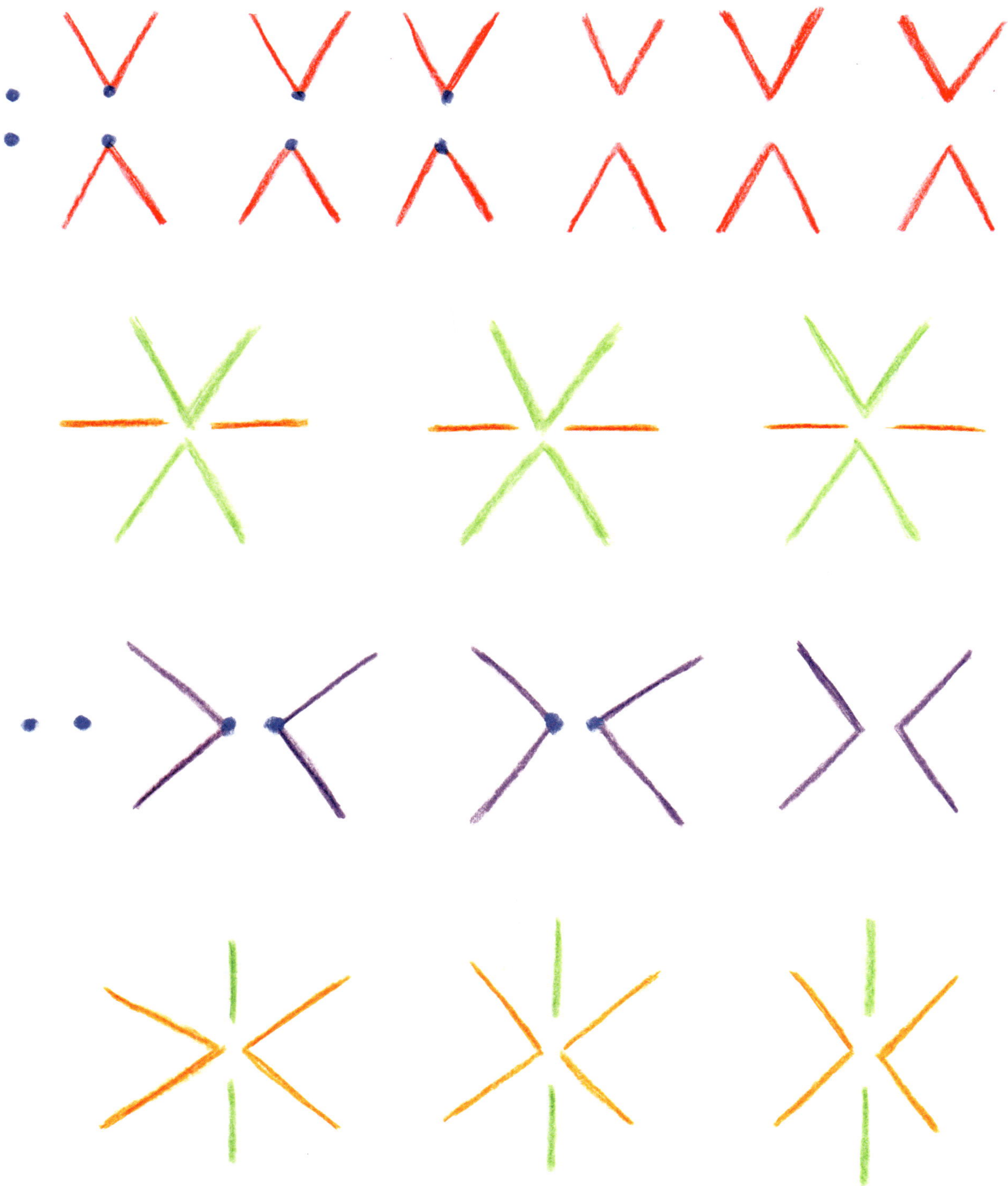

In these angle forms, the angles begin narrow and then step-by-step become wider. Here the children are learning:

- How to compare
- How to draw a progressive sequence
- How to relate one form to another.

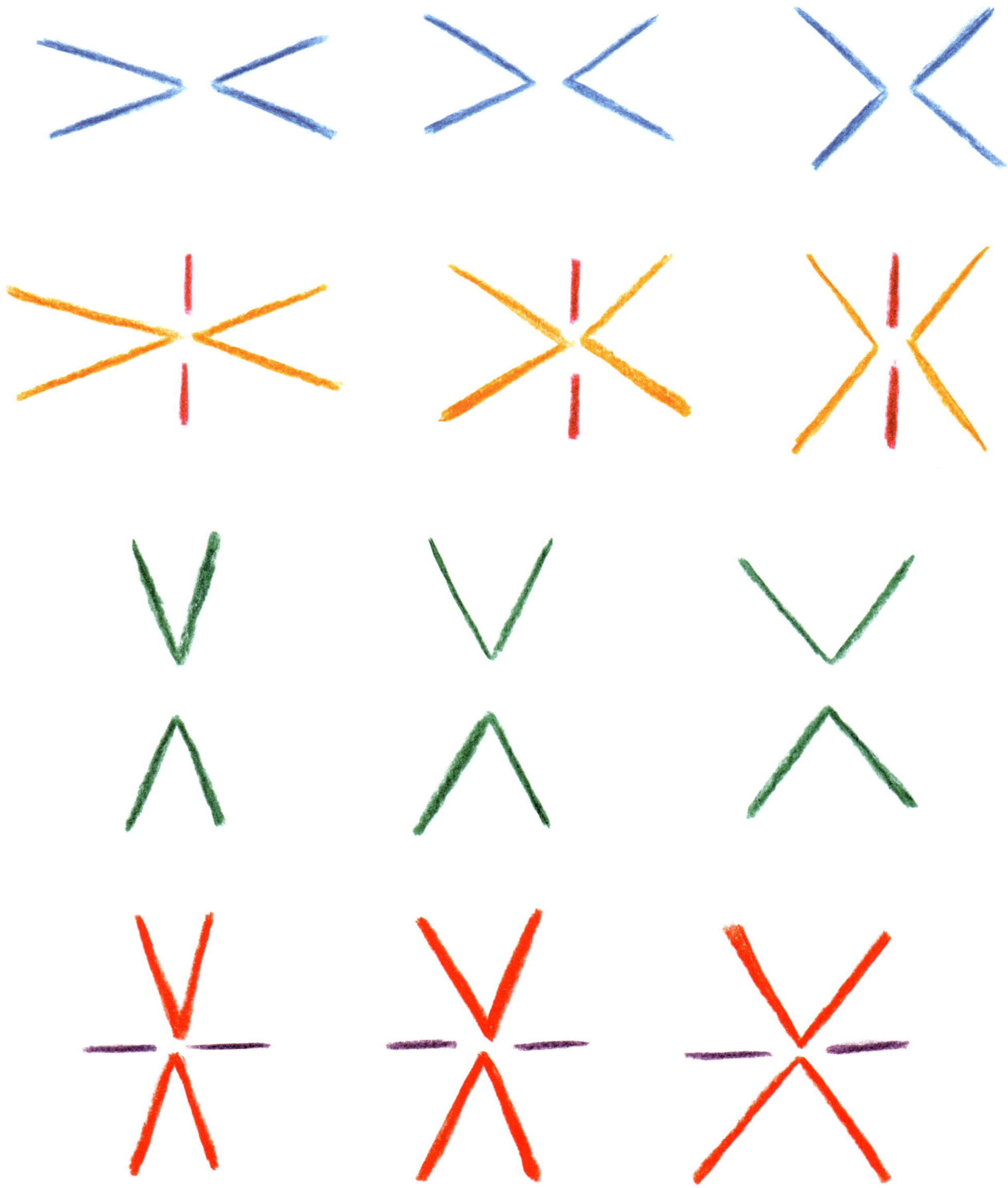

Now the children draw the angles with the wide part of the angles near to each other and the points outwards.

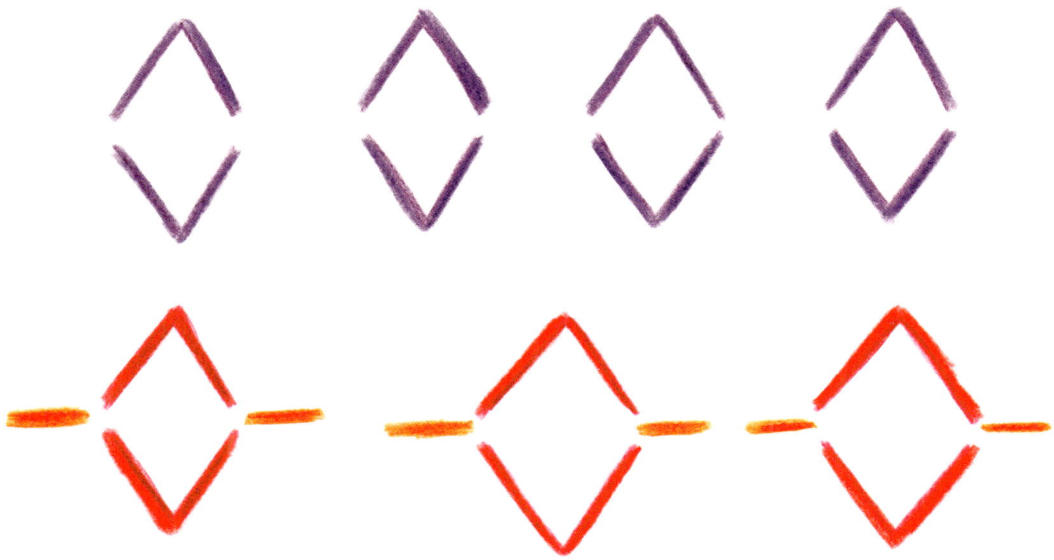

Here the angles fit inside each other:

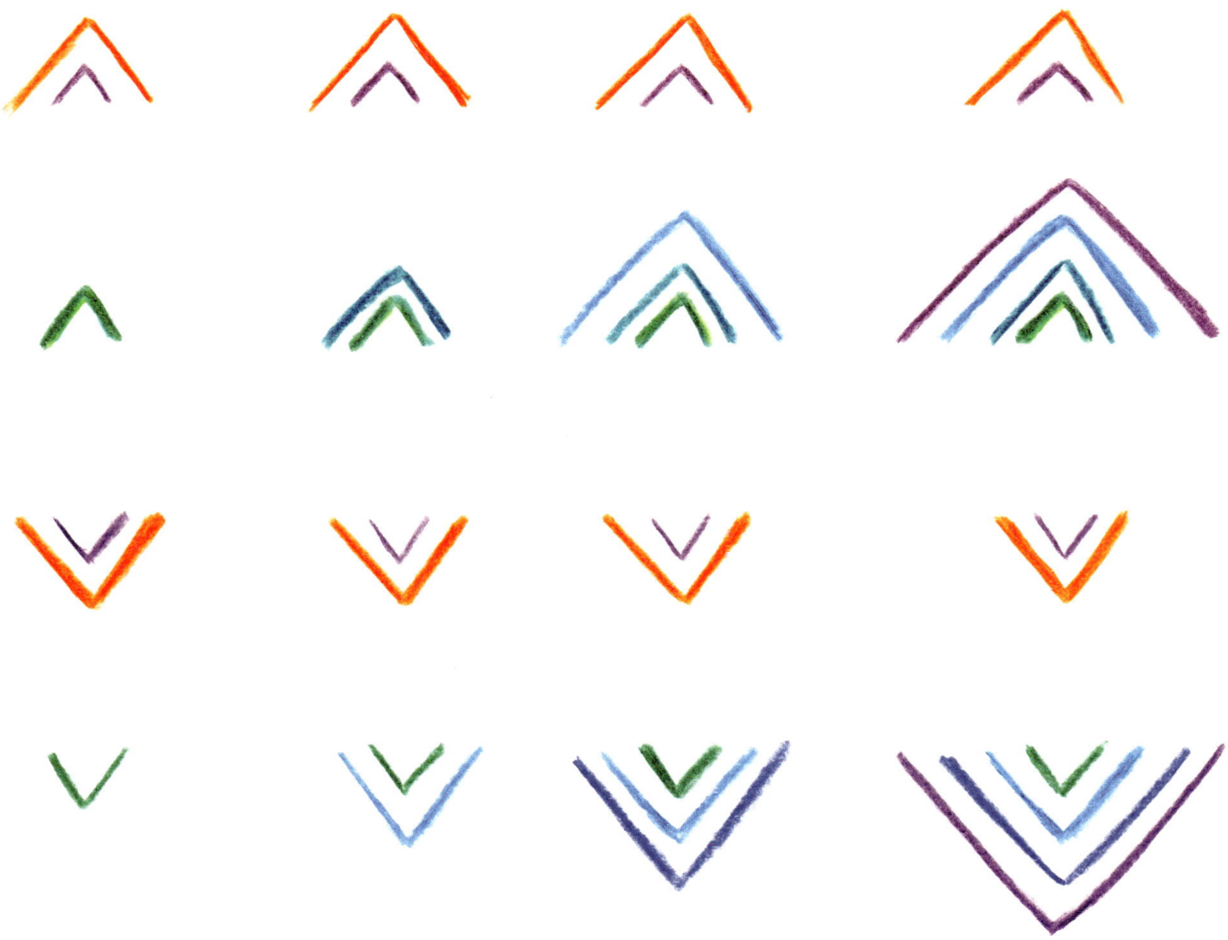

Diagonal Lines

The children can practise drawing diagonal lines, placing them in various relationships. Firstly they can experiment with 'free' forms, drawing lots of diagonal lines to make interesting patterns:

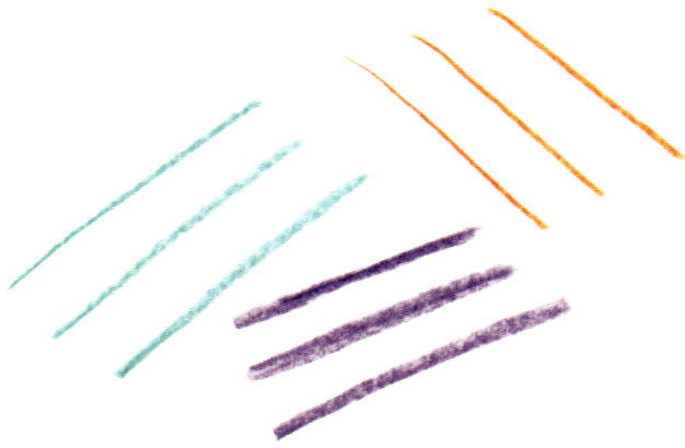
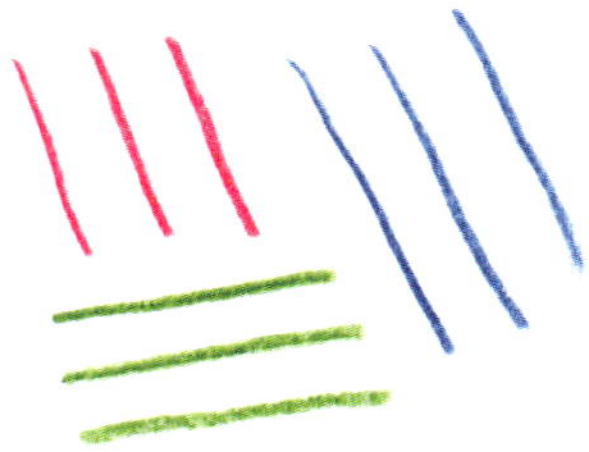
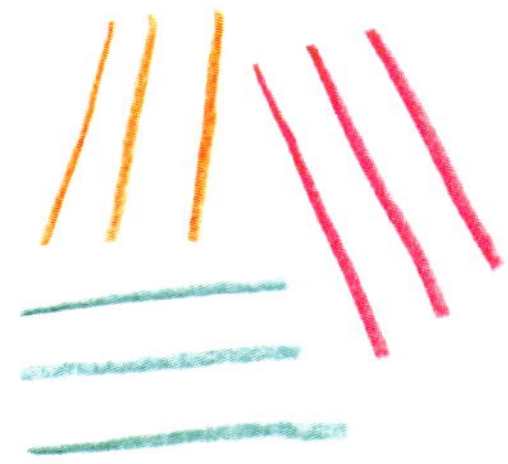

Then the diagonal lines can be placed in definite ways:

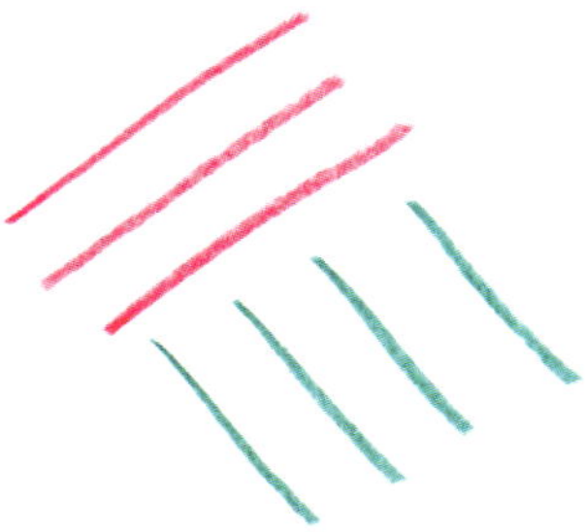
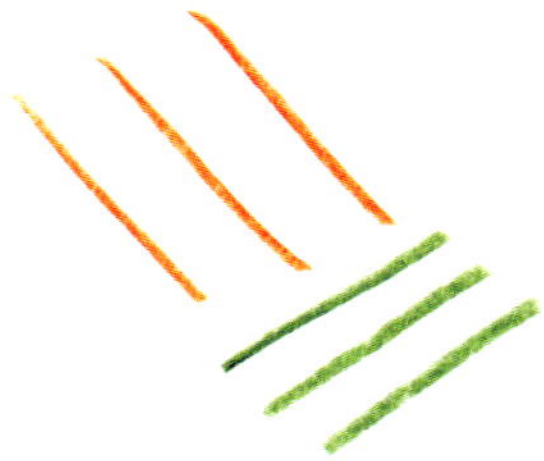
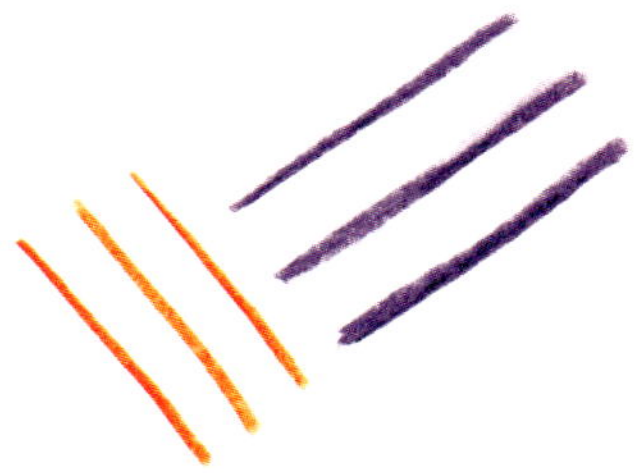

Drawing different lengths can create balanced forms:

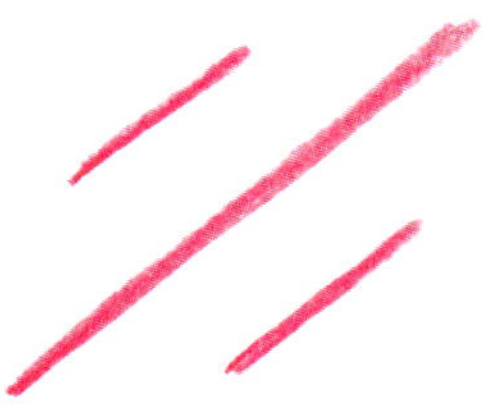
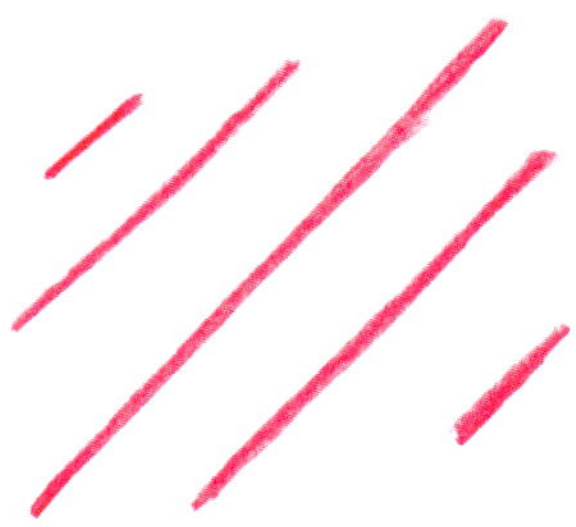
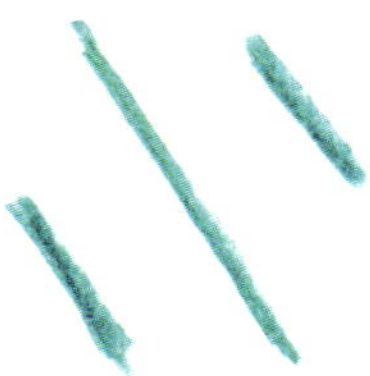
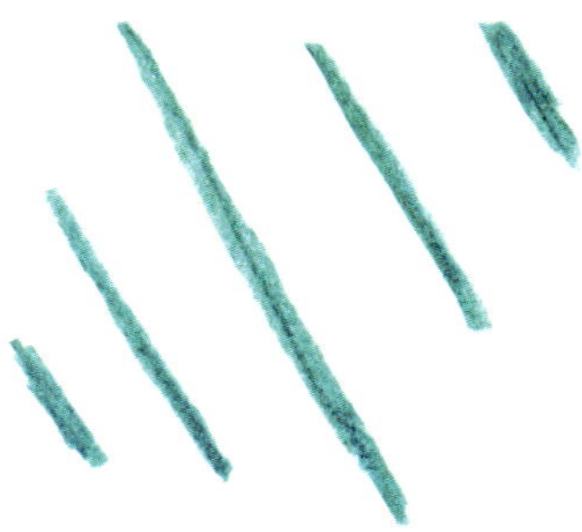

Circles and angles

Draw a whole row of evenly spaced circles, quite close together. Draw over each circle four or five times in both directions if wished.

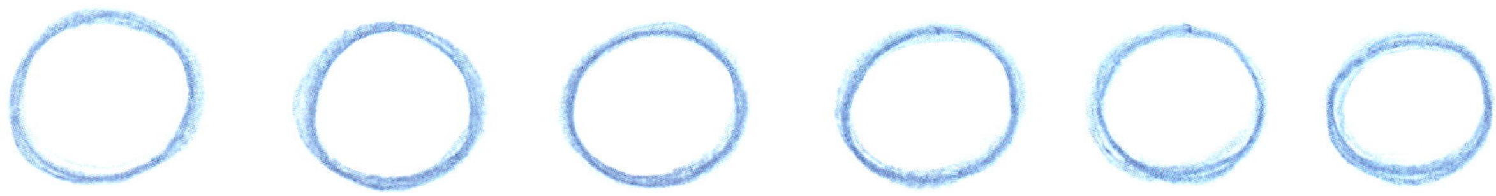

Draw a second row of circles.
With a second colour draw angles above them. Each circle has a roof! The children may need to draw over the circles again, to get them under their roofs.

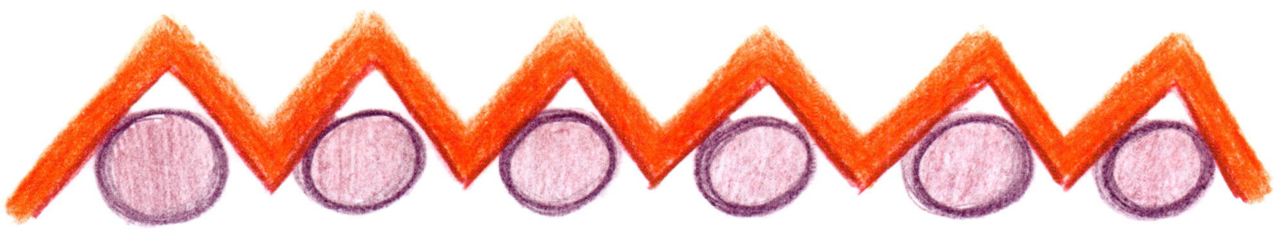

Draw another row of circles.
Draw the angles below in one continuous zig-zag line. Now the circles seem to sit inside the angles. Draw over the circles again if necessary.

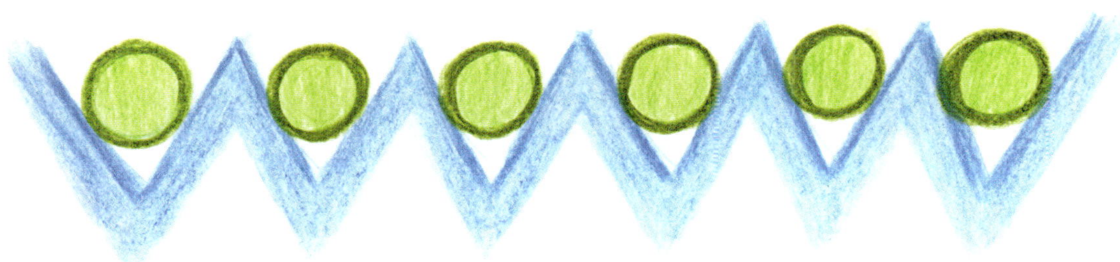

Draw two circles standing on top of each other.
Next draw angles above and below the circles.
Now the circles are inside a diamond form.

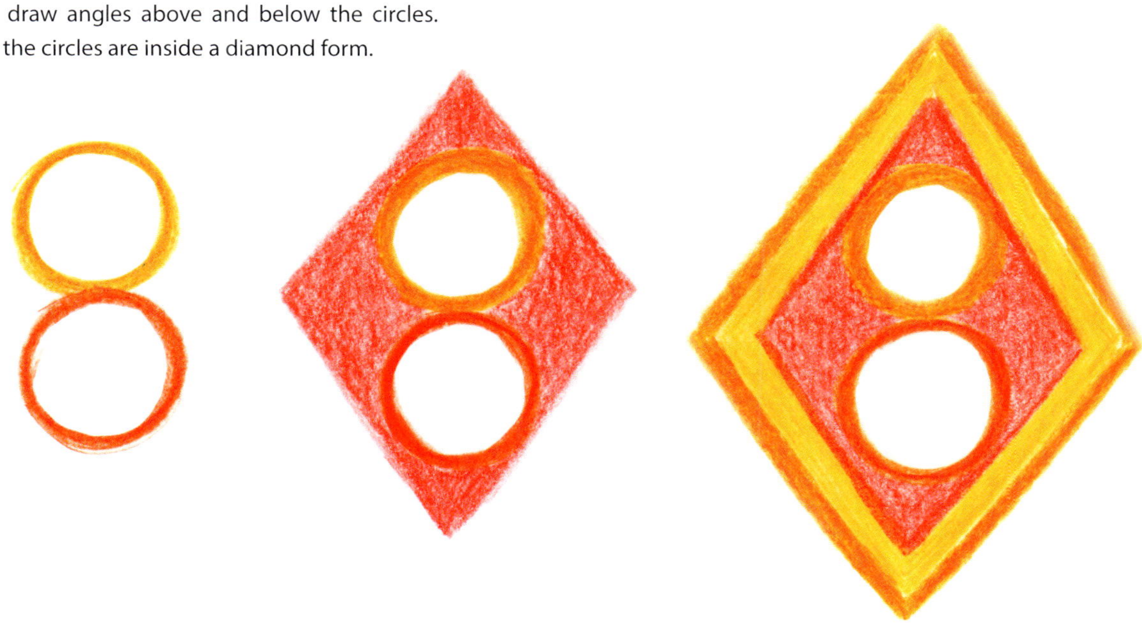

Circles and triangles

The children draw a continuous line to make a triangle, drawing over it several times in both directions. They need to 'feel' their way into the shape of the triangle. 'Tri' means three, so the children will be able to count three connected lines which create three angles. Then they draw the circles, inside the triangles, then outside. Again, they can draw several times over the circles, in both directions, so that they experience the circular forms.

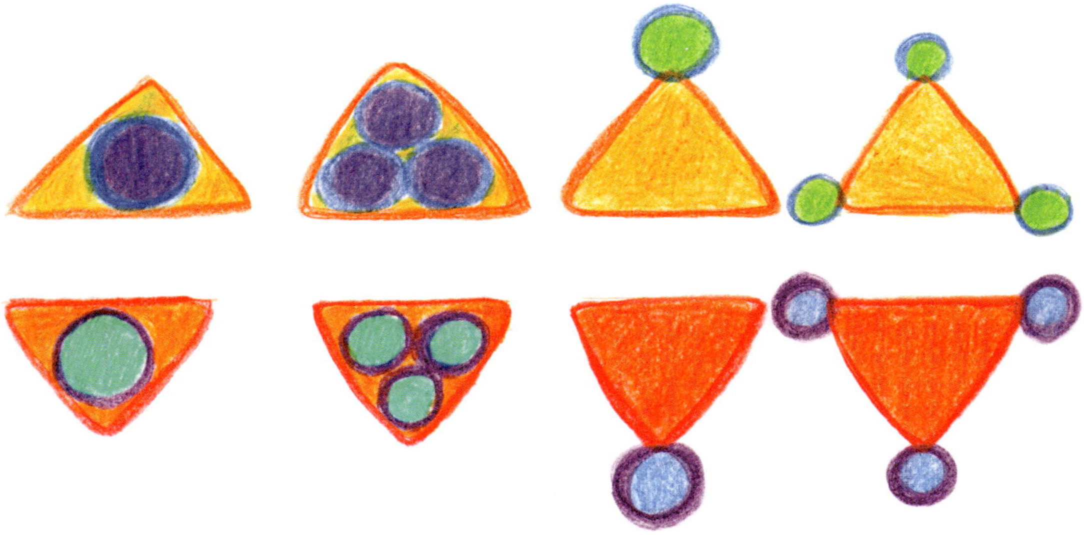

Can we change a circle into a triangle?

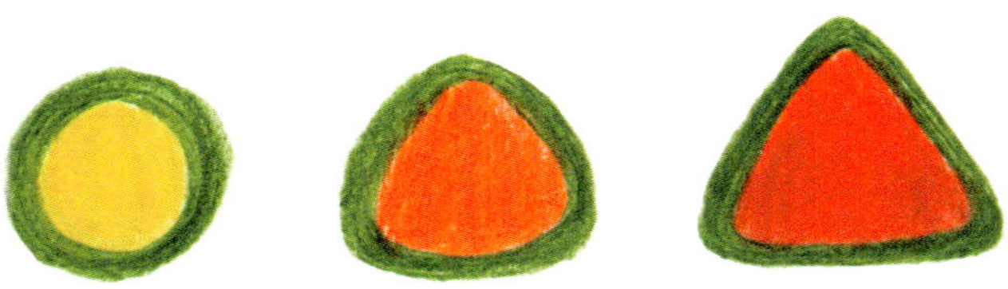

And a triangle into a circle?

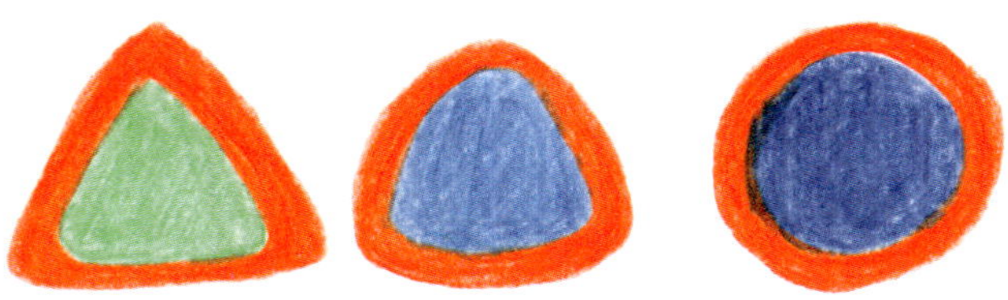

Can we change a circle into a triangle then back into a circle?

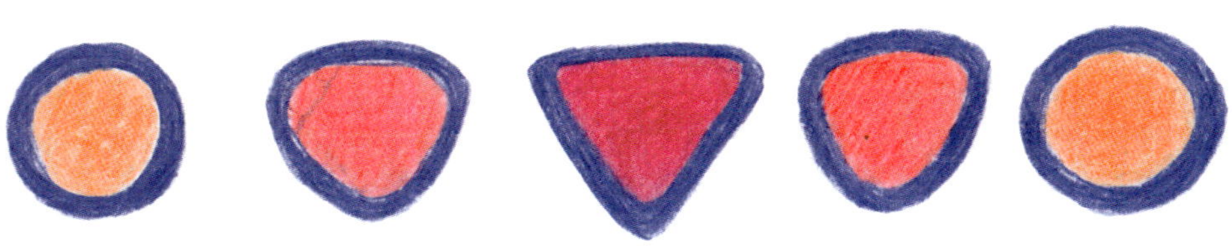

When the children have drawn their forms, they can enjoy colouring them in. This can be done during the lesson, in their spare classroom time or for homework. Colouring these forms will consolidate and strengthen the children's experiences.

Flowing lines crossing over

The children can now return to flowing lines that create figures of eight (8) or lemniscates. It may take many times to practise the lines crossing in the centre of the forms. It is important that the children experience walking these forms, and drawing them in the air. This will provide spatial orientation (in walking the form) and an experience of rhythmic movement (when drawing in the air). The forms can be drawn many times over in a very flowing way.

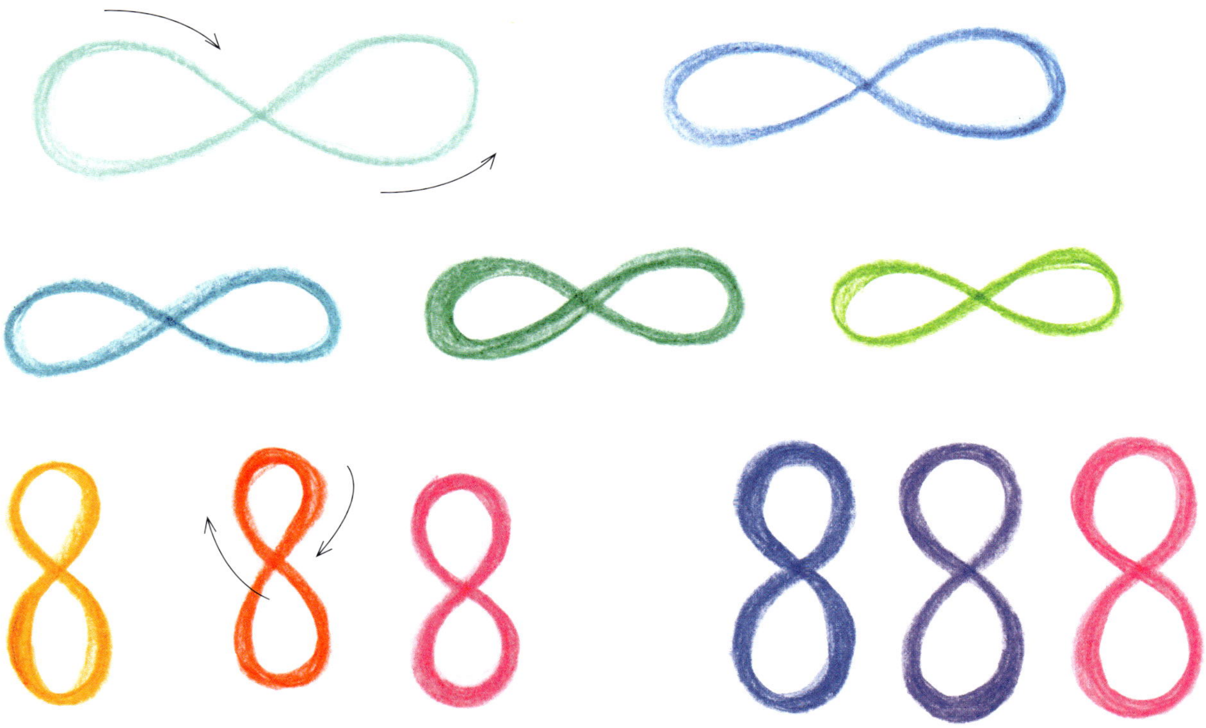

Two separate forms which cross over in the centre.

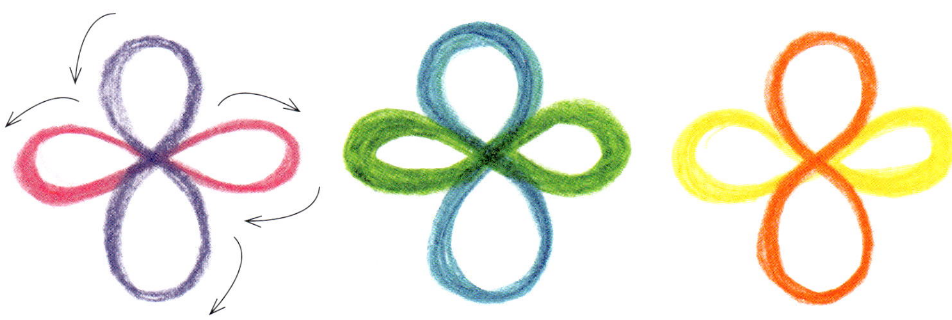

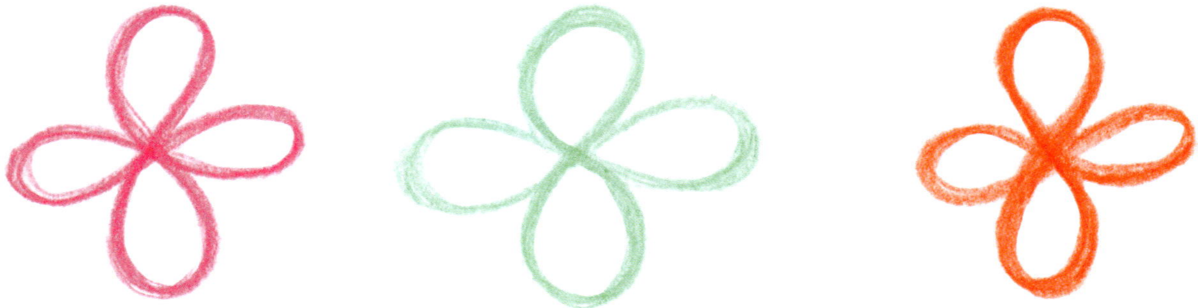

These forms are drawn in one continuous flowing movement which begins either on the horizontal or the vertical form, but always crosses over in the centre. Some of the lines might also cross over on the diagonal. Allow the children to experiment, and to enjoy the harmonious rhythm. They will hear this in the sounds which their pencils make when they are drawing!

Draw different sizes and colour them. The children can create many different colour combinations so that the forms look like brightly coloured flowers.

Flowing forms

In these flowing line forms the children are learning:

- Fine-motor skills
- Linear spatial orientation
- Observation of how a form changes.

They are experiencing the processes of inter-related change, that the changes which occur are in accordance with another form and that the forms are similar but not identical. The children can draw the forms in both directions, from left to right and from right to left, tracing over each form two or three times.

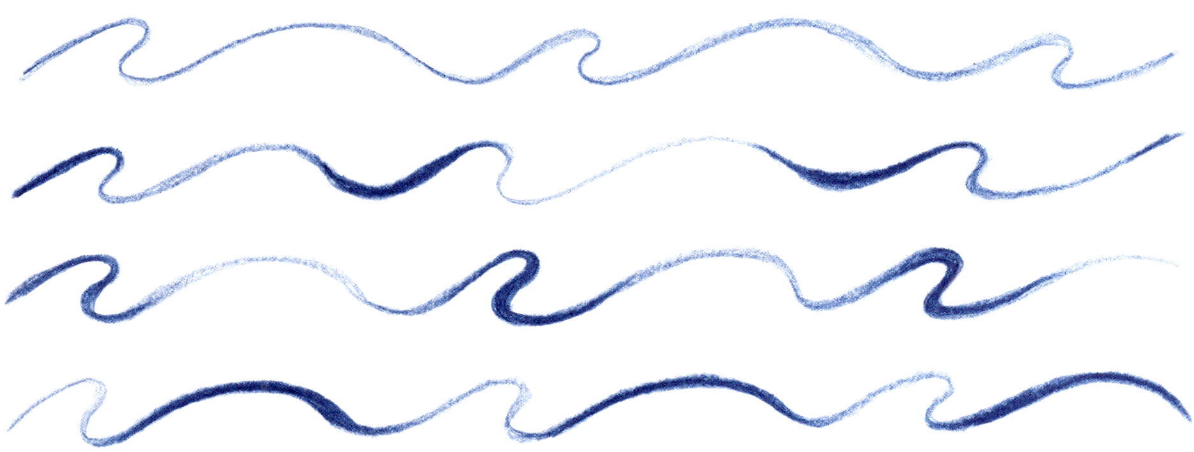

Pressing more firmly with the pencil, and then softly, brings accent and rhythm to these forms.

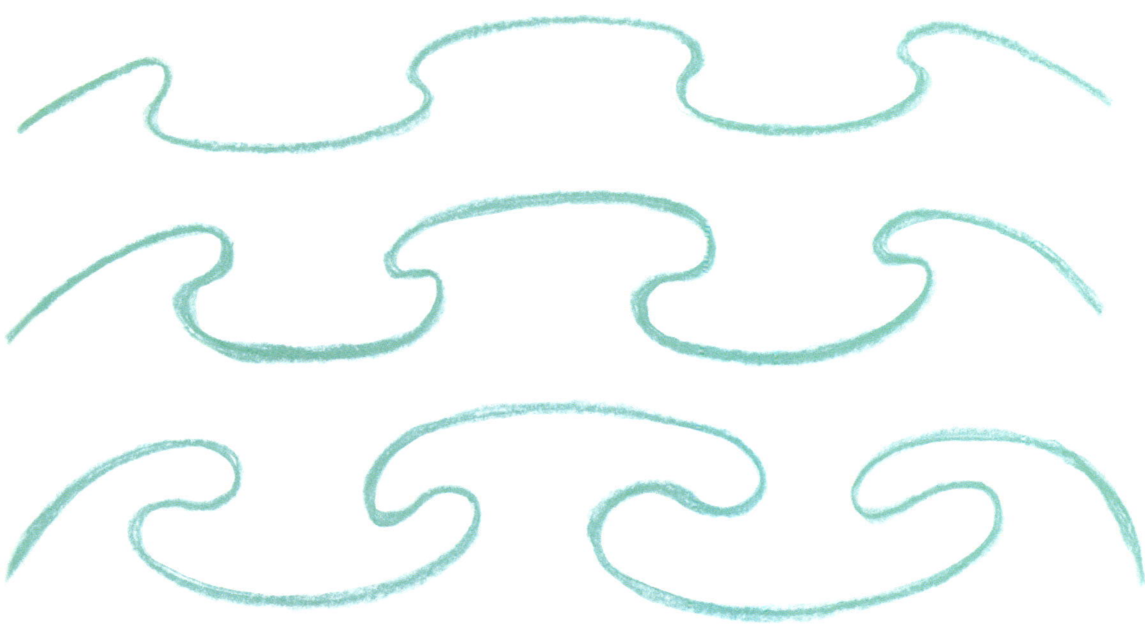

In these forms a gradual transformation of gesture is happening. The forms are changing in an organic way, which develops the movement in a gradual and connected process from one form to the next. This is known as metamorphosis. What do we see when we turn our books upside down?

In these forms the size of a gesture is growing larger. The size is increasing but the form does not change. Draw each form once only so that the movements are very flowing.

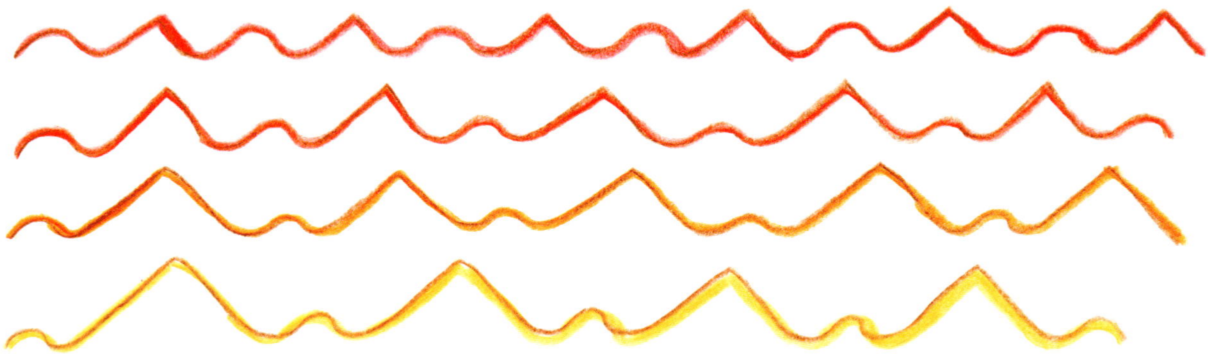

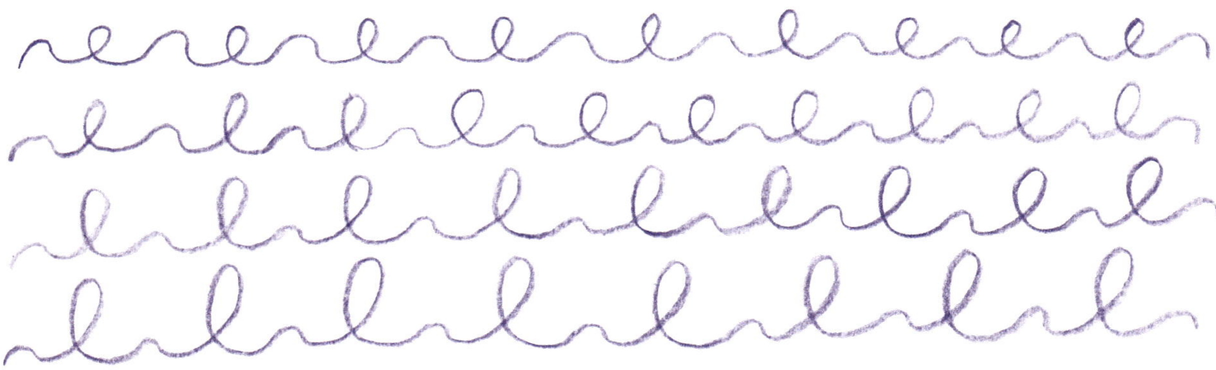

Remember to leave plenty of space between each line so that the growing forms can really grow taller! These forms need to be drawn carefully and not too fast. Although they are flowing they need to be accurate.

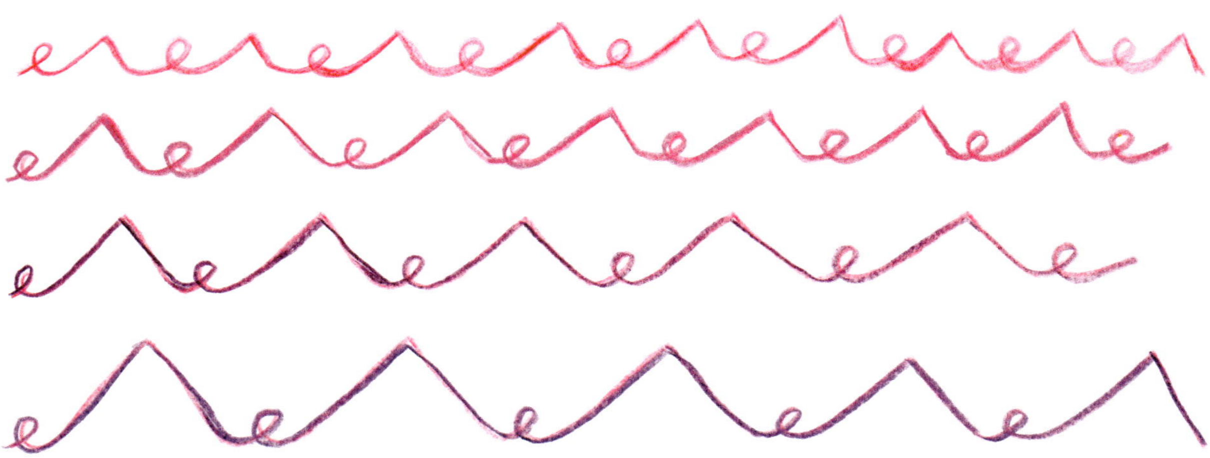

In these flowing lines, two processes are happening. Firstly the forms are balanced above and below – they mirror each other. Secondly, the inner form is changing – it is growing larger. Although the forms are flowing, the children will need to draw them carefully so that they experience these two processes. The children are balancing above and below as well as 'growing' the middle form.

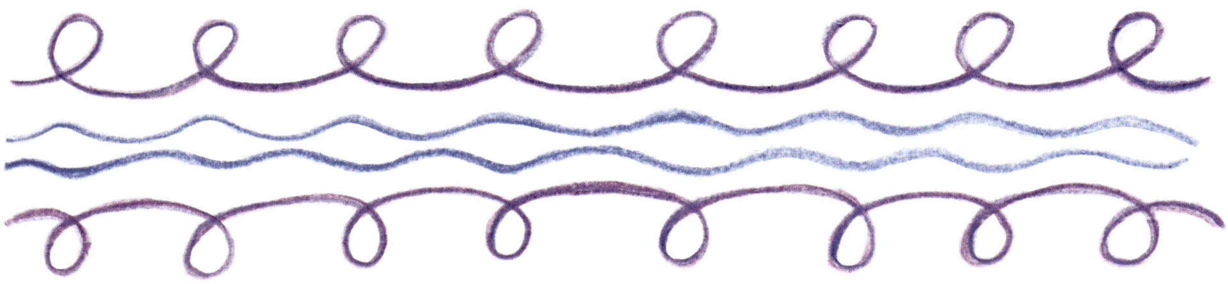

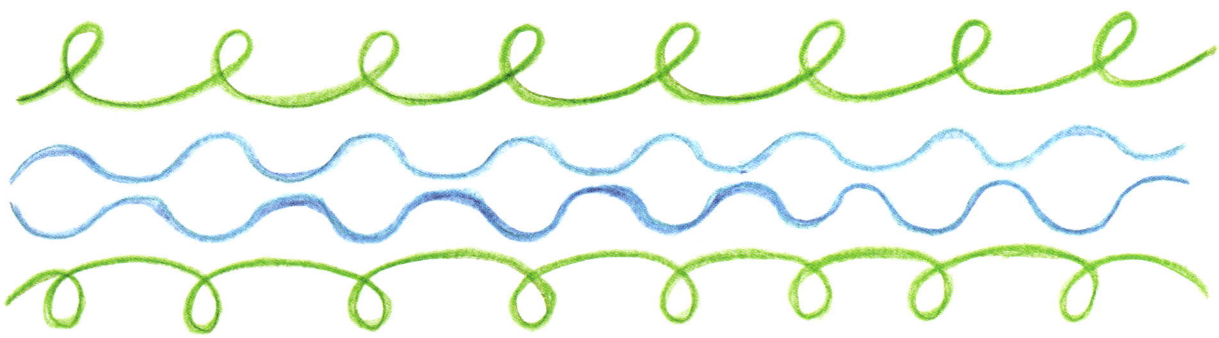

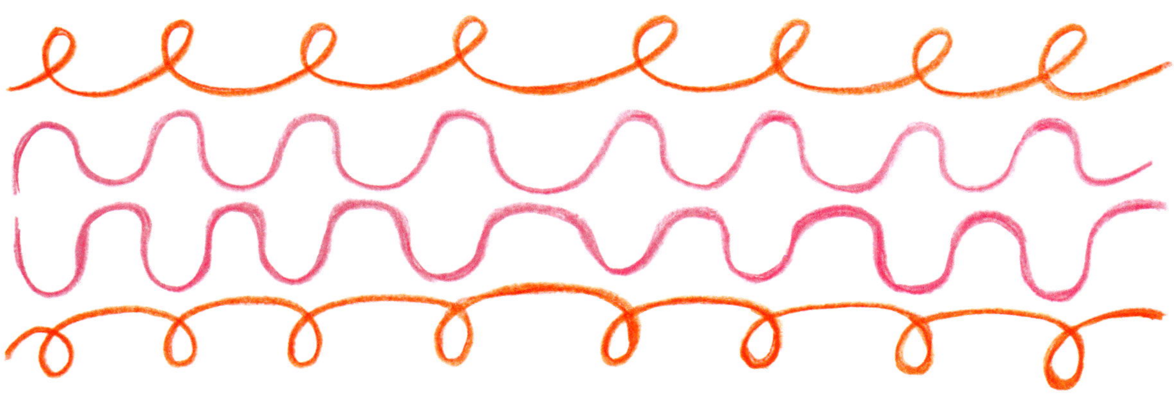

Now the forms change so that the wavy line is outside and the looping forms are on the inside. They need to be drawn carefully so that they reflect, or mirror, above and below.

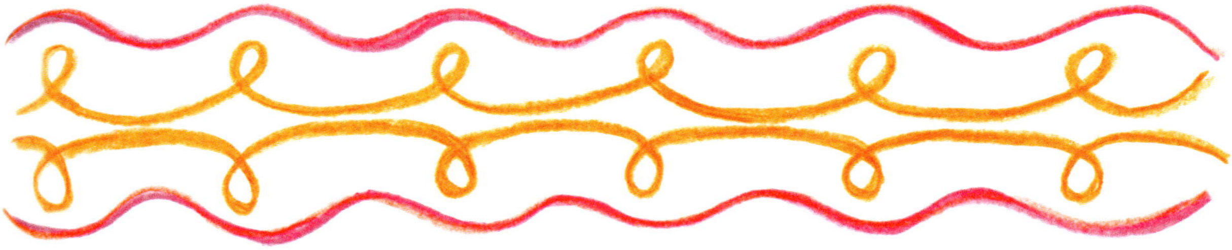

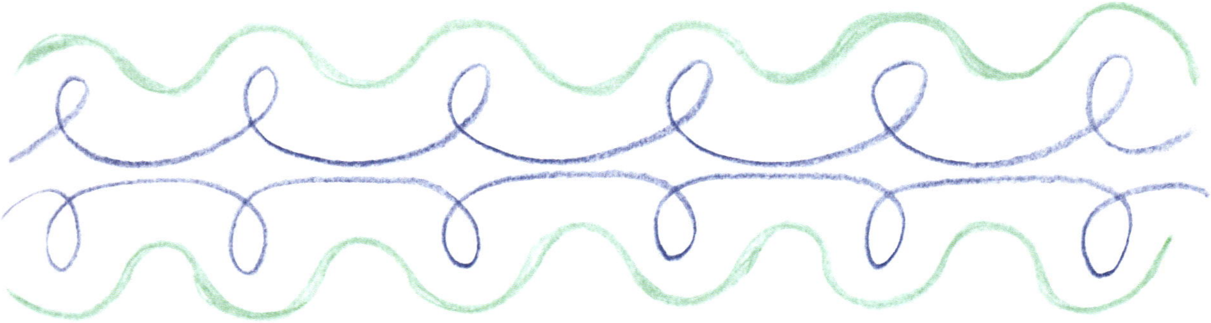

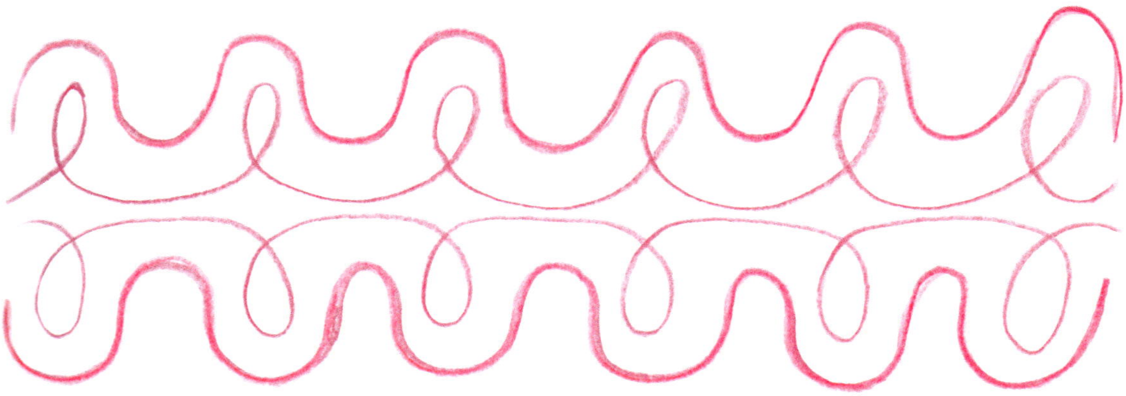

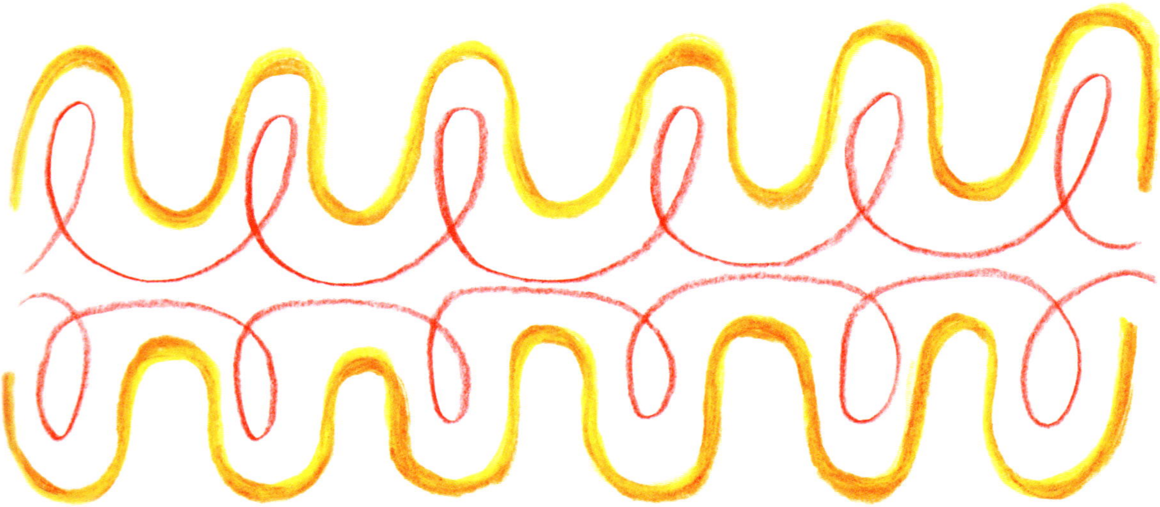

Developing patterns

This basic diagonal leaf-form can be decorated in different ways to create patterns as a border. These forms are also suitable for Class Three.

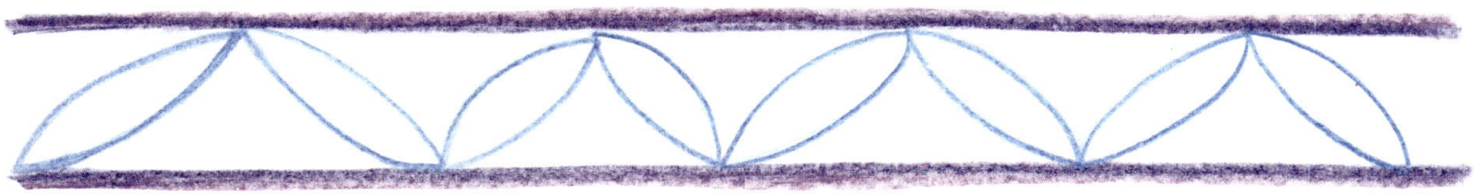

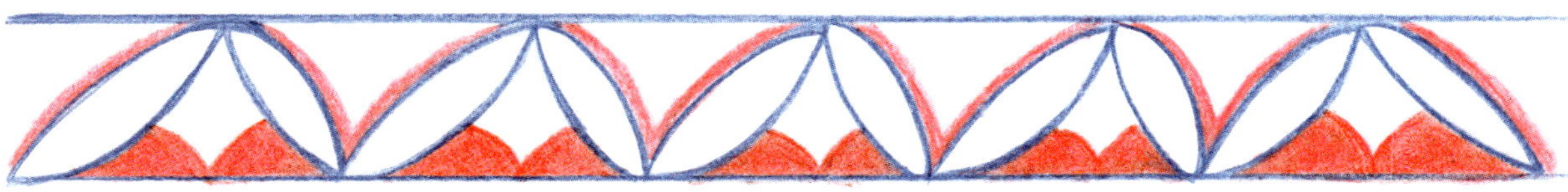

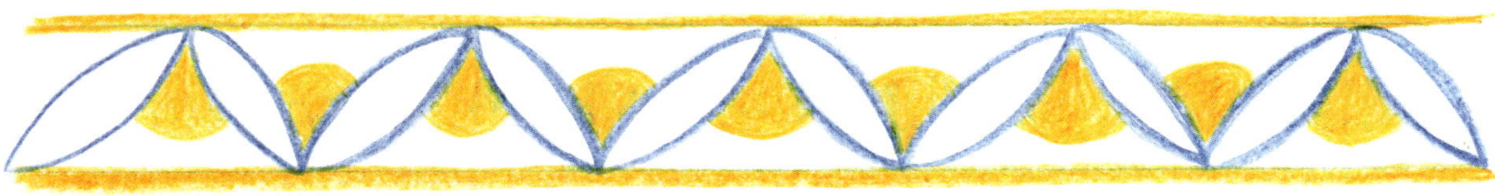

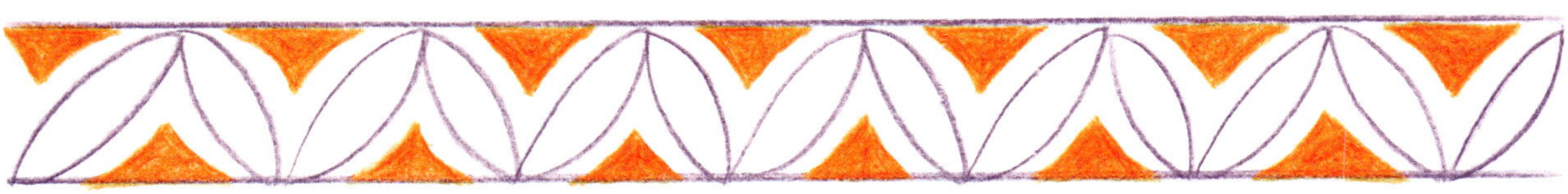

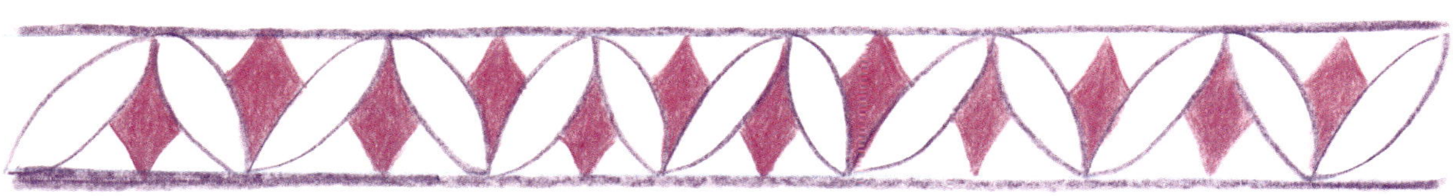

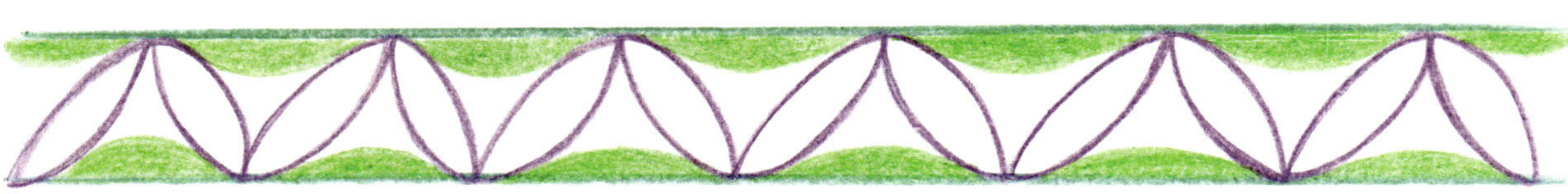

Further patterns arise when a new form-gesture is added, with the repetition creating a lively rhythm. These borders can be drawn to decorate a page.

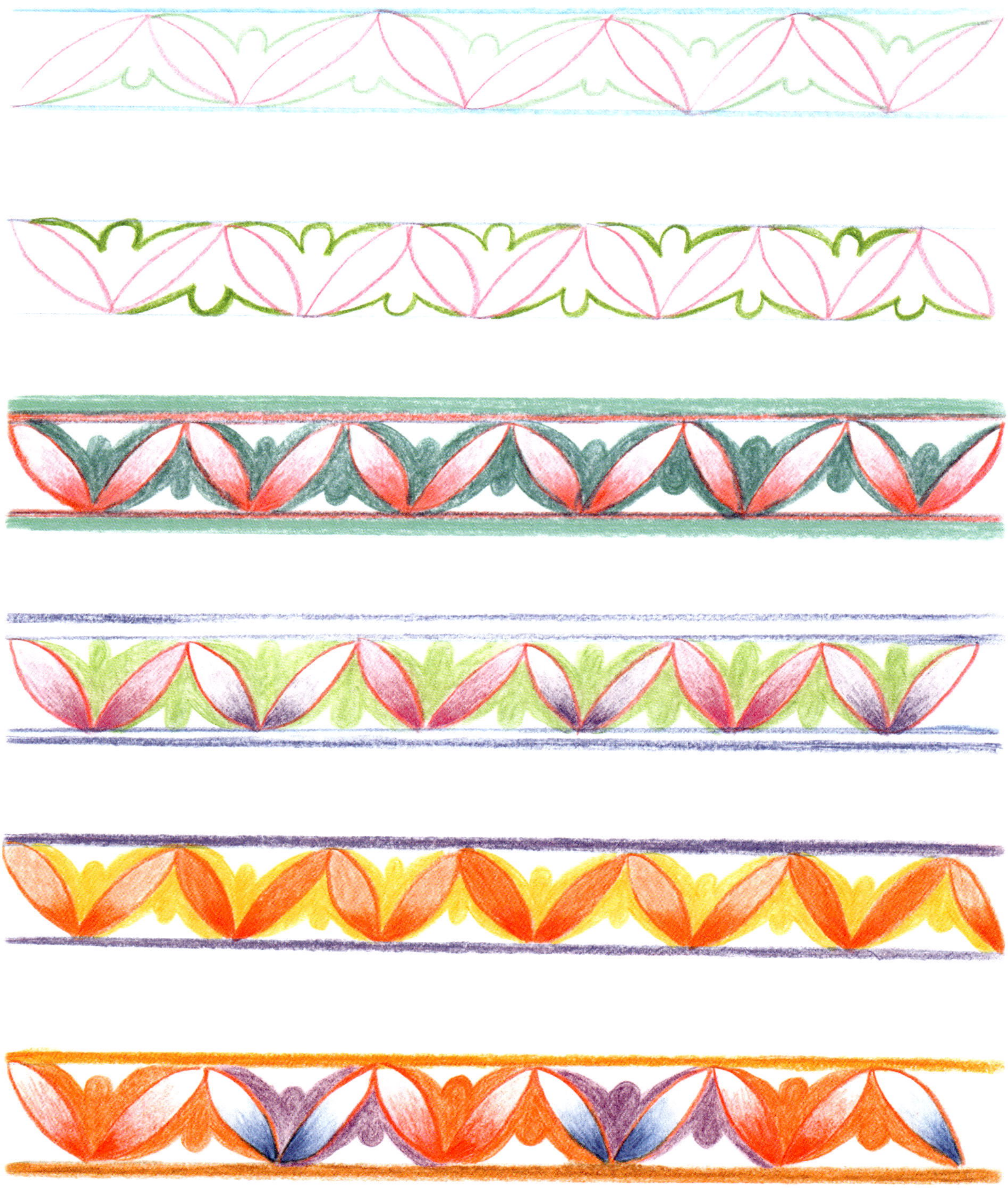

Lines and curves

The curving lines weave through the horizontal and vertical crossed lines, crossing carefully through the centre.

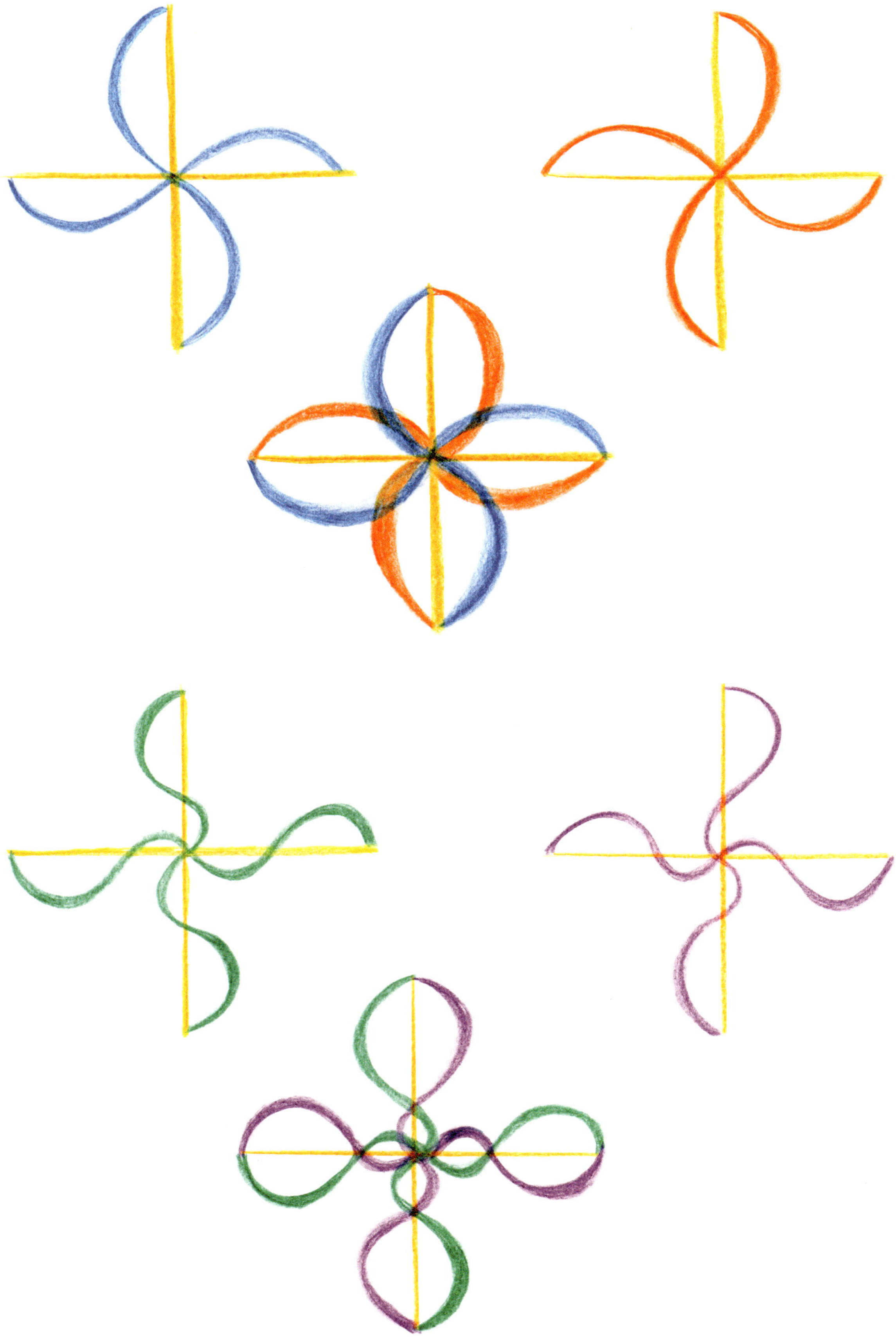

Dividing a circle

The circles are drawn freehand and divided in half, either vertically or horizontally. How many different combinations of half circles can we make?

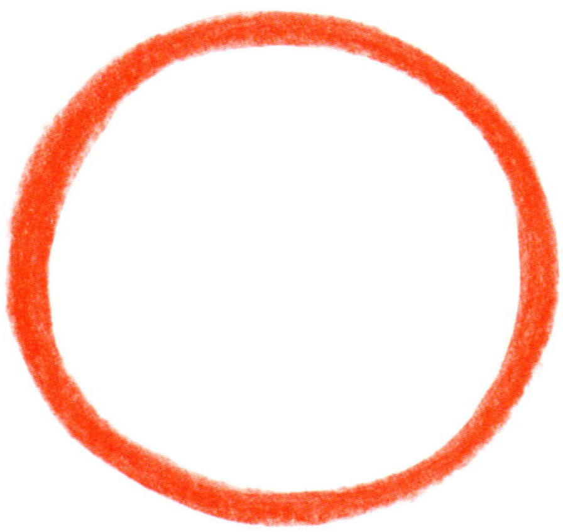

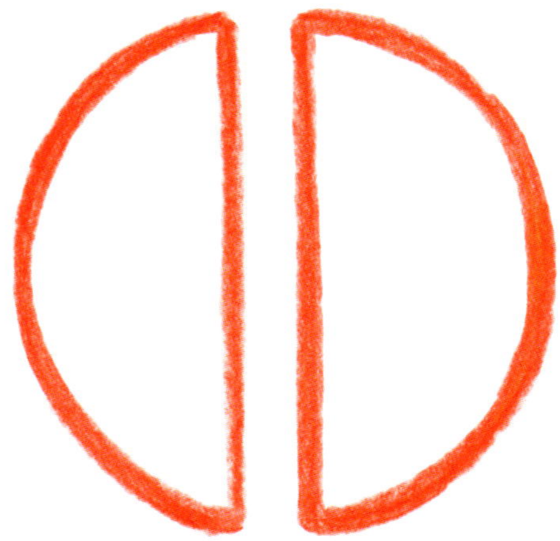

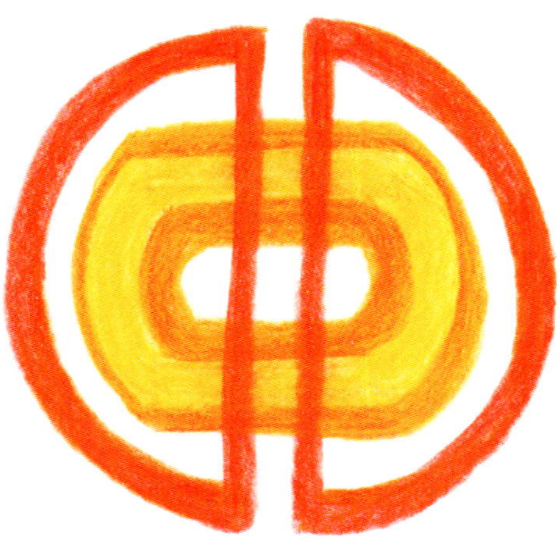

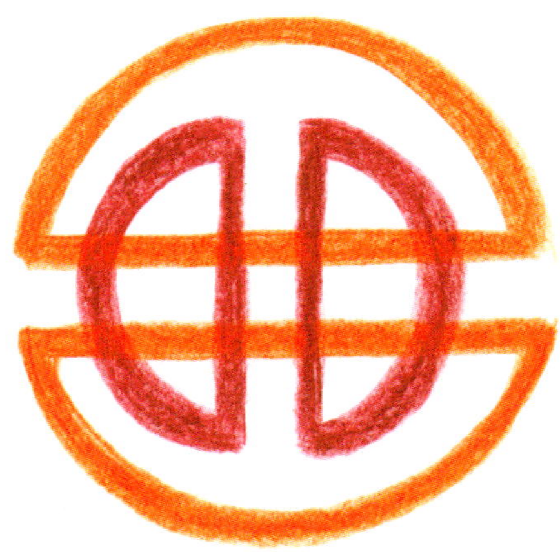

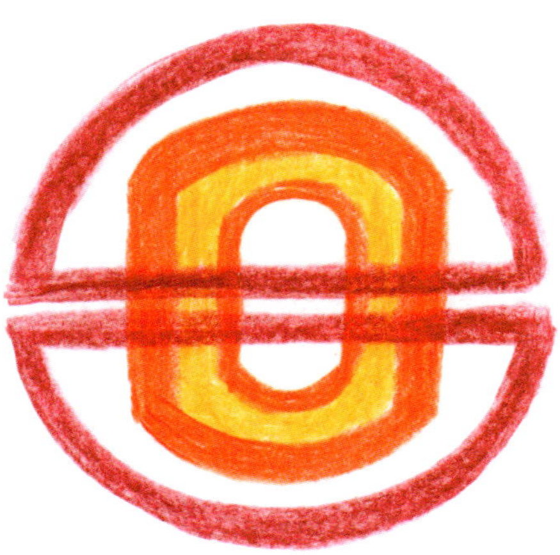

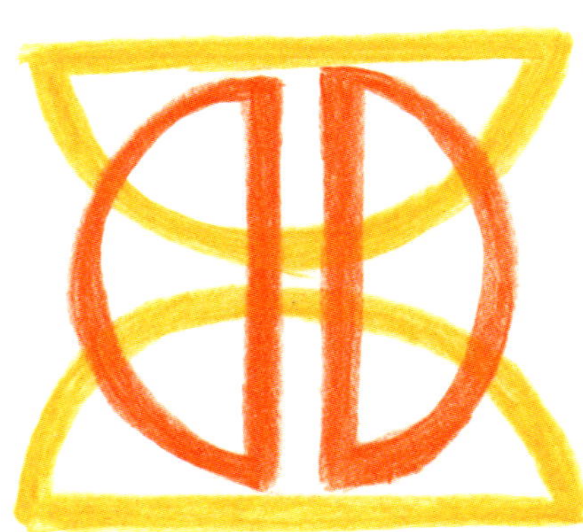

Mirroring

It is necessary for the development of a correct conception of reality that accurate observation and clear perceptions are exercised and trained. Symmetrical forms will provide the most suitable processes for this. Firstly, the children grasp in a subtle way how a form is shaped by observing the teacher drawing the form.

The children draw the teacher's half-form several times in the air, in large movements using their whole arm, following the form in both directions. They then copy the form into their books. Now they complete the form. By completing something which is incomplete the children are exerting themselves independently, which in turn strengthens their thinking activity in a lively and healthy way.

Drawing the reverse (or mirror image) of the given form requires concentration, flexibility and accuracy. In a way, the form is created anew, which is both challenging and satisfying. The children themselves can assess their accuracy by comparing the two halves and they may need to draw over their form several times in both directions, correcting and adjusting it as necessary. Throughout this whole process the children are exercising and enlivening their senses of sight, movement, balance and life.

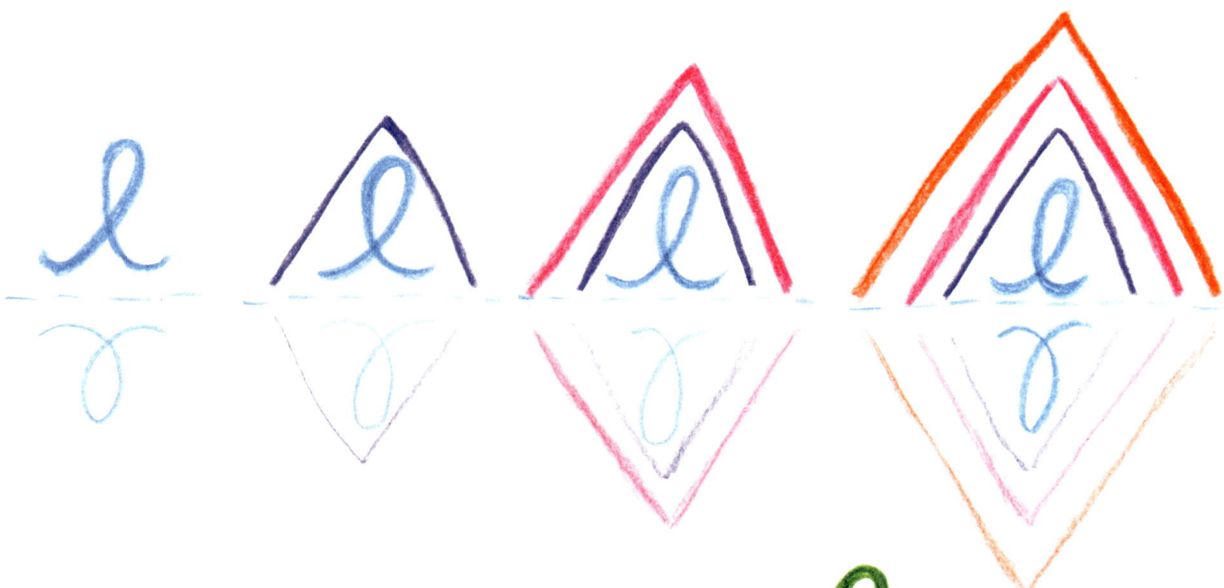

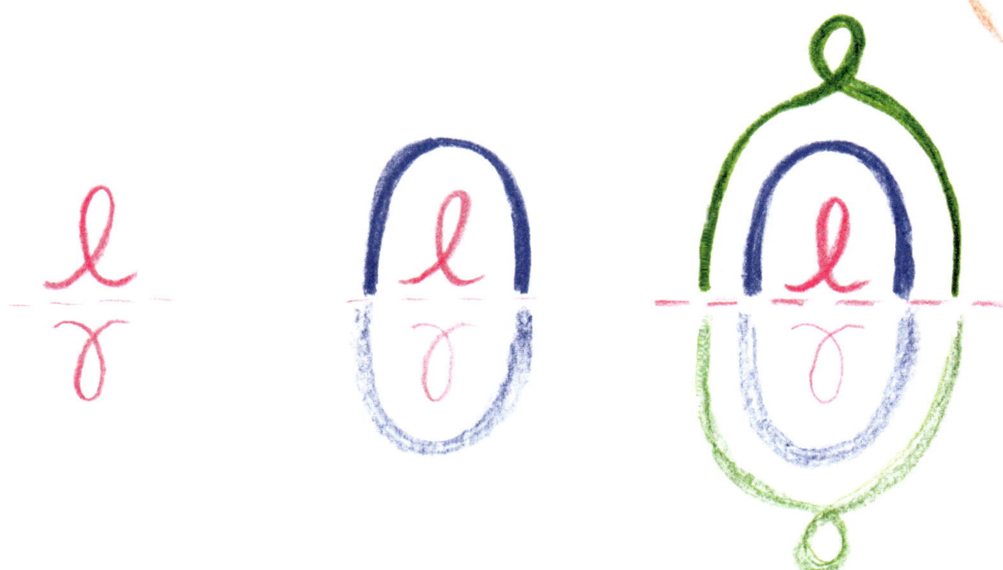

The teacher draws the upper form on the board as the children are watching. The dotted line indicates an area above and an area below. The children copy the form with the dotted line and complete it in their books (without turning their books upside down). The children can create their own forms.

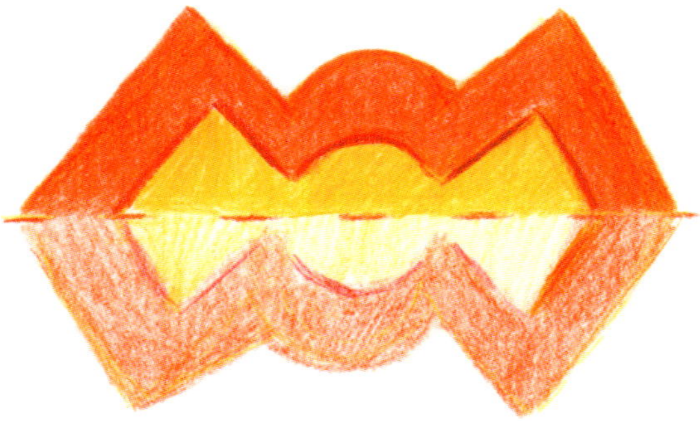

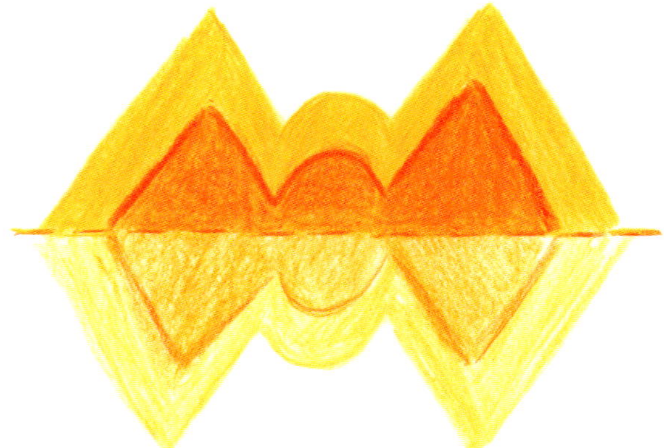

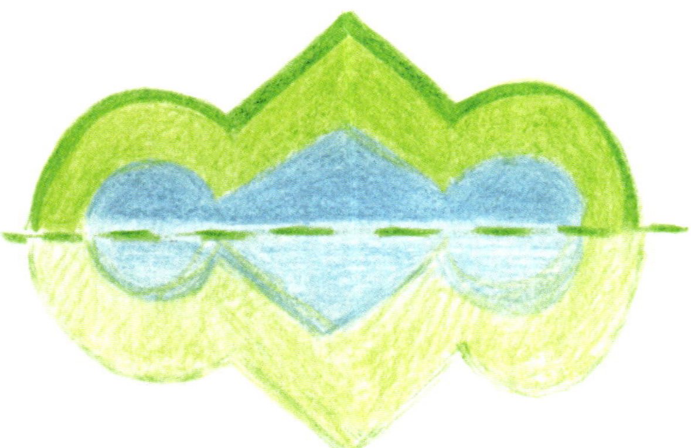

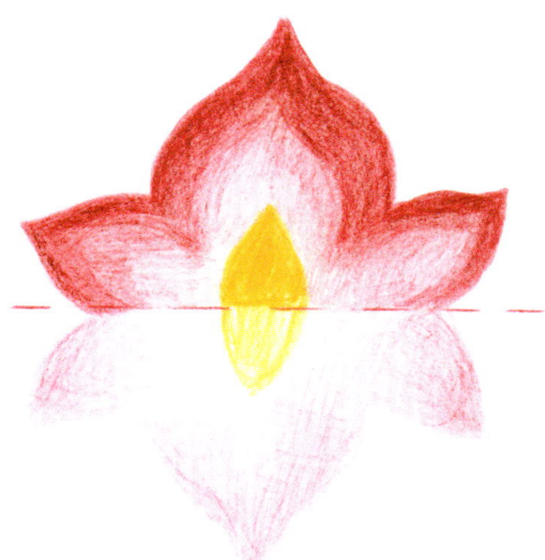

These forms mirror from left to right. Once again the teacher draws one half of the form for the children to see. The children then draw the form in the air with both arms, mirroring to create the whole form before drawing in their books. They can also create their own forms, beginning with simple then more complex drawings.

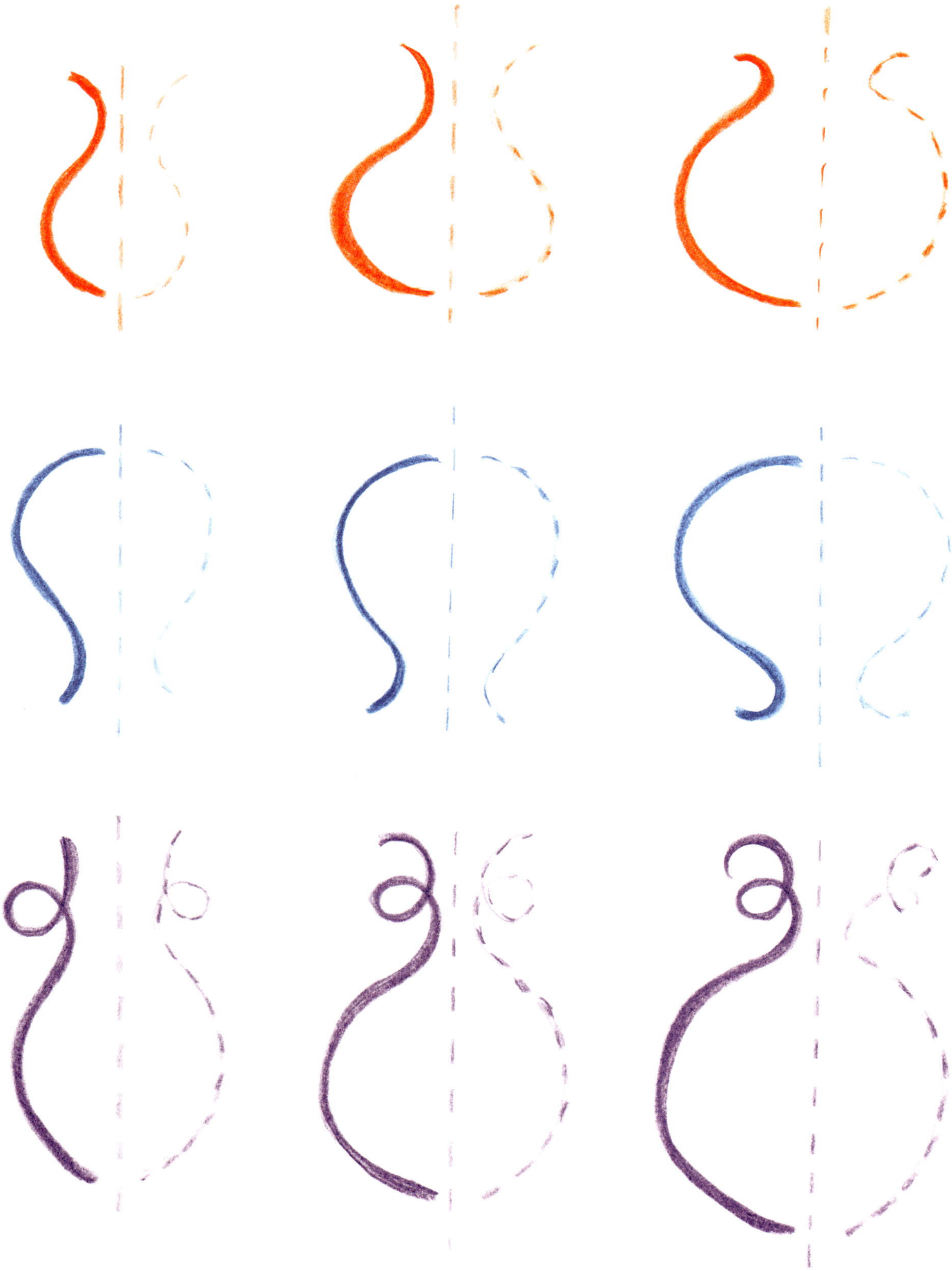

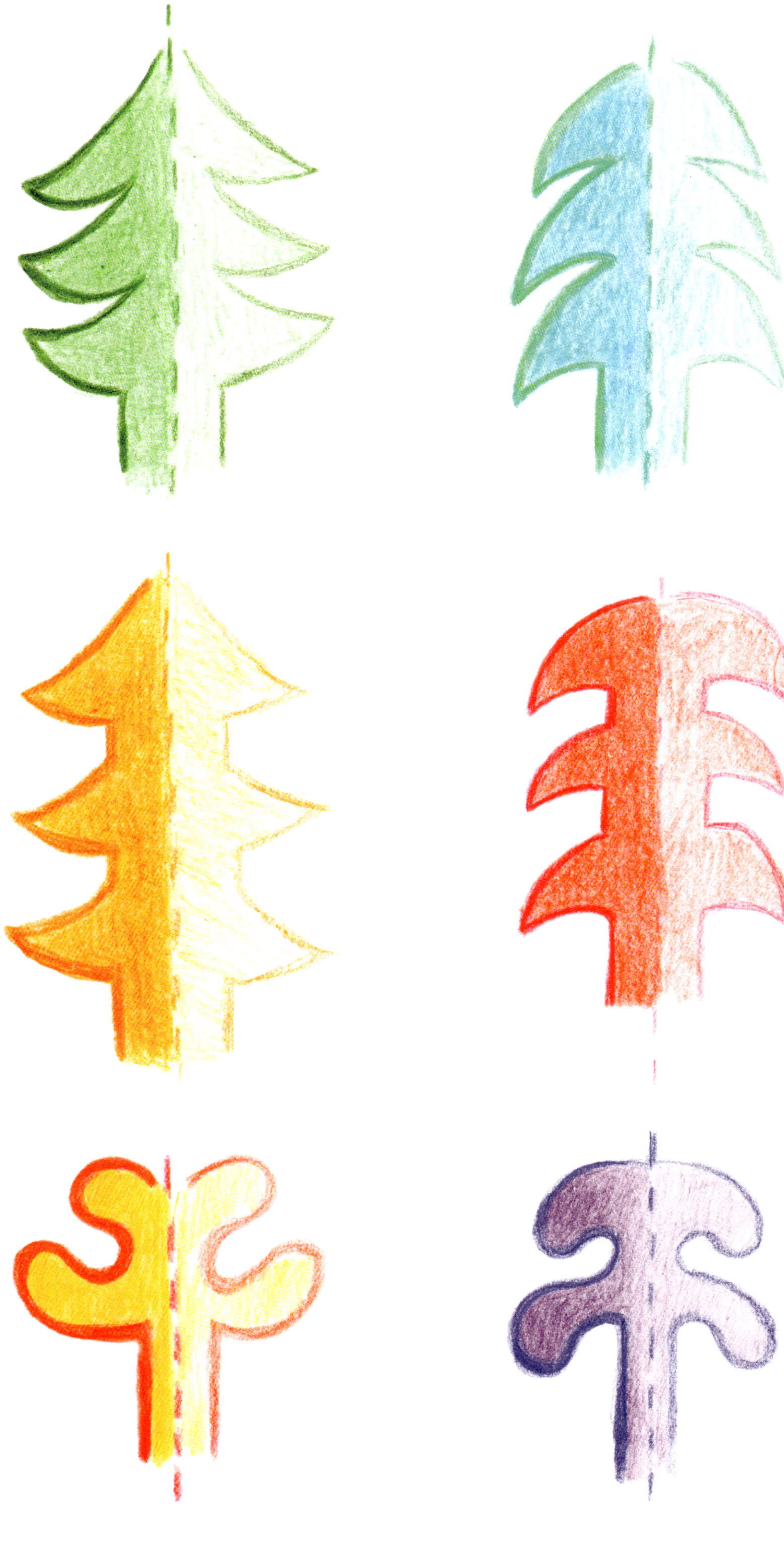

Evaluating the children's work

The children should be able to complete all the exercises in this chapter. Where problems exist, provide extra drawings to deal with the specific weakness. Remember that everyone learns at their own pace and some children will take longer to master a process. Exercises from Part One can also be repeated and the children will enjoy re-discovering something that they already know. This helps to build up their confidence and provides a sense of security. Encourage the class to create their own forms, especially towards the end of the year, by which time they will have their own ideas to express and the skills to do this.

Part Three

Class Three

9–10 years old

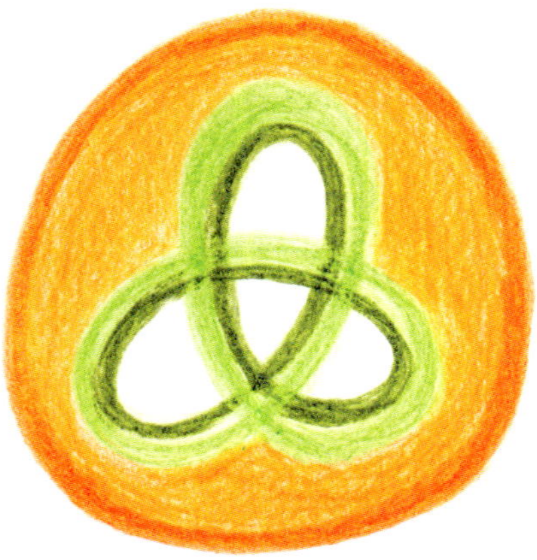
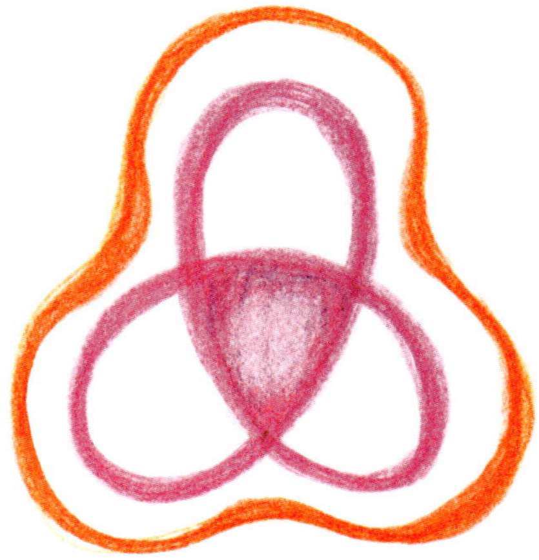
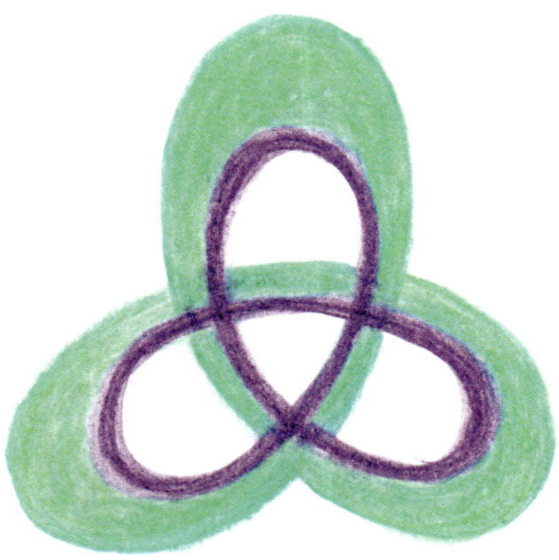
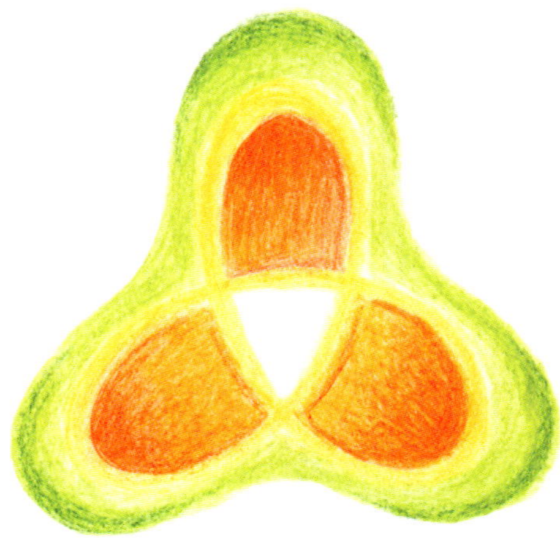
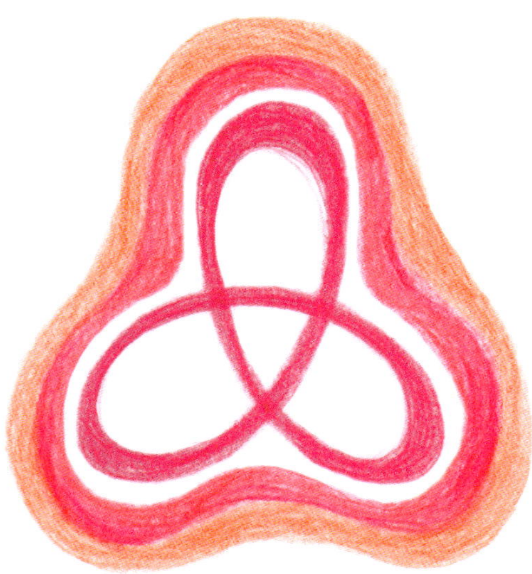
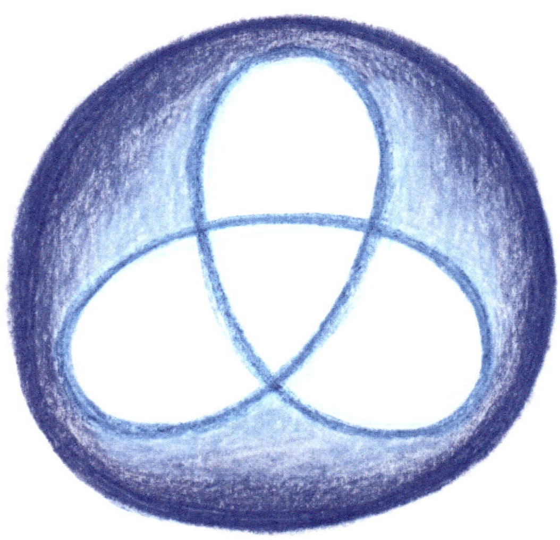

Exercises for Class Three (9–10 years) support, strengthen and develop:

- Handwriting skills
- Perception of form relationships
- Seeing things from different points of view
- Problem-solving capacities
- Creative thinking processes
- Sense of aesthetics
- Independence.

Examples included here provide experiences of:

- Relationships
- Polarities
- Completing what is incomplete in a relevant way
- Static and dynamic movement
- Transformation processes (metamorphosis)
- Integration.

In the ninth or tenth year children have a deep experience of the distinction between themselves and the world, between their inner or individual self and the outer world. They may wonder whether the circumstances into which they have been born are really theirs: Who are their parents? Who are their teachers? What is the world 'all about'?

Sensitivity, reassurance and respect towards the newly experienced sense of self growing within the child are needed at this phase of transition. Children need to cultivate an inner sense of security, trust and well-being. They also need to transform their earlier childhood senses of wonder and curiosity regarding the world into a new, more conscious grasp of the various phenomena in their outer surroundings, encompassing both people and nature. At the same time they need to consolidate their own place and existence within the world around them.

Form drawing in Class Three can help to integrate and balance this sense of duality, providing supportive confidence, strength and inner security through this time of change and consolidating it in a healthy way. The form drawing gives expression to the natural forms and rhythms of life which the children are experiencing within their own lives, and which they are now beginning to discover all around them.

Forms that have both contrast and stability between inner and outer, between centre and periphery, will be of great benefit to them. The children at this age also need to strengthen their inner capacities for imaginative thinking, especially in the processes of inner picture-building. This should not lead to abstractions, but to an enlivened imaginative thinking which is relevant and related to the form. Imaginative thinking should also not be one that 'flies away' in its own unrelated way, but that remains mindful of the actual circumstances and situation to which it is connected.

In this instance form drawing has a two-fold benefit:

- It protects against dry abstractionism in thinking.
- It provides a balance to prevent any tendency towards disconnected flights of fantasy.

Curved forms in three spatial directions

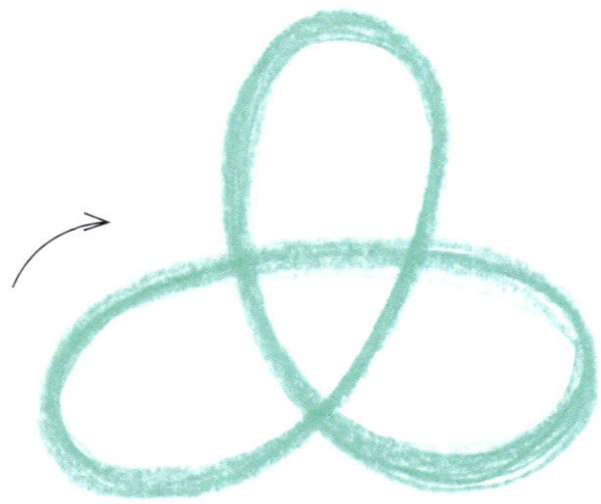
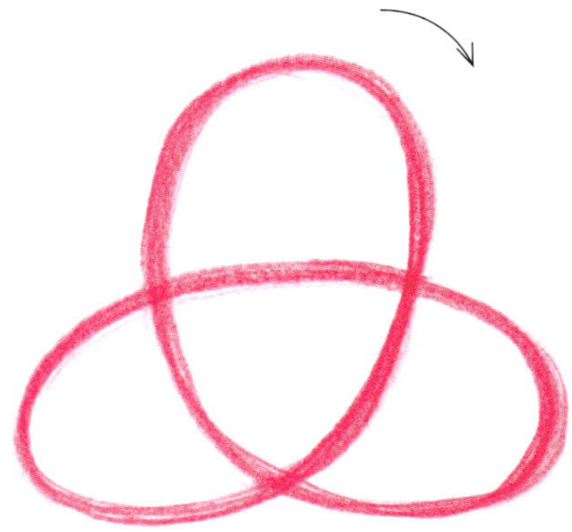

The children draw over the form several times with a continuous flowing movement. They can begin the form in different places, which will result in different directions in the movement, from left to right or from right to left.

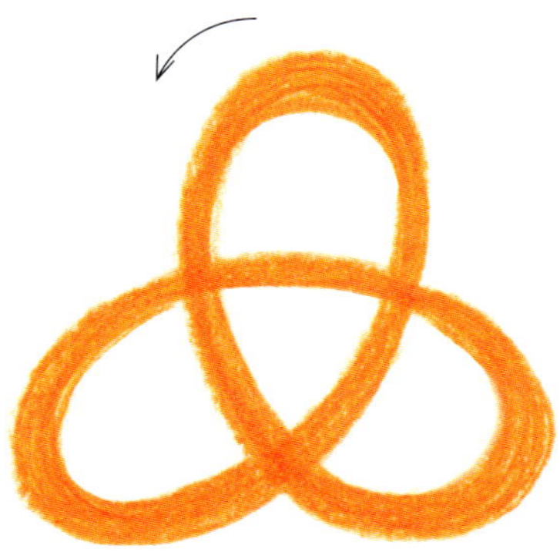
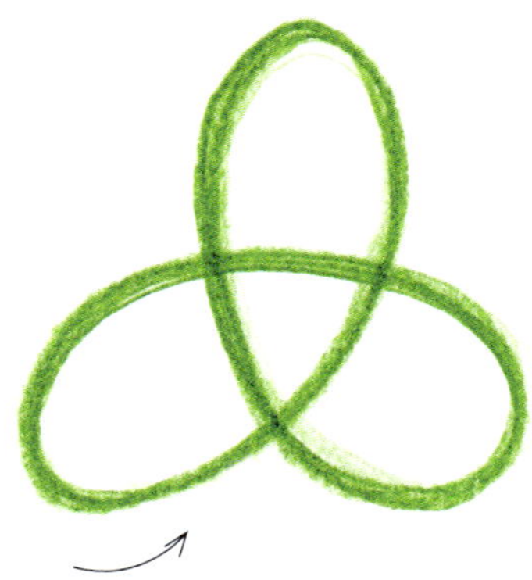

These forms are very harmonising and the rhythm is soothing. The children can hear this rhythm if they listen to the sounds that the pencil is making on the paper.

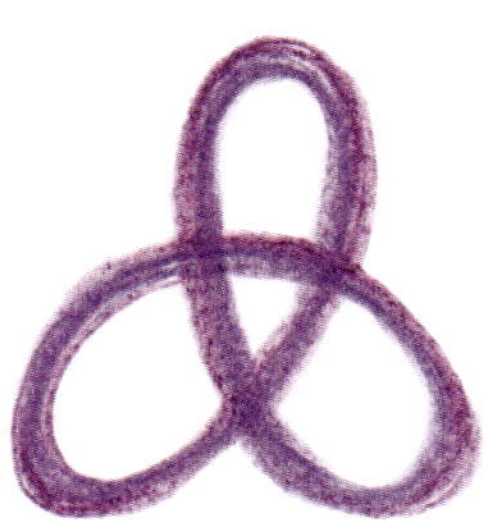
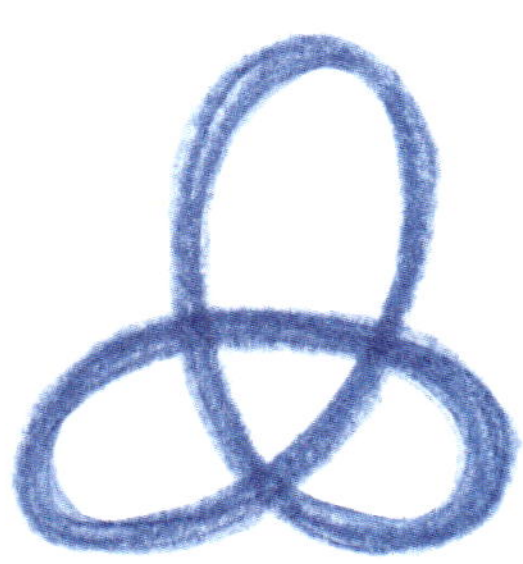
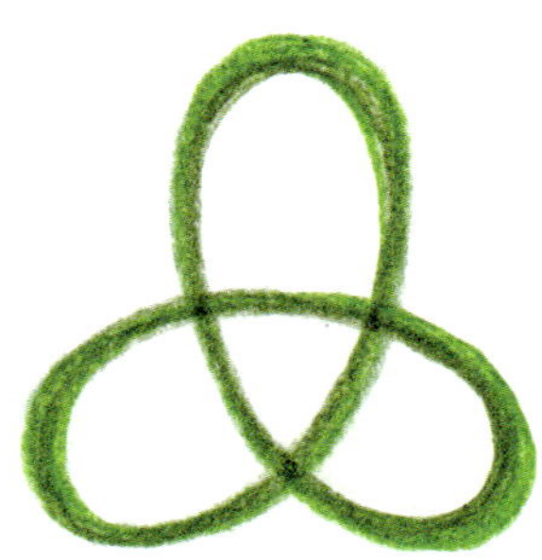
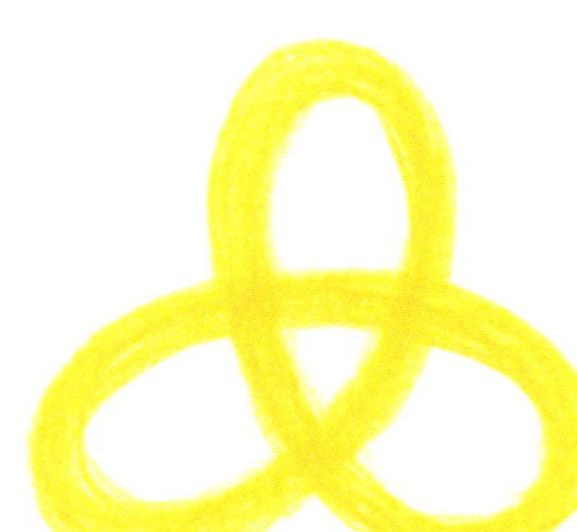

The curved forms can be developed further by adding flowing lines around them and by colouring them. The outer lines are also continuous. By drawing around the forms many times the surrounding colours build up to be quite thick, as well as flowing. The colouring is simple in order to enhance the simplicity of the forms.

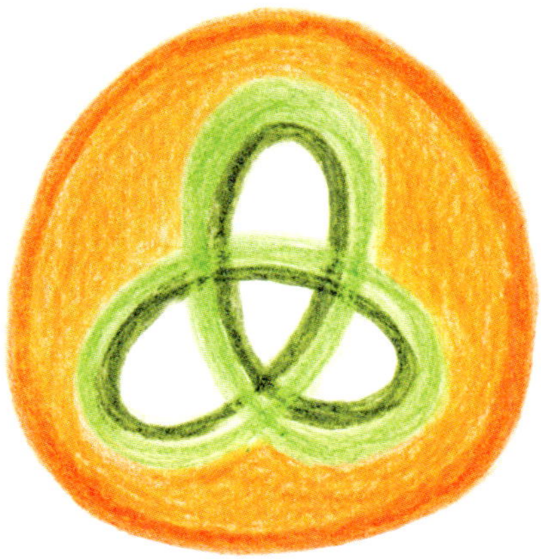

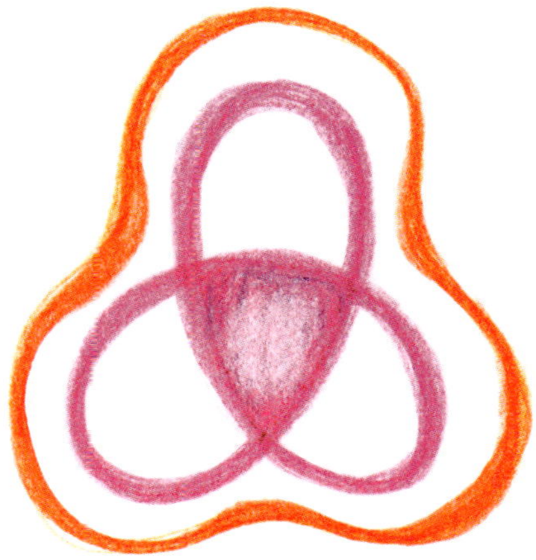

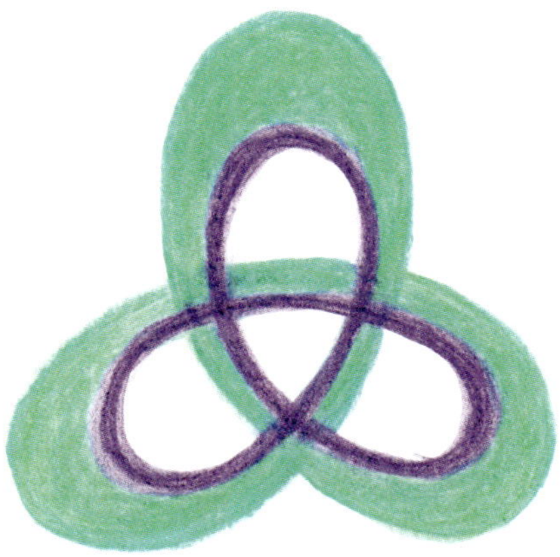

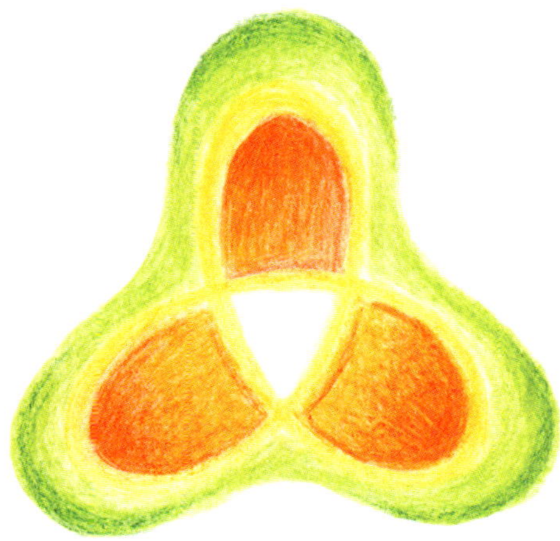

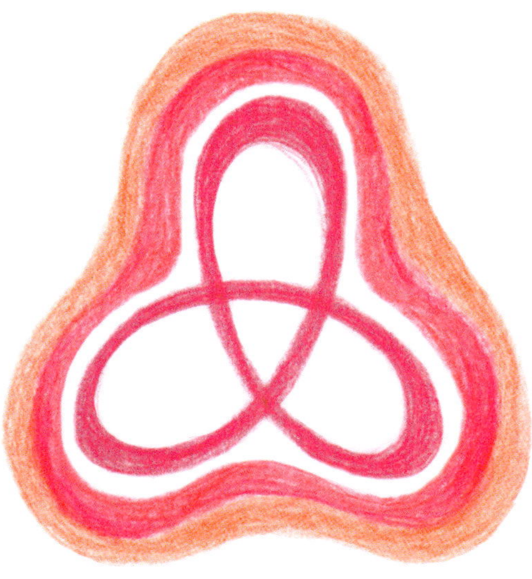

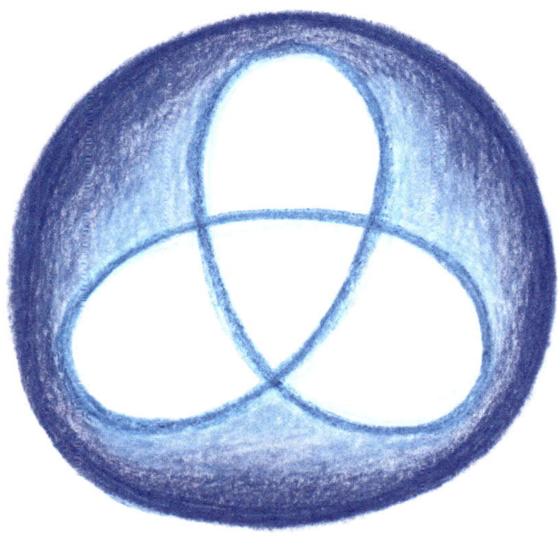

The children draw the helpful dots first. They begin the curving lines very gently at first, so that they feel their way into the form, then strengthen the form by drawing over it several times in both directions.

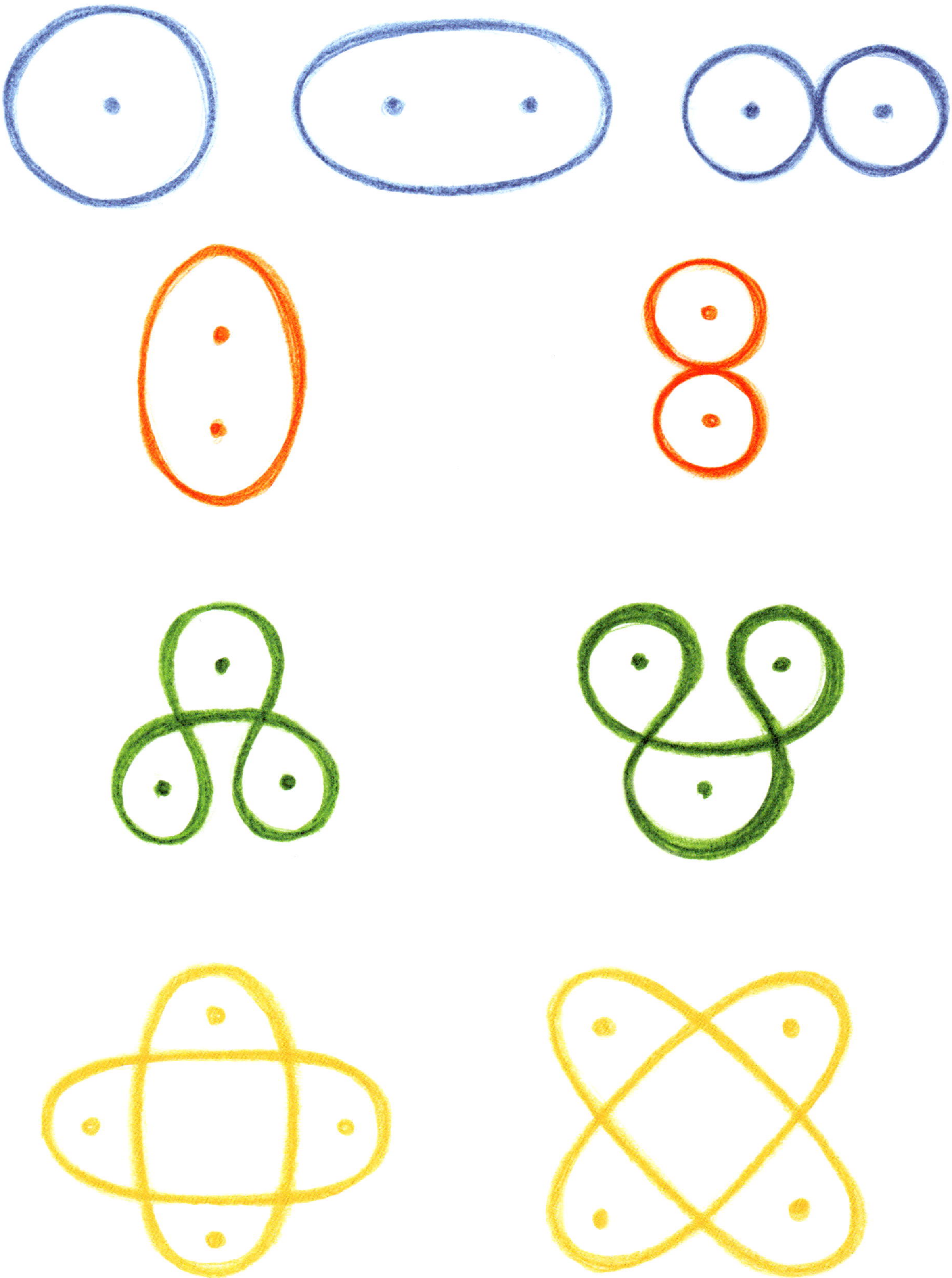

Flowing forms with four directions in space

These are all variations of forms which have flowing lines. To help the children create the shapes 'helpful dots' can be used. They are drawn freehand. The dots are drawn first, then the lines around them. How many different form possibilities are there?

Remember: the line must be continuous, and it can be drawn in both directions, beginning very lightly and slowly pressing more firmly.

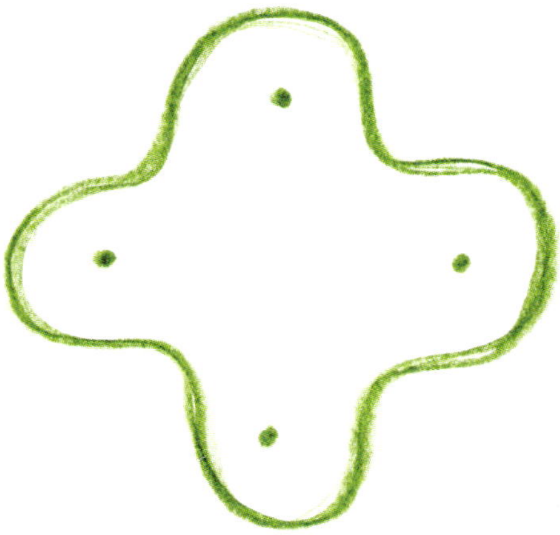

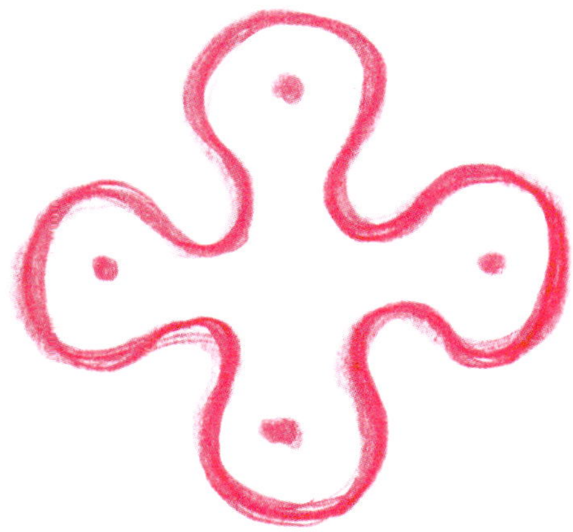

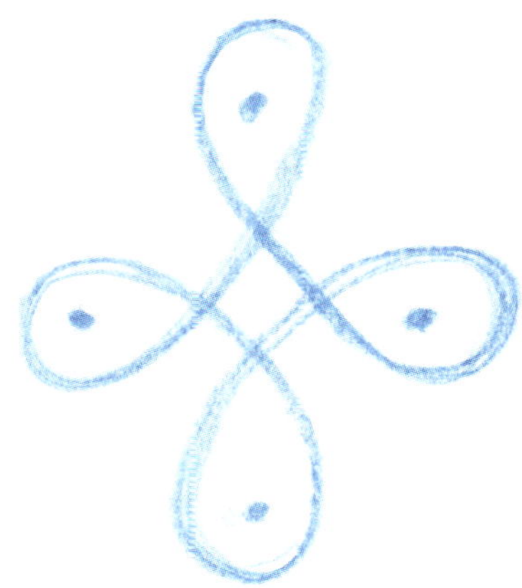

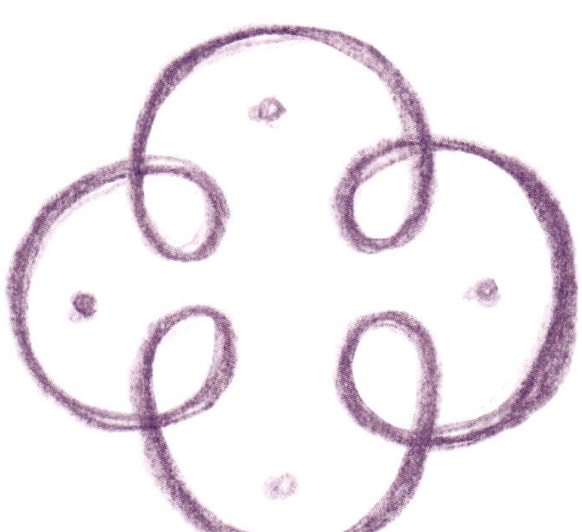

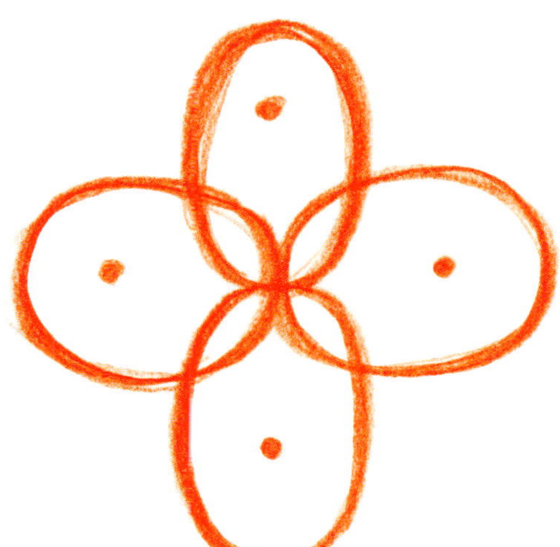

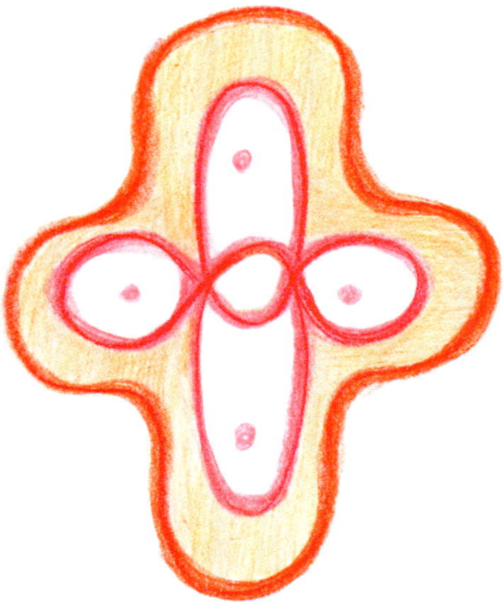
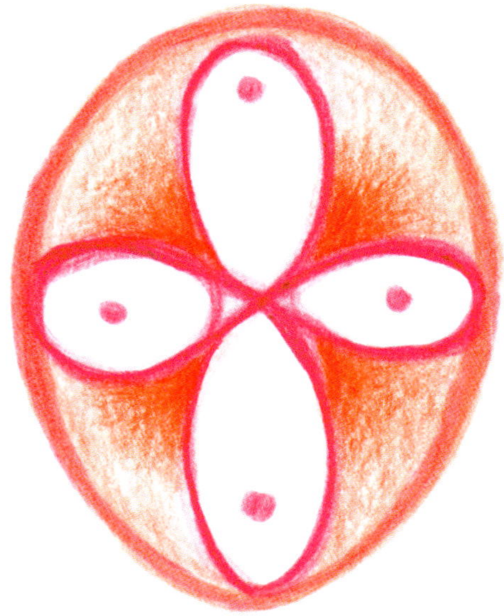
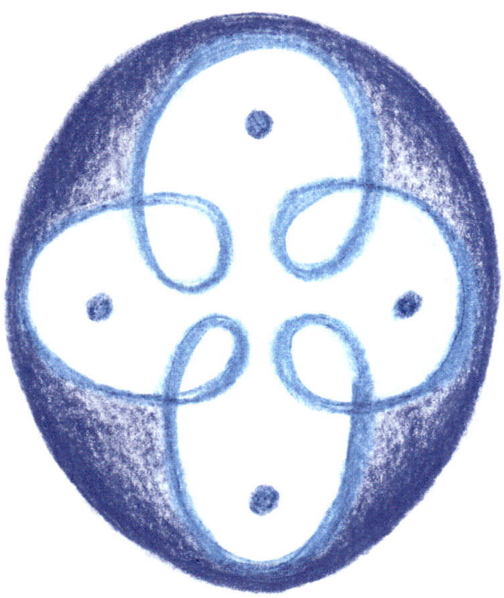
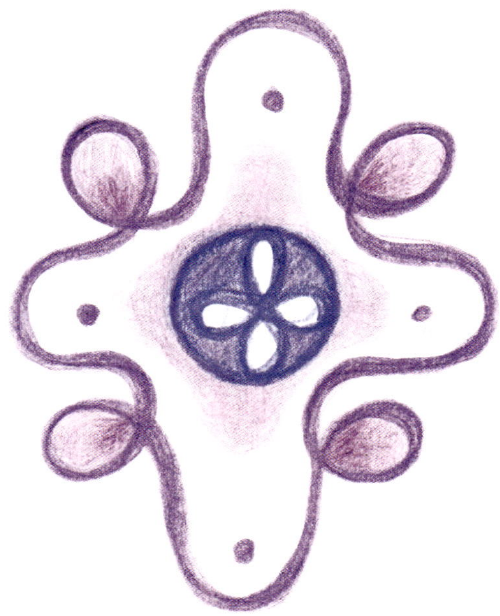
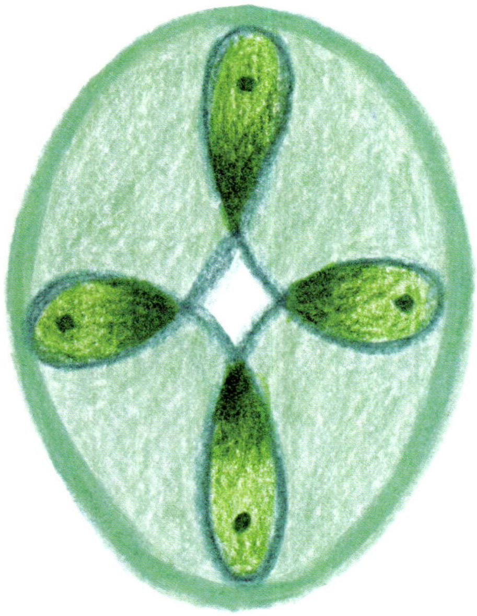
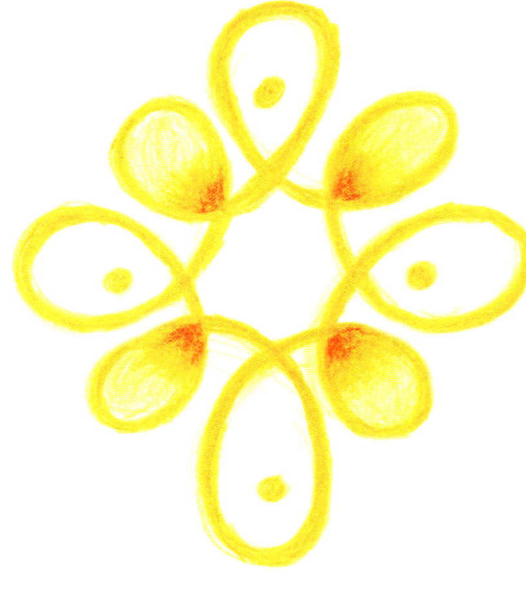

Lemniscates with circles and ellipses

The two crossing forms, or lemniscates, can be drawn separately and then combined into one form with a central crossing.

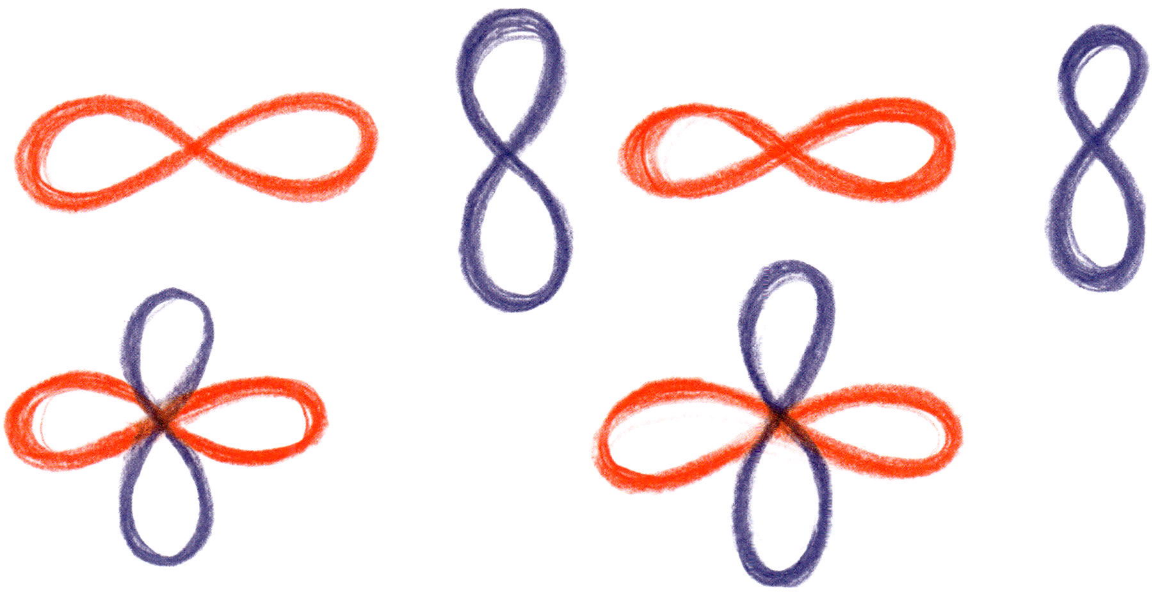

The form can be drawn in a continuously flowing line. The children can experiment with different ways of doing this, crossing through the central point, and drawing in different directions.

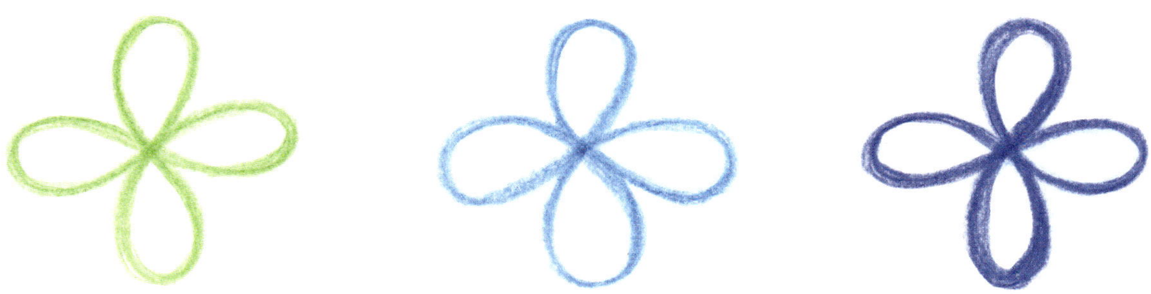

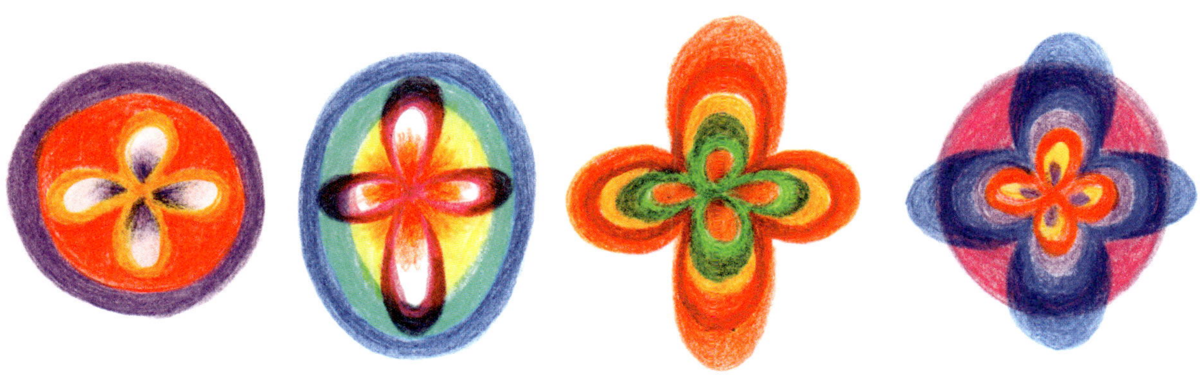

The children can develop this form in different ways. It will be familiar to them from Class Two so they will enjoy adding circles and ellipses and colouring them.

Straight lines and curves

Draw the straight lines first, followed by the 'helpful dots'. Then the curved lines are drawn in one direction, then retraced back again. These forms are quite challenging, and may need practising on paper before being drawn in the books.

These forms bring the experiences of:

- balancing four directions in space on a linear form
- balancing four directions in space on curved forms
- orientation on the horizontal line
- orientation on the vertical line
- judging spatial distances
- using the eyes to measure a balanced form (no rulers!)
- mirror drawing.

The forms can then be developed in different combinations (see following page).

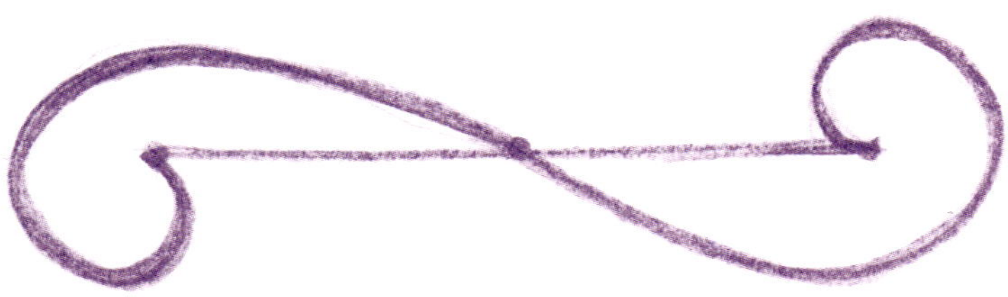

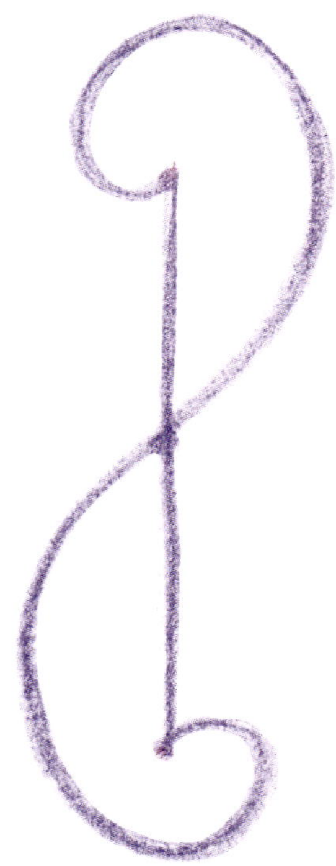

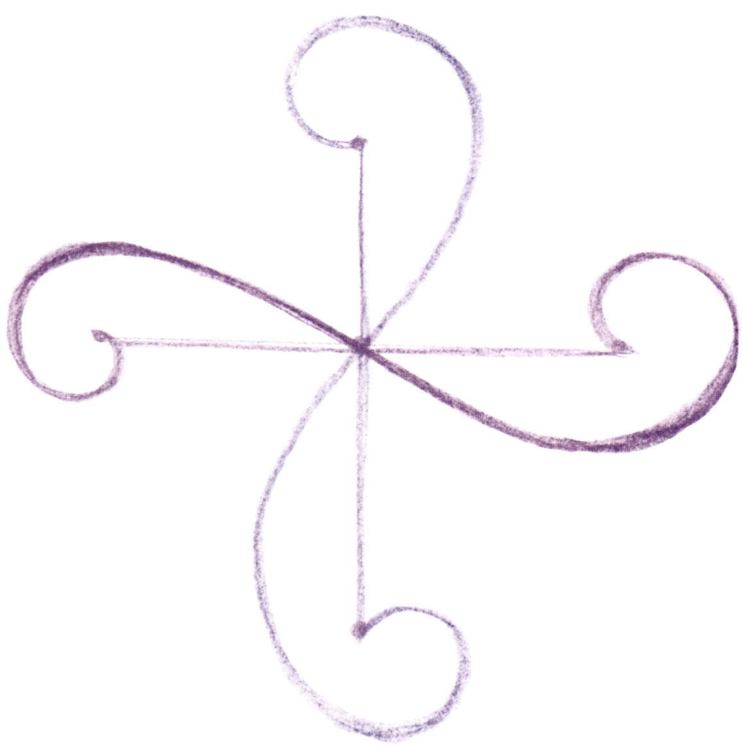

Straight lines and lemniscate curves

Firstly the children draw the straight lines and put the helpful dots on evenly spaced places along the lines. The curved lines are drawn through the helpful dots, weaving through the straight lines.

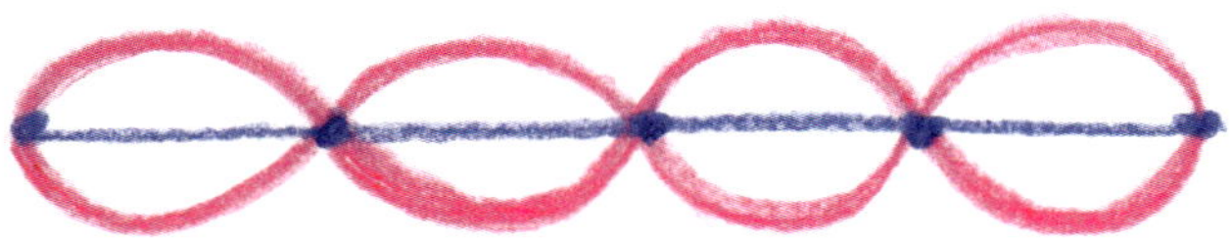

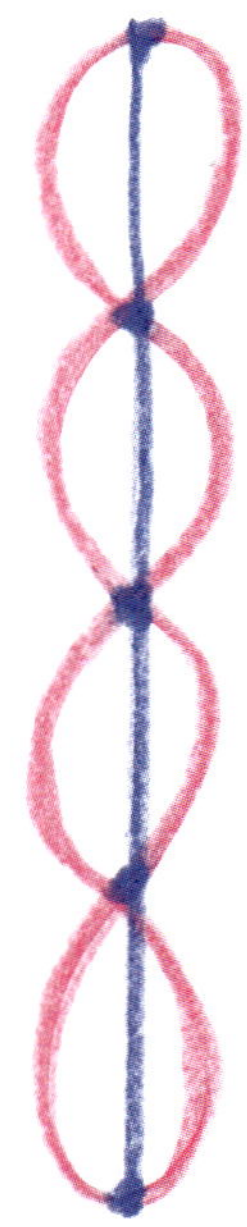

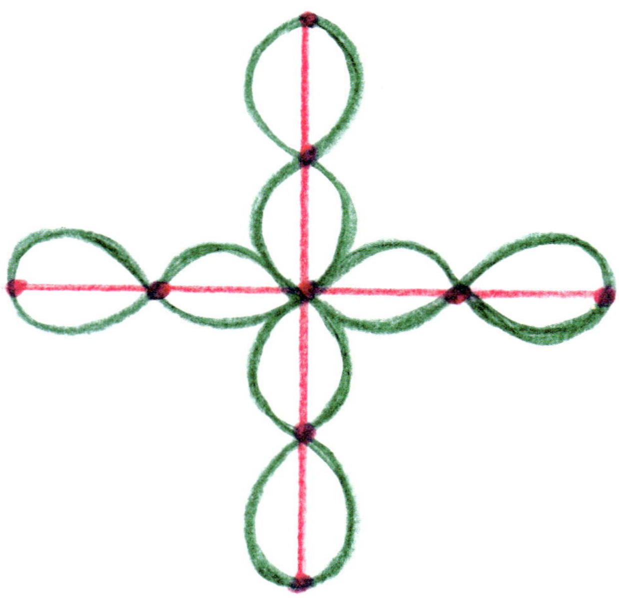

This beautiful form can be drawn in a continuous l ne which begins in the centre and returns to the centre, as each radial line (reaching out line) is completed. The curved lines near the centre cross over each other. They can be coloured in.

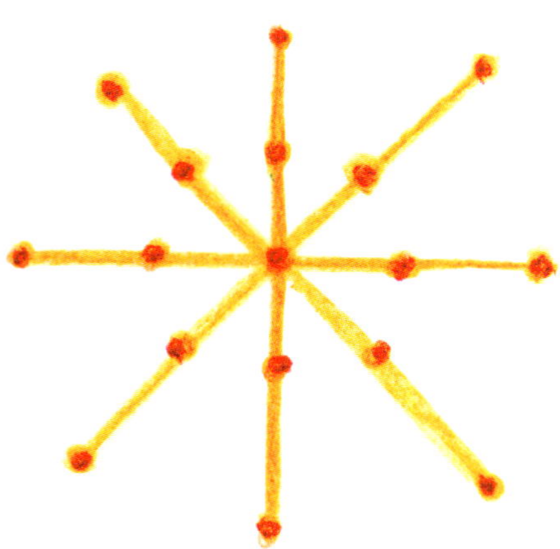

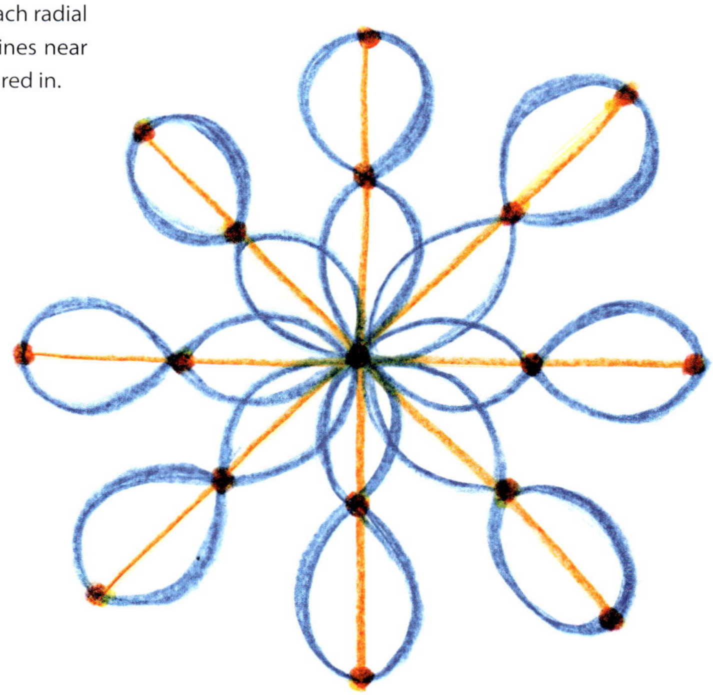

Transforming a straight line into curves

Because these forms 'grow upwards' the children will need to draw the straight line halfway down the page and gradually transform the straight line to a curved line.

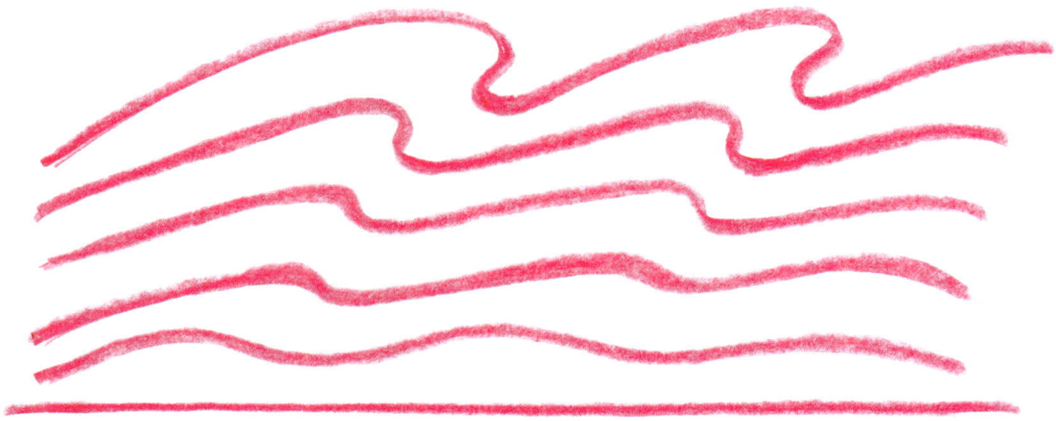

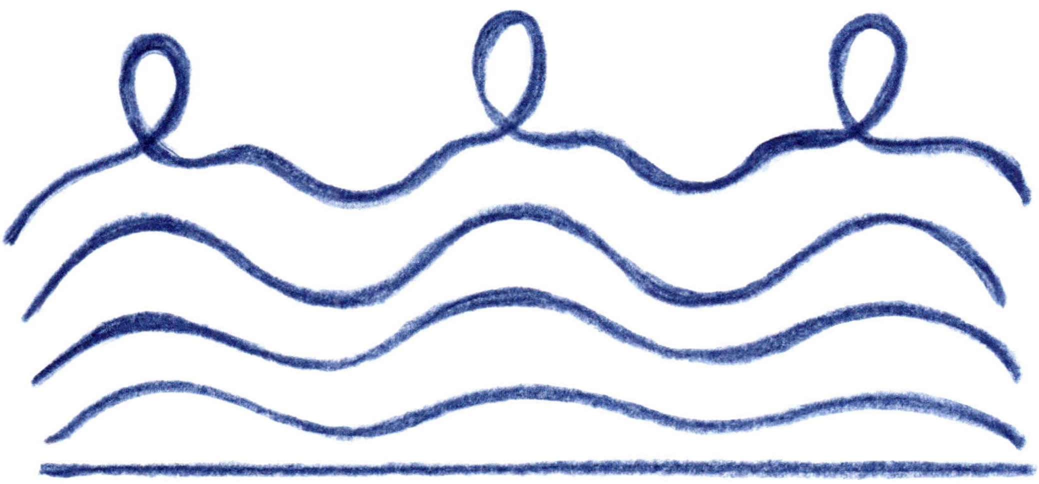

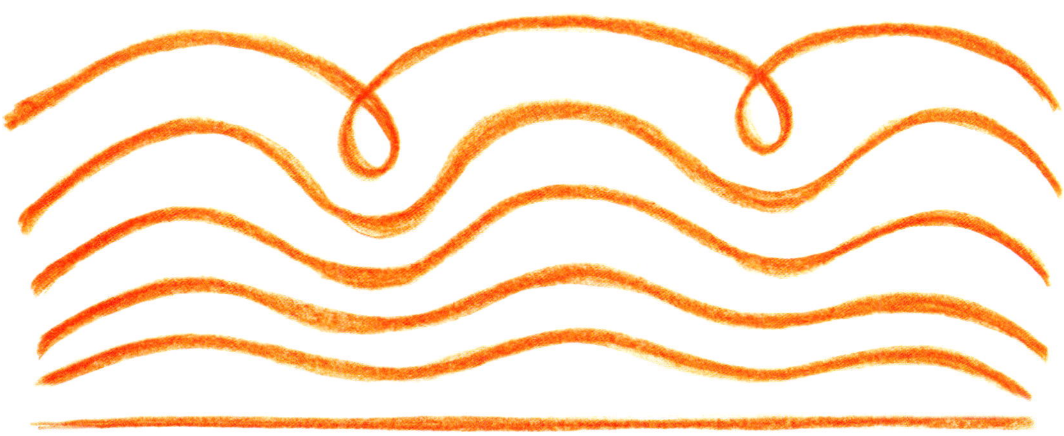

They can then begin with the curved form and step-by-step transform it into a straight line, showing each stage of change.

In these forms the children are learning how to relate one linear movement to another, and how to connect a sequence of forms in a logical progression. They can create their own transformation forms which show a clear sequence.

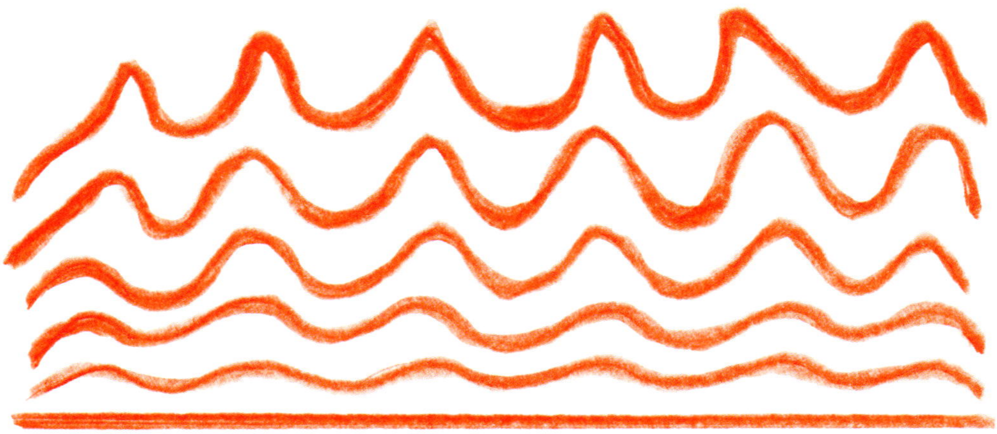

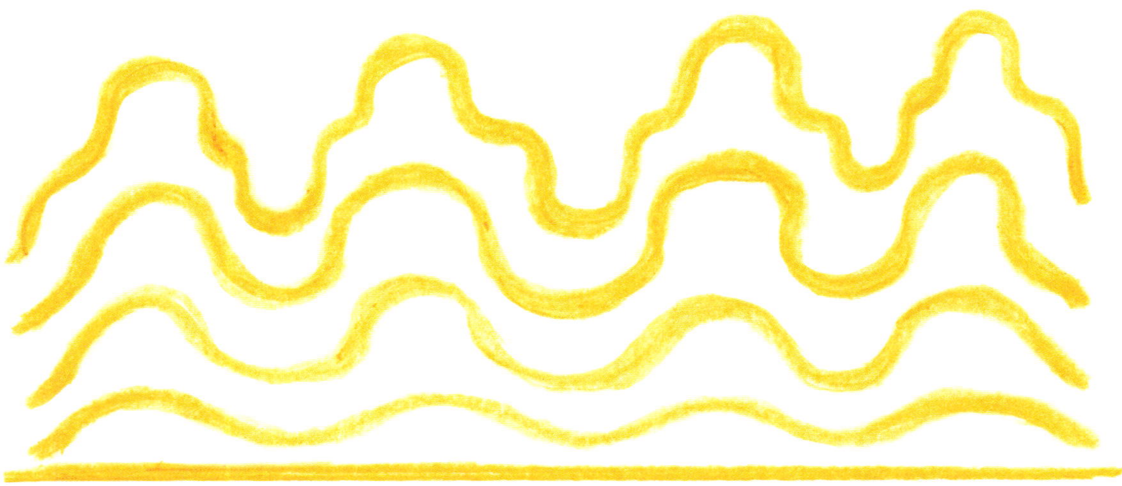

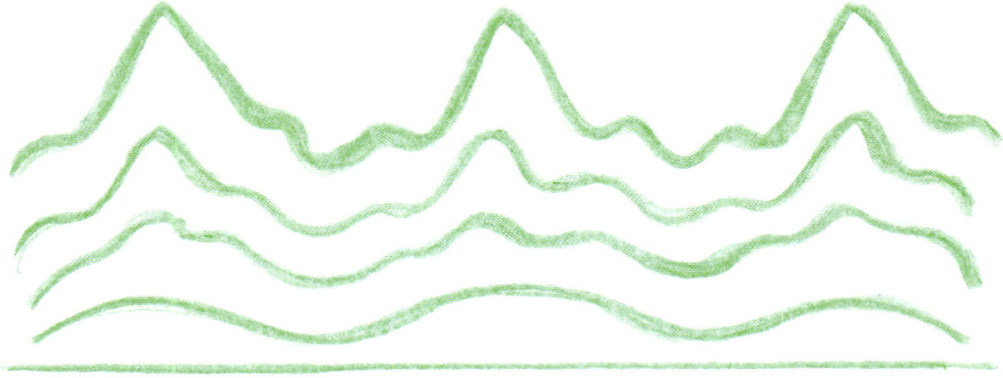

Sequences which grow

In these forms each row shows a slight change, developing one aspect of the form so that it seems to grow. A clear progression from one row to the next can be seen. Leave plenty of space between the rows to allow the form to grow taller.

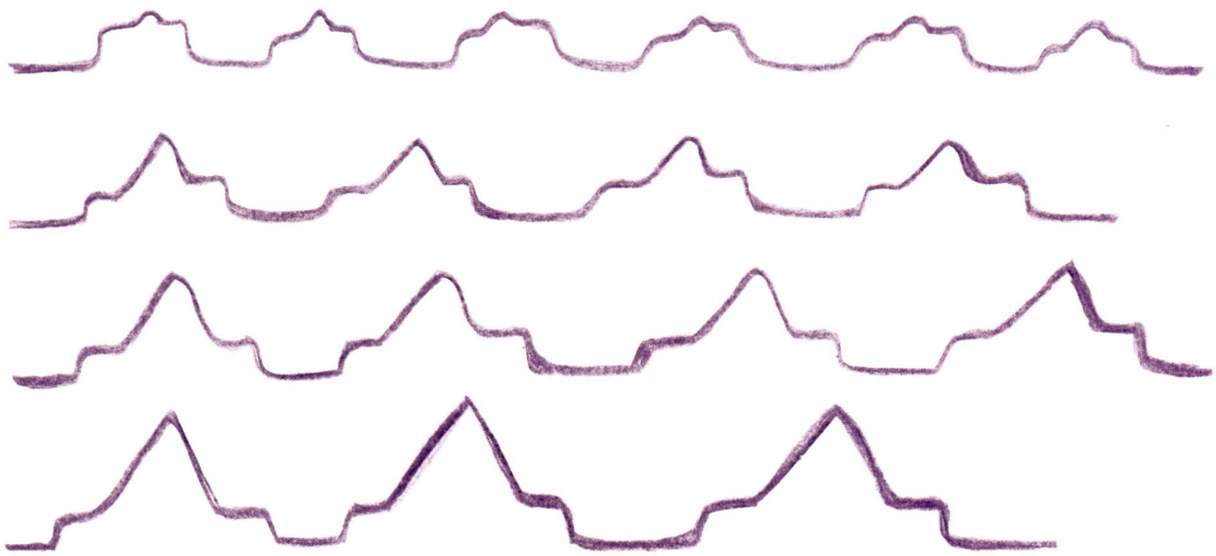

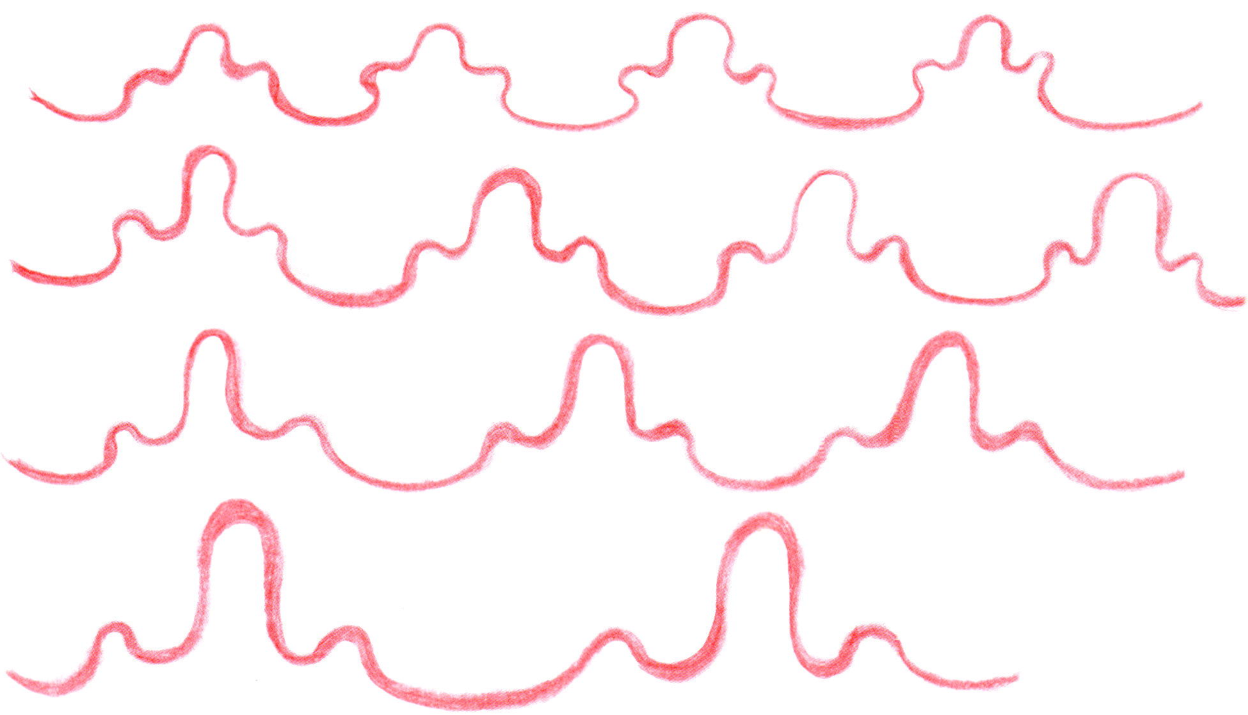

Transformations

These forms also change in a gradual step-by-step sequence, so that the children can experience transforming the shape and movement of the line into a new form. When the page is complete they should be able to see the changes from one row to the next. (It is not necessary that the forms are identical.) The children are learning:

- How a simple form becomes a complex form.
- How forms are related to each other.
- How sequences can develop.

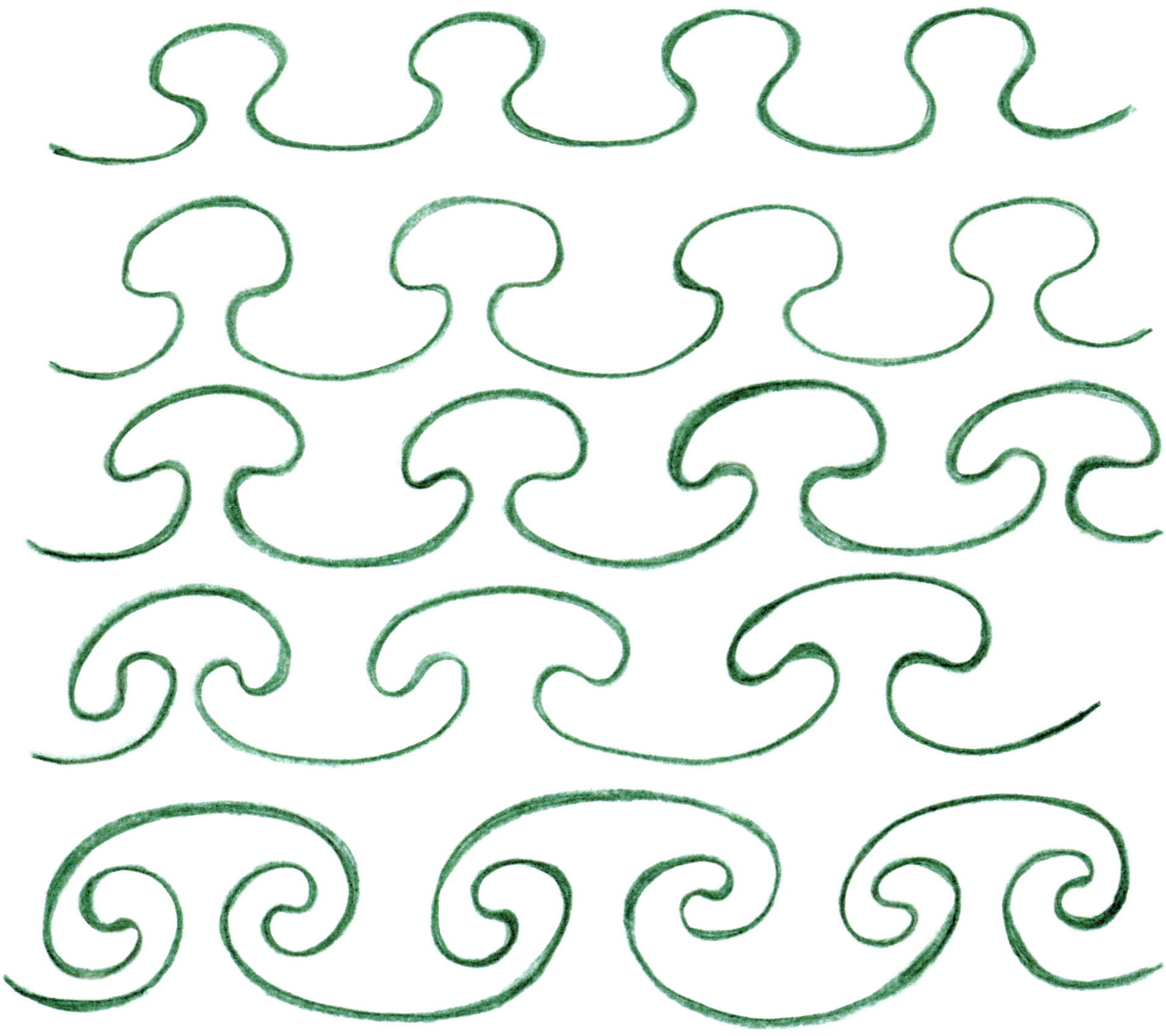

What do we notice when we turn the page upside down? Do the forms appear similar in both directions?

Sequences with angles

After working with the curved forms, the children can now draw forms which are angular. The angles change as the forms grow taller.

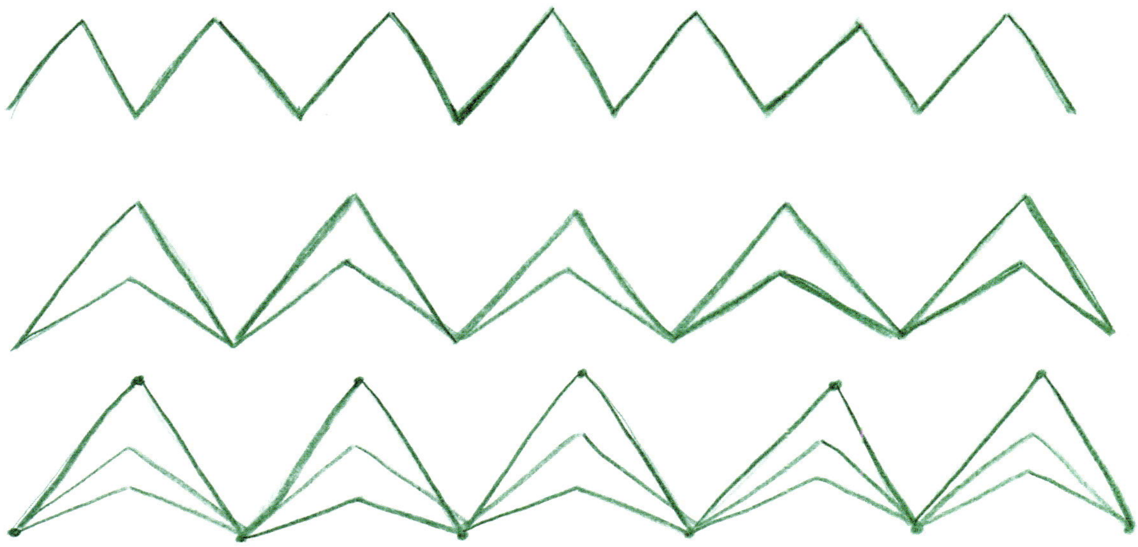

These forms may need helpful dots on the base-line as they have a tendency to slope upwards on the page. Stay with one colour to begin with so that the experience of the structure is foremost.

The children are experiencing :

- forms which are regular
- repetition
- spacing which is even
- strong structures
- angles
- clear spatial directions.

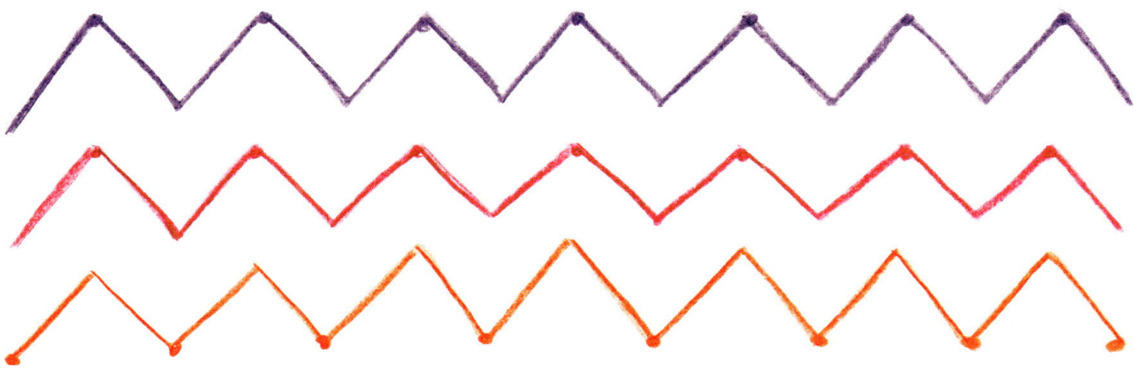

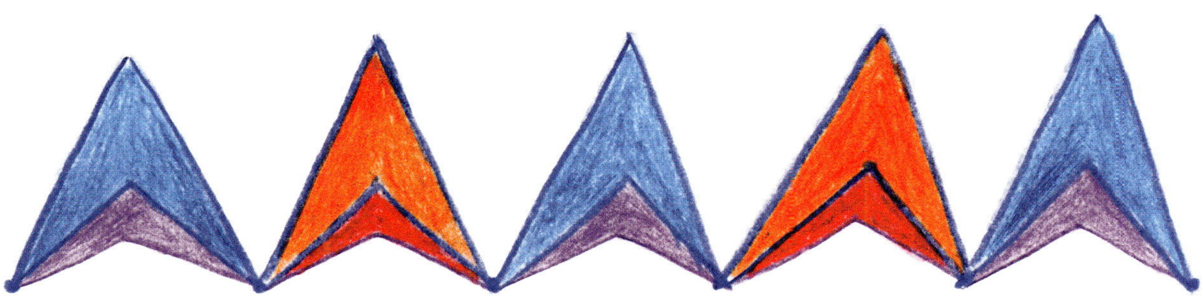

When the basic drawings are completed the children can then use different colours to define the structures.

These exercises can begin from the lower row of angles followed by drawing the central and upper rows, then in the opposite way beginning with the upmost row and working downwards. Allow plenty of space on the page for them.

These forms need a certain amount of forethought so that the spacing is even. They are mirror forms, each drawn in a continuous line.

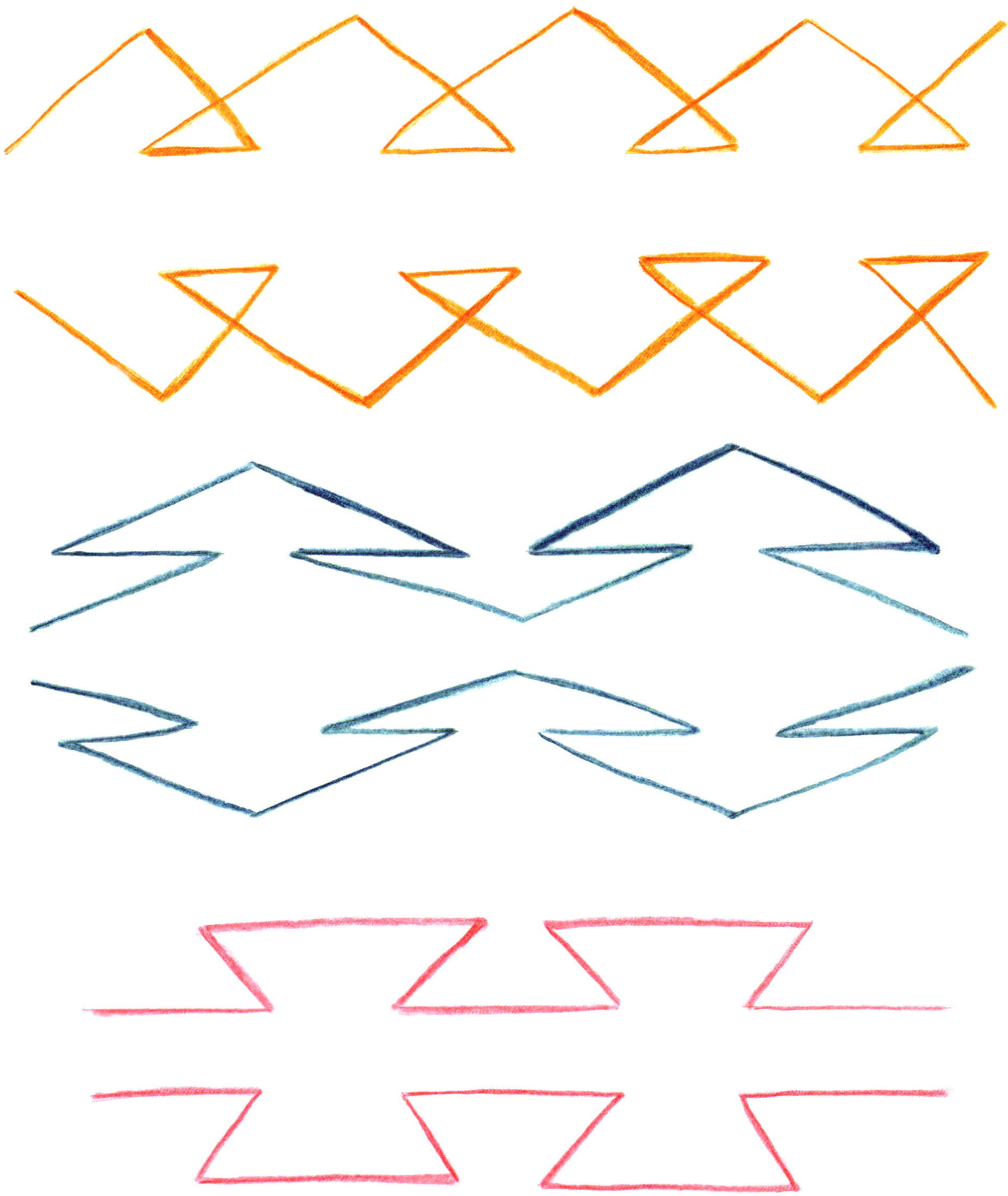

The forms can be reduced in size to create geometric patterns, using helpful dots.

The children are learning how to :

- draw in different directions
- plan ahead
- compare one form with another
- sustain a repetitive form
- observe from different points of view.

When the children have drawn the forms, they can turn their books upside down. The forms look the same from both sides!

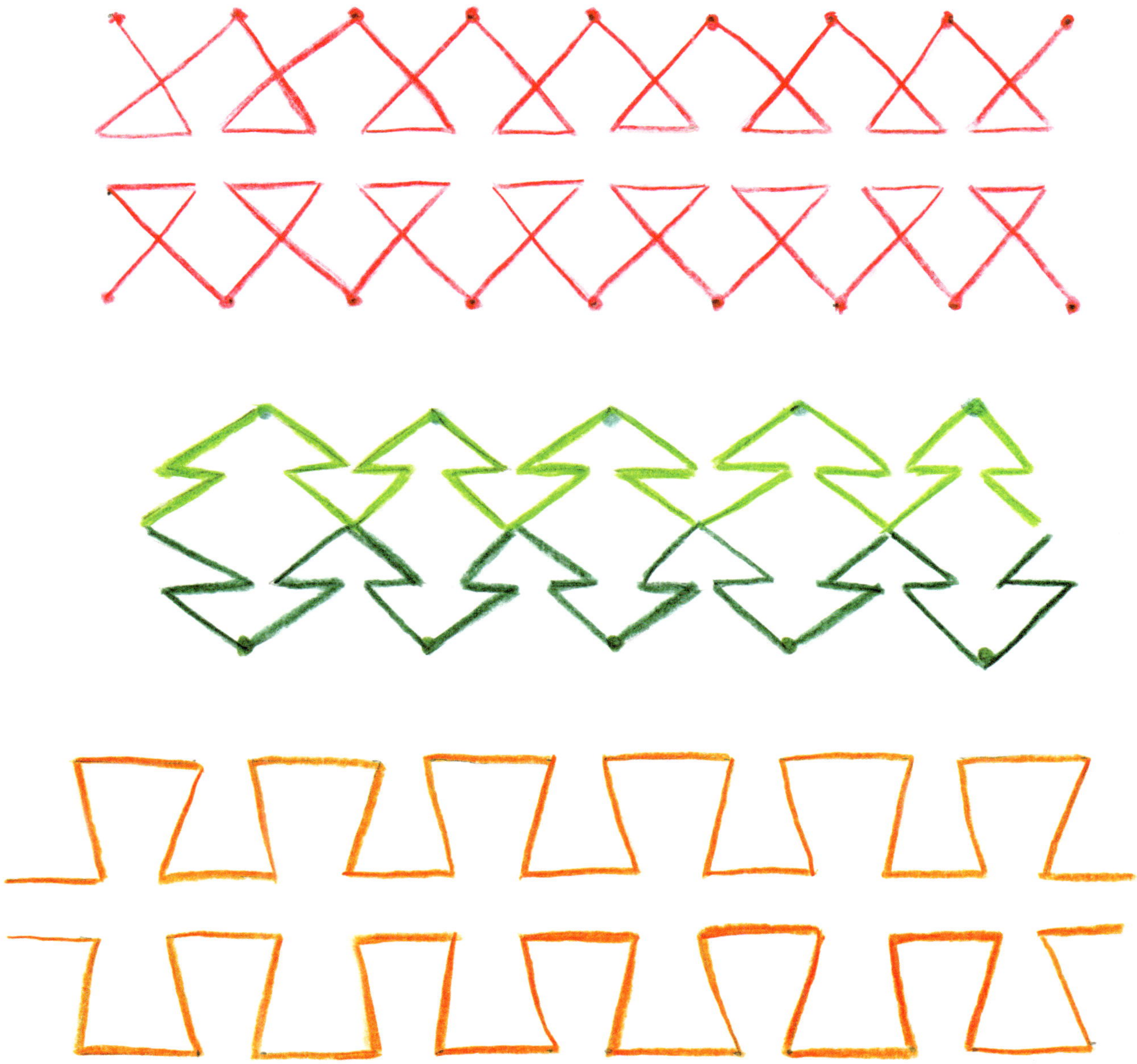

Diagonal lines

The children have already drawn diagonal lines in a free way in Class Two. Now the diagonal lines can be arranged in more formal ways in definite relationships. The diagonal lines need to be evenly spaced so that they form definite patterns.

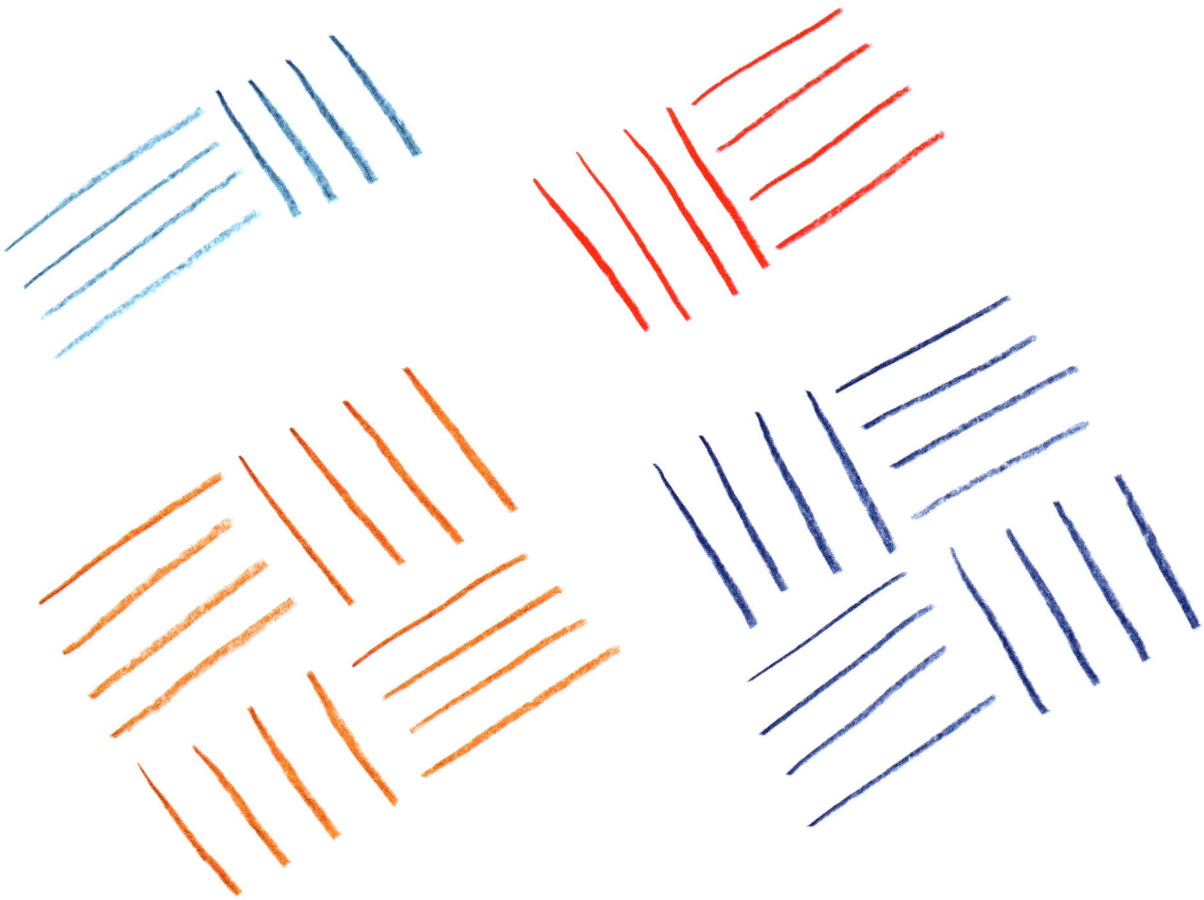

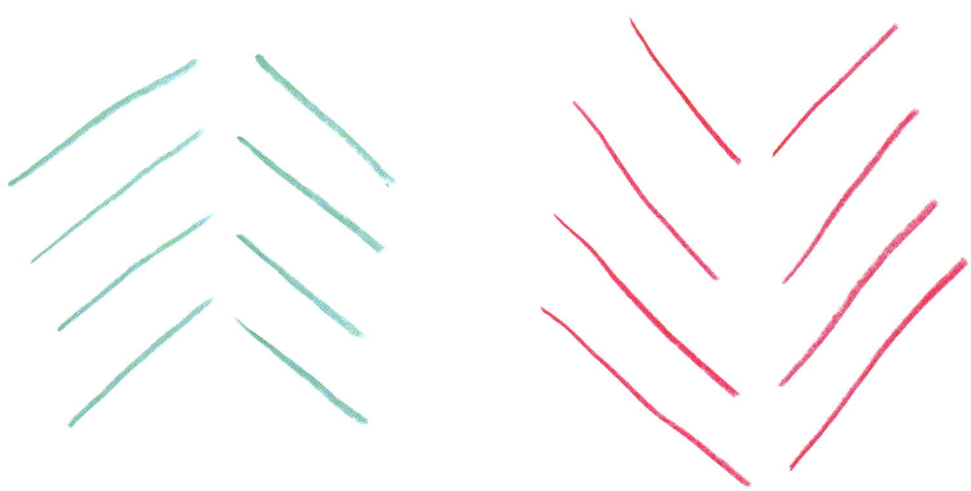

The diagonal lines can also be drawn to give shape to more definite structures. Children will need to draw the vertical and horizontal lines first and then carefully draw the diagonal lines, beginning in the corners.

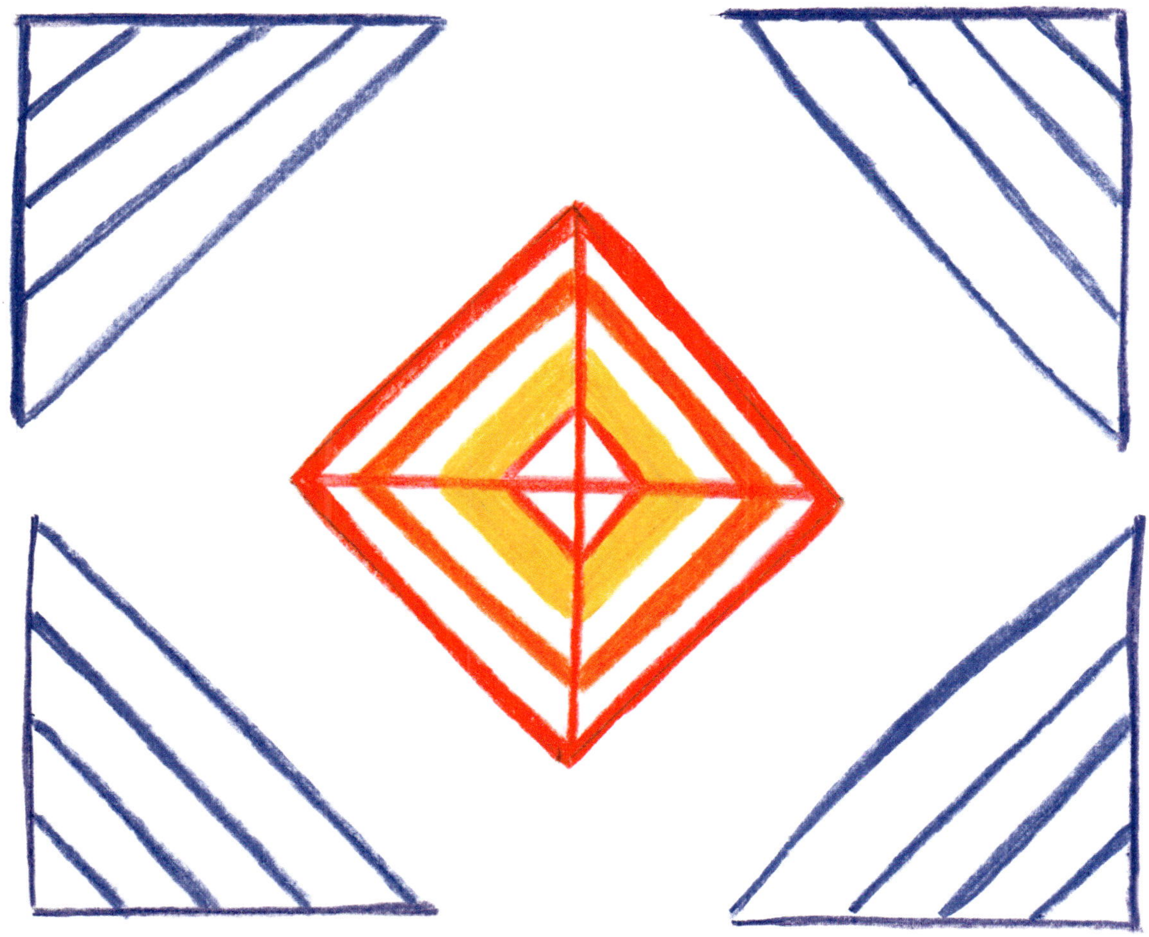

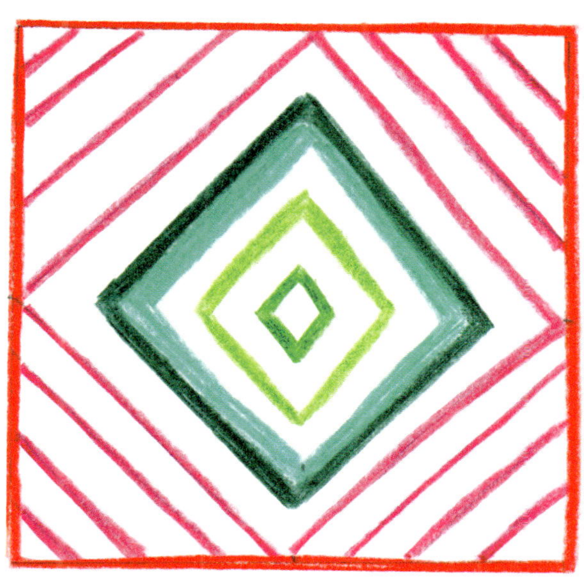

Radiating diagonal lines

Many beautiful radiating forms can be created by varying the lengths of the diagonal lines and drawing with careful, even positioning. The children can experiment with diagonal lines to create their own forms.

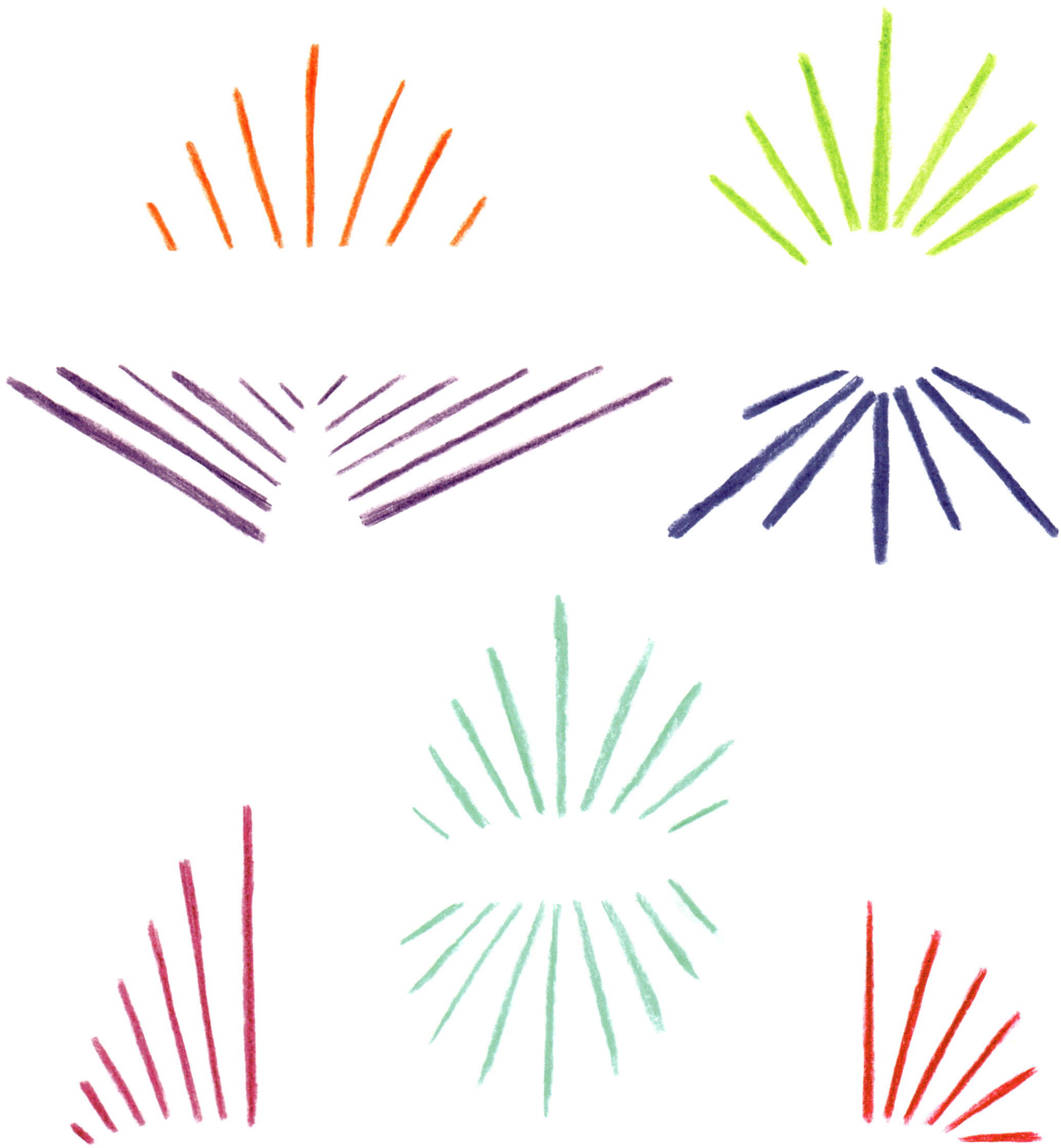

Symmetrical drawings

Eight carefully spaced lines create snowflake forms. Different geometric shapes can be added to them.

The children are learning about:

- form
- structure
- symmetry
- balance
- linear relationships
- optical effects
- patterns.

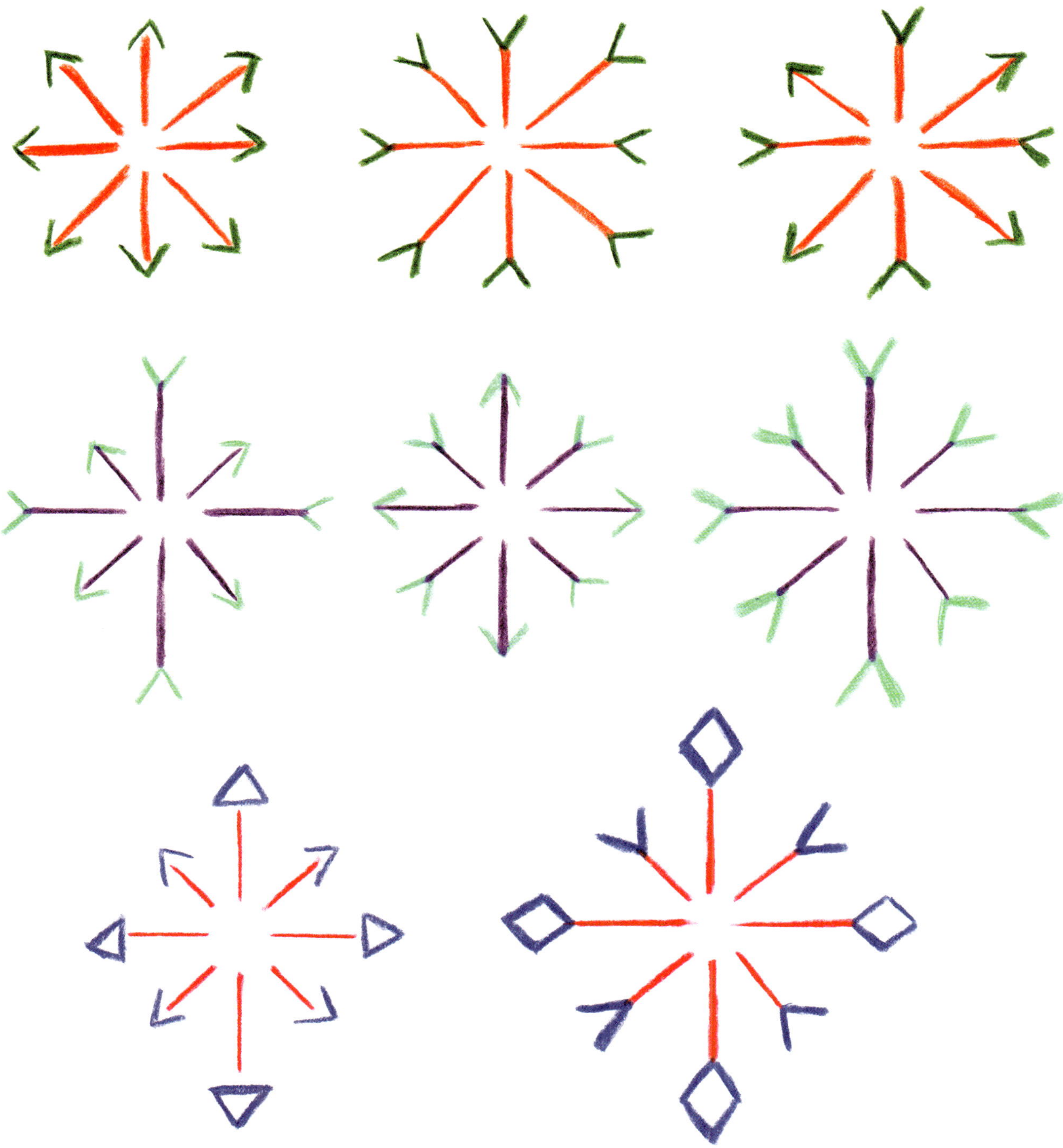

Symmetrical sequences

These drawings are all symmetrical and have two central lines which cross in the centre. The outer forms relate to each other in a sequence, which is regular and harmonious.

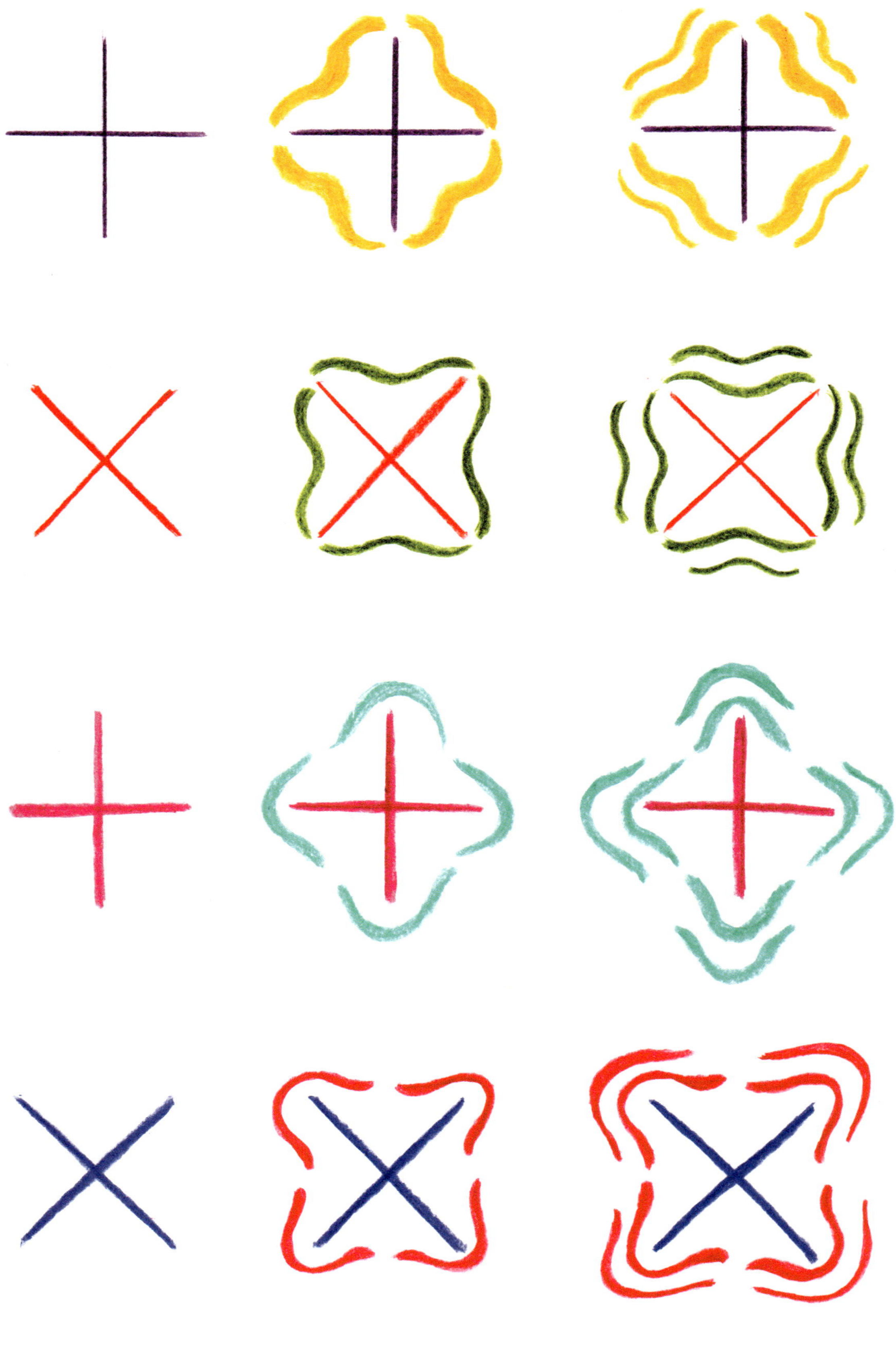

Shapes: Triangles, squares and diamonds

The children can draw shapes which have a clear structure, and yet are drawn without rulers. The helpful dots drawn first help the children to visualise where the lines should go.

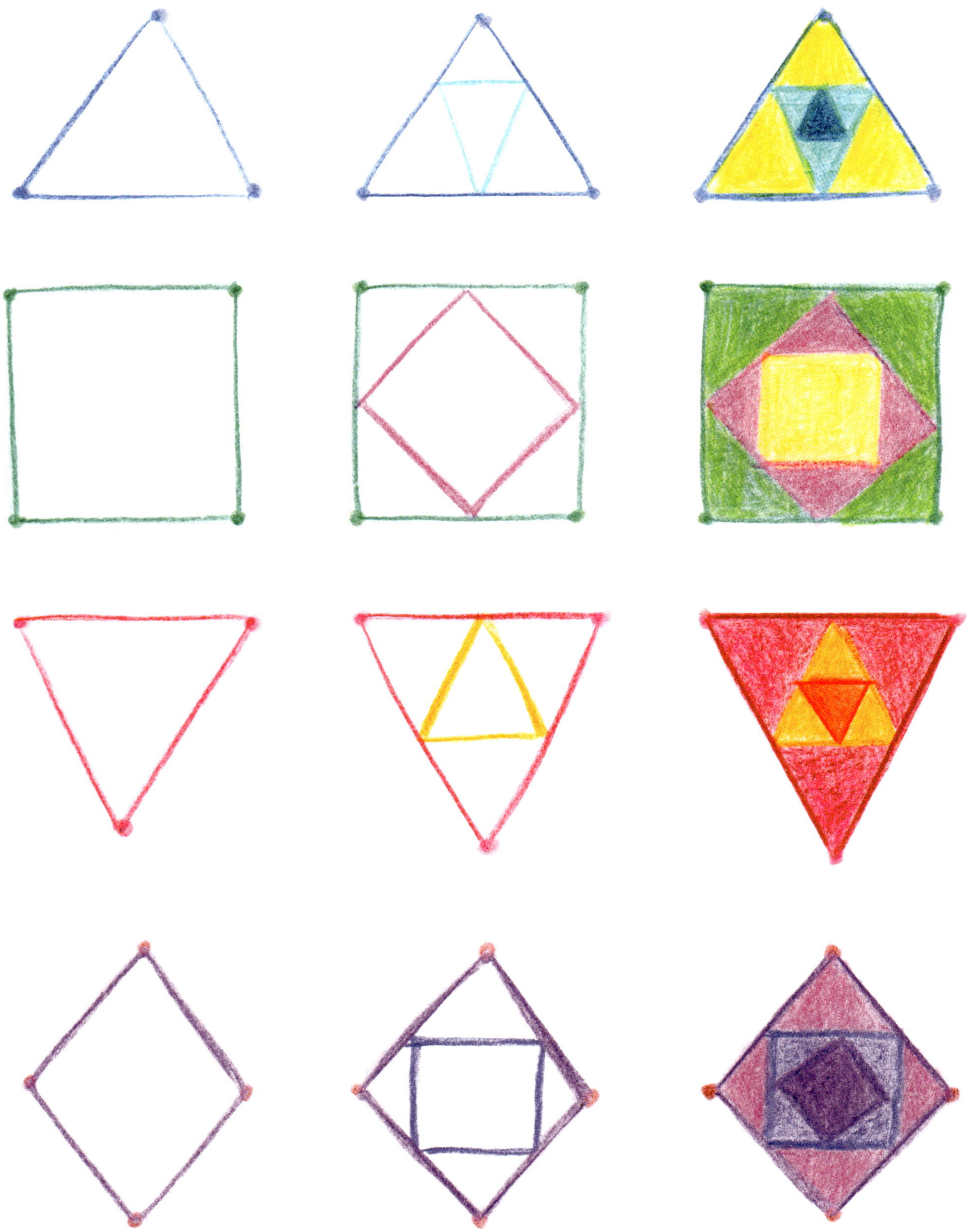

Forms with diamonds

These forms are evenly spaced and balanced in their symmetry. They require a lot of concentration, and can be drawn lightly at first to get the diamond angles lined-up. In the first row the diamonds are wider and by the last row the diamonds are narrower.

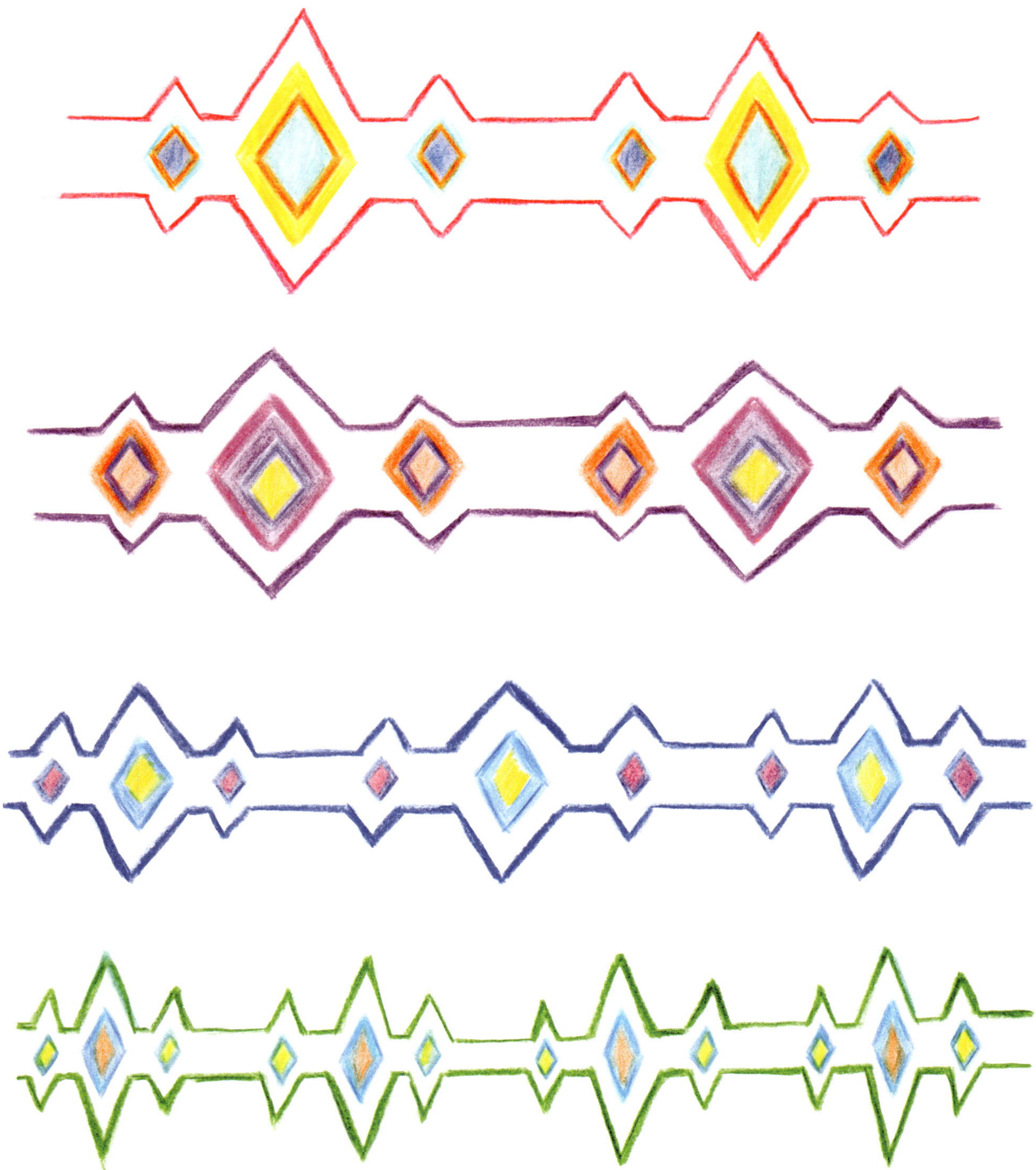

Forms with rectangles

These forms are quite striking in their symmetry and structure. The children will need to work carefully and to take their time so that the forms are as regular as possible.

These forms give the experiences of:

- structure
- stability
- regularity
- strength
- solidity
- verticality combined with the horizontal.

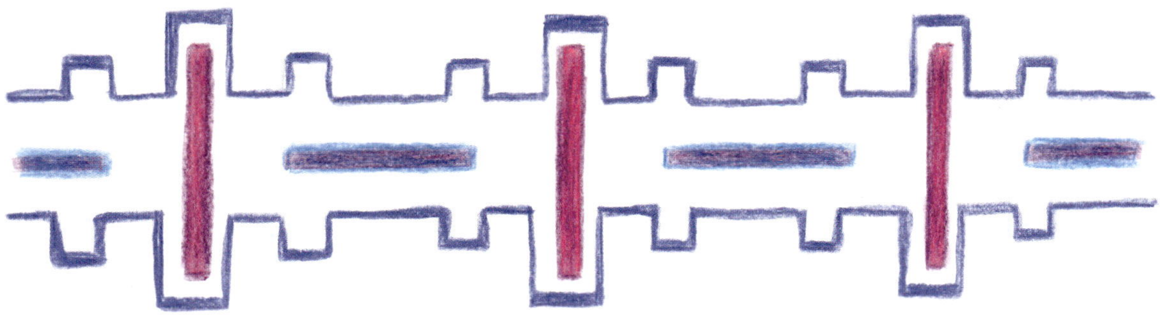

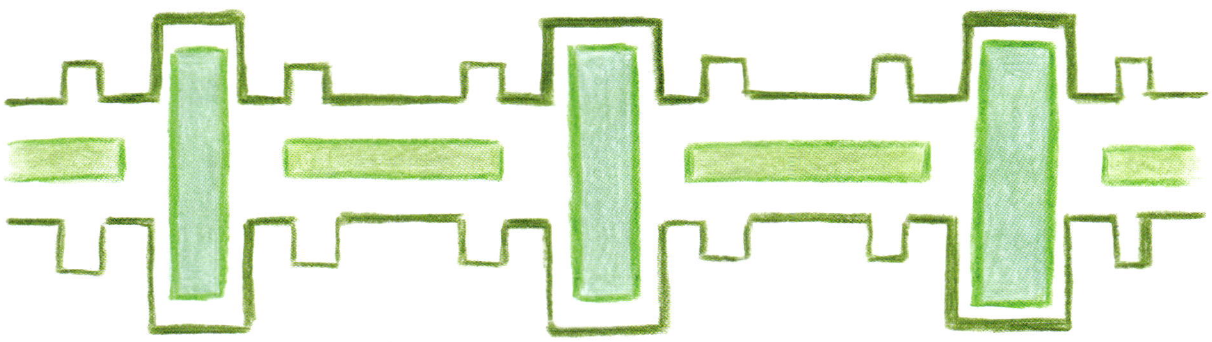

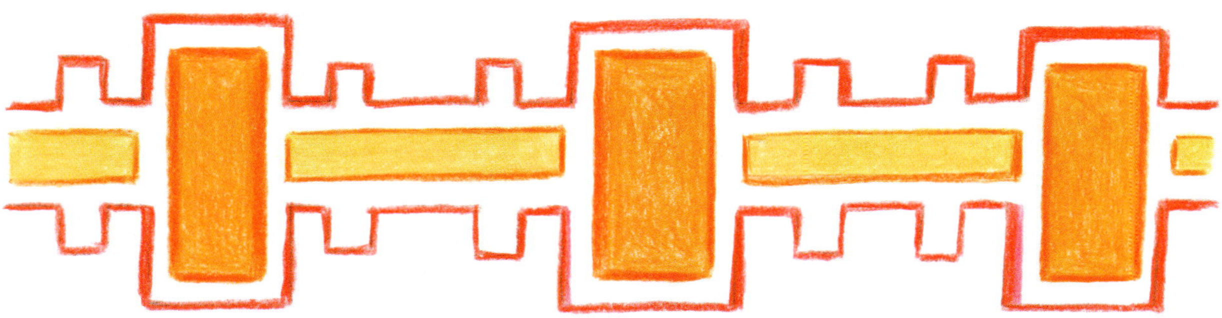

Forms with lines

These forms need to be drawn carefully and spaced evenly. The children will be surprised when they turn their books upside down. The first three forms look the same!

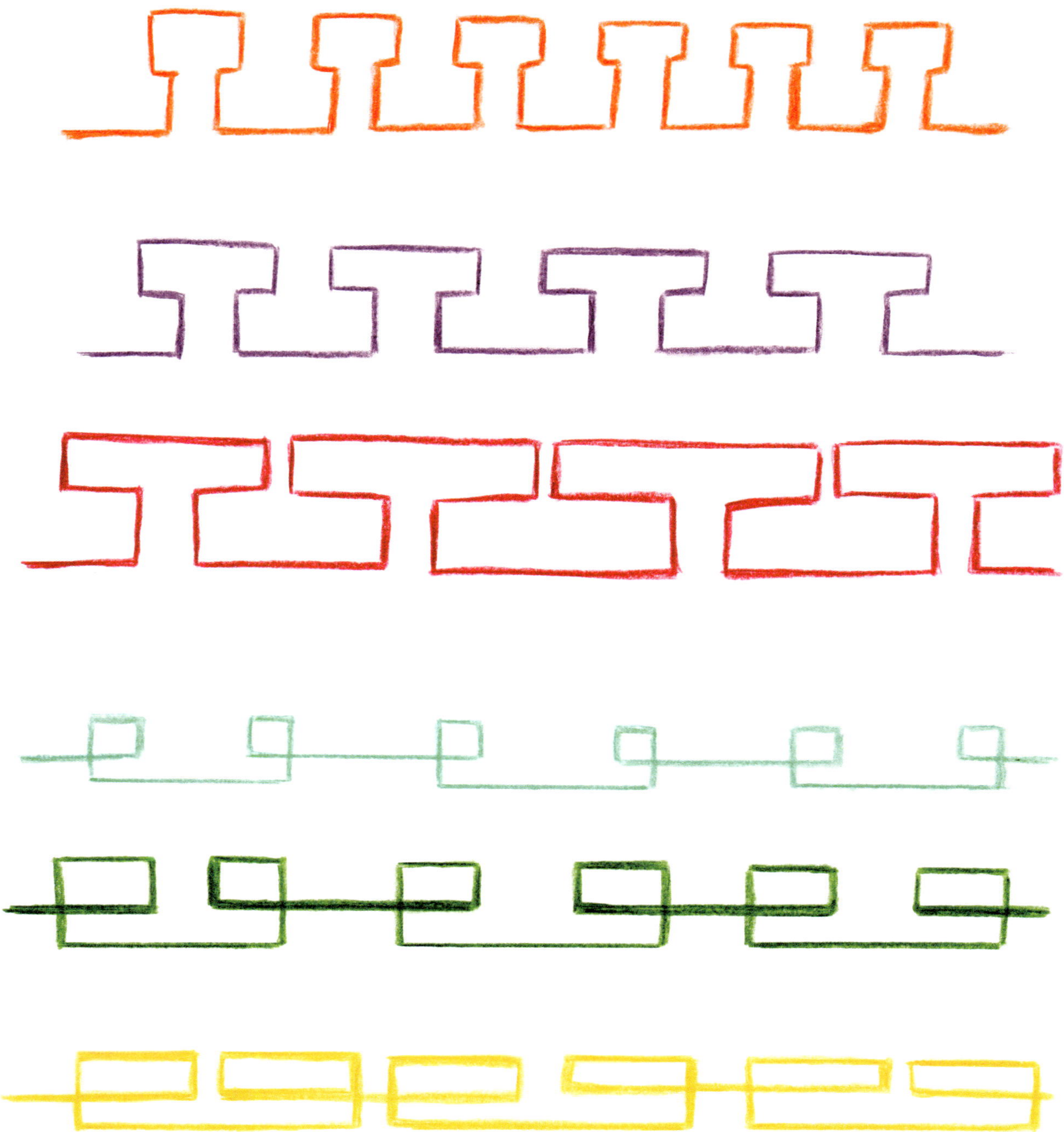

Rhythmic forms

The world is full of rhythm and the following forms are based on the rhythms of movement, speech, poetry, music and dance. The children will need to clap, nod and step the rhythms before drawing them. They may be familiar with poems or songs that have a strong rhythm and they can say or sing them at the beginning of the form-drawing lesson. Clapping hands can be done singly and also with an opposite partner, crossing the hands over (i.e. right hand to right hand, left to left for the shorts; both hands together for the longs). The class can move in a large circle when stepping the rhythms, and also stand singly at their desks moving from one foot to another. This can be accompanied by clapping and nodding!

When the children are drawing they will hear the rhythms in the noise that the pencil makes on the paper. Rhythmic forms will support:

- listening skills
- movement experiences
- multi-sensory integration
- co-ordination
- appreciation of poetry and music
- development of timing and tempo in speech.

The children should also invent their own rhythmic forms.

Starting with a short beat:

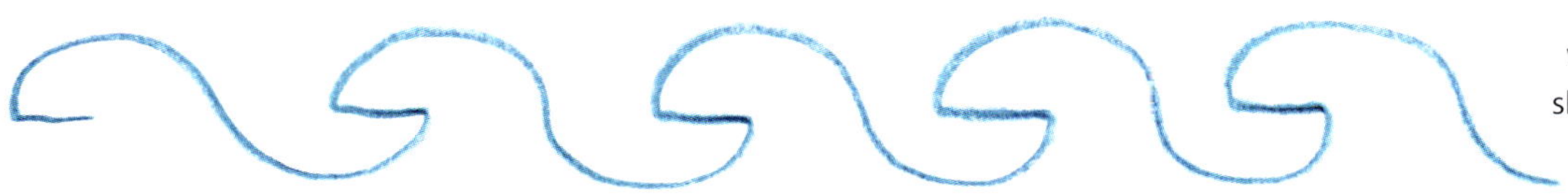

◡ —
short long

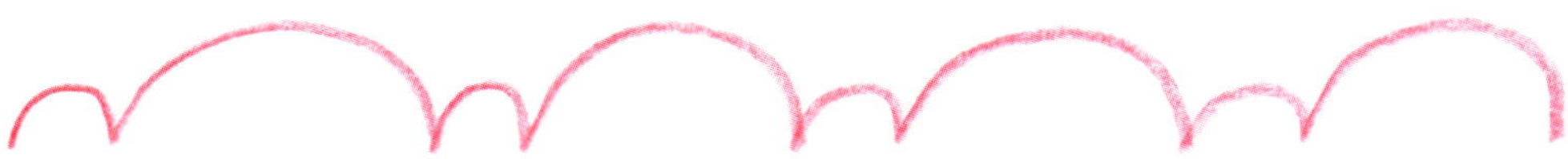

◡ —
short long

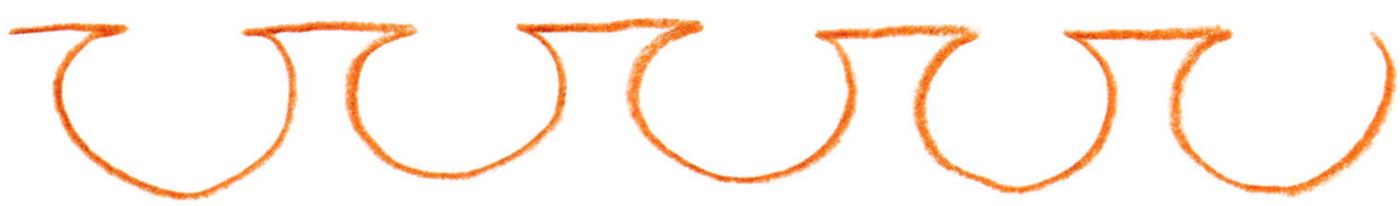

◡ —
short long

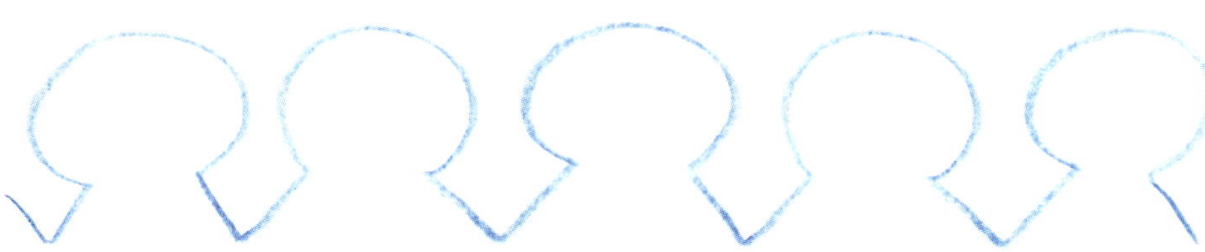

◡ ◡ —
short short long

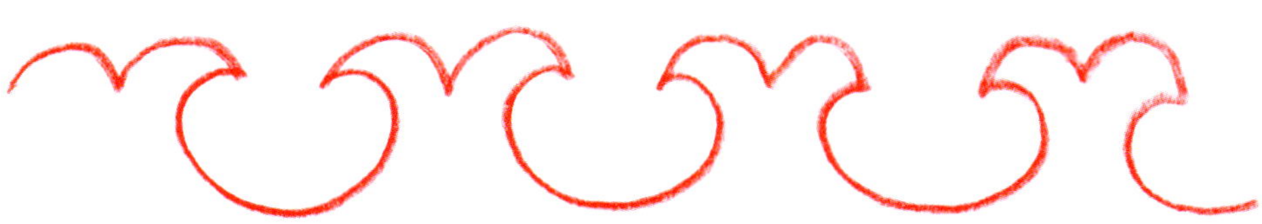

◡ ◡ —
short short long

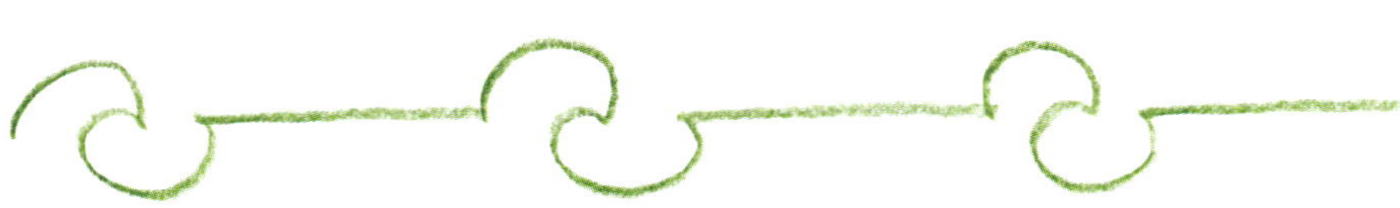

◡ ◡ —
short short long

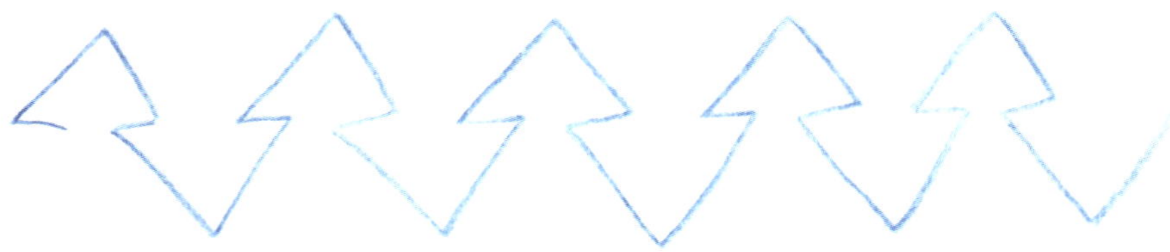

short long long

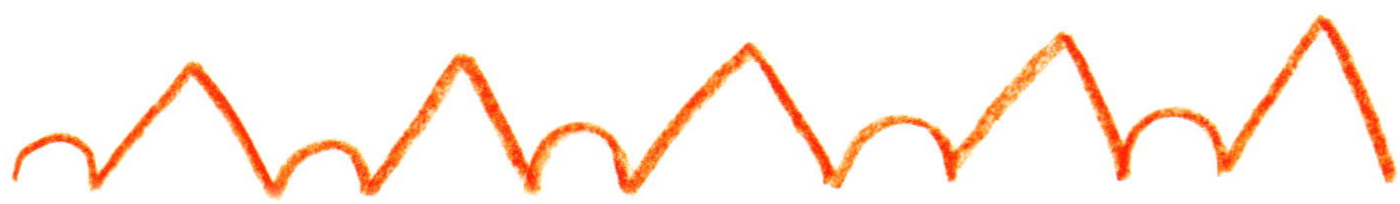

short long long

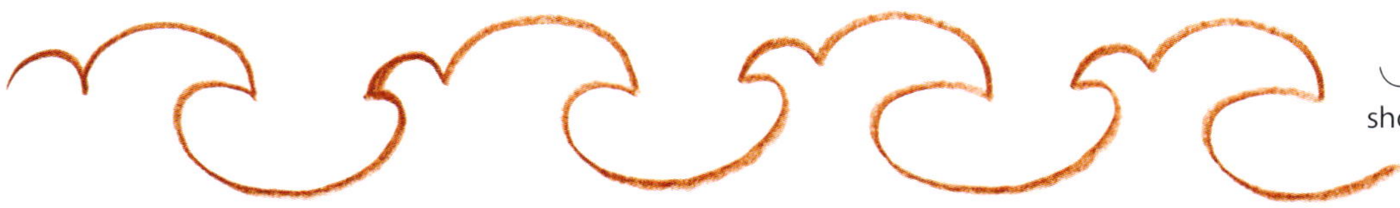

short long long

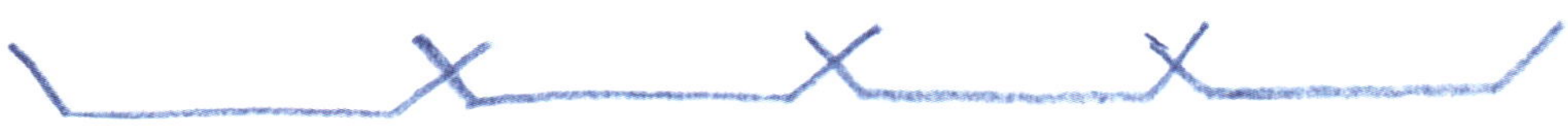

short long short

short long short

Starting with a long beat:

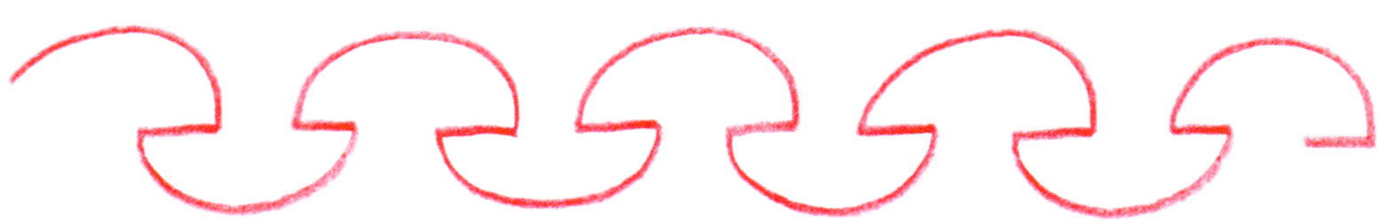

long short

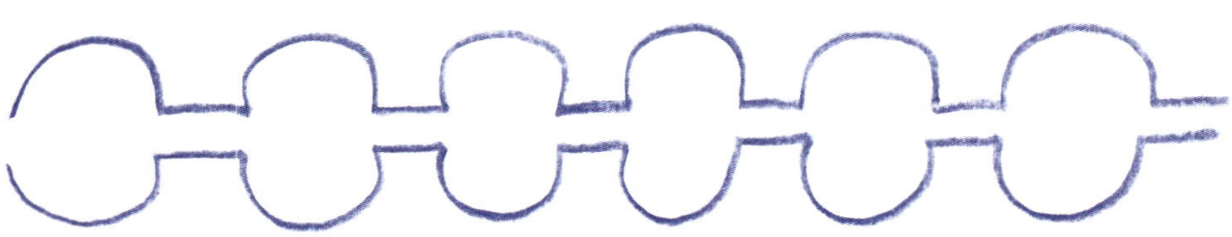

long short

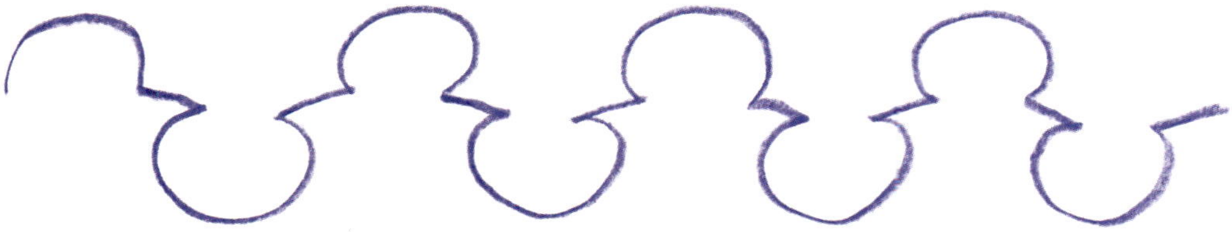

long short

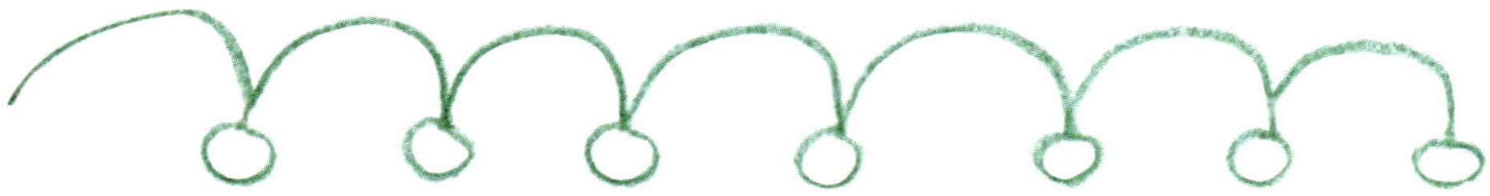

long short

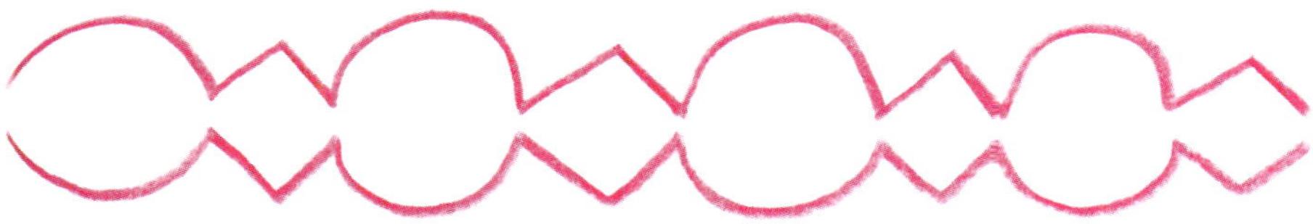

long short short

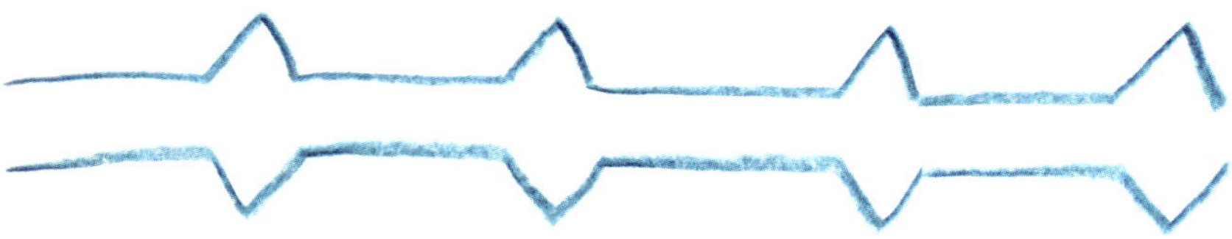

long short short

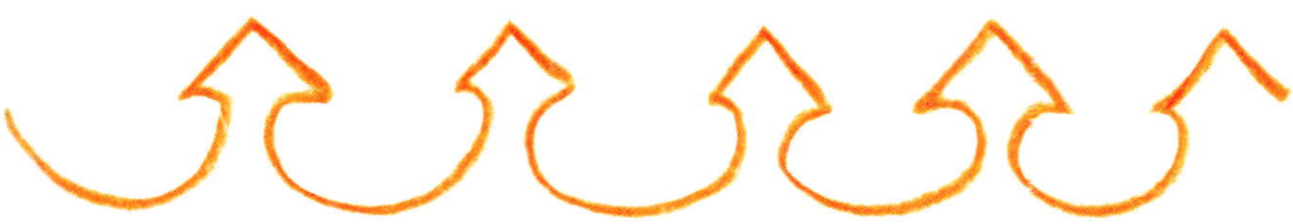

long short short

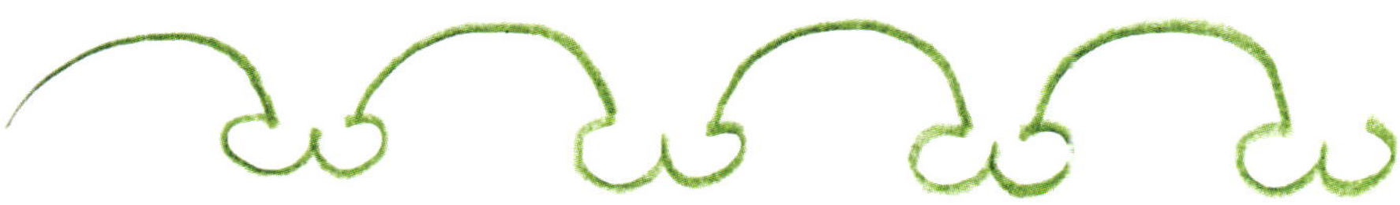

long short short

long short short

Rhythmic circles

We see rhythmic linear forms everywhere in nature:

- in leaf veins
- in tree bark
- in the rings of a cut tree trunk
- in rippling water surfaces
- on sand blown by the wind.

A living material substance senses the influence of water, of heat, of air, of light, and responds in its own way.

Nature's growth patterns fluctuate in rhythms of expansion and contraction created by living-sensing processes which give rise to extraordinary gestures.

These circles seem to be filled to bursting point with dynamic movements created by lines responding to the influence of other lines. Forms echo forms and create new elements of tension or harmony.

The children can experiment with linear rhythms in this way, creating their own patterns within a circular form, which provides a boundary for the lines to respond to.

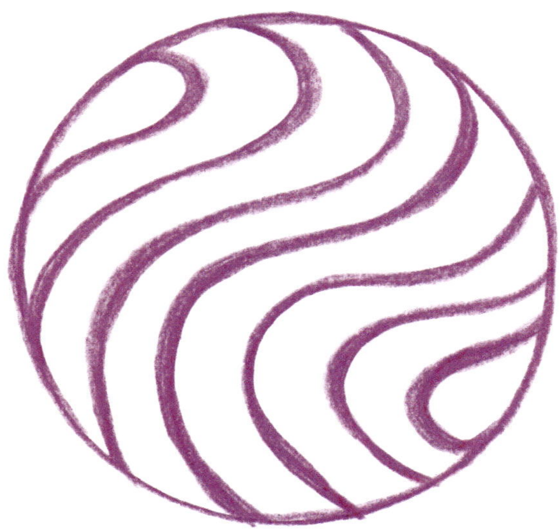

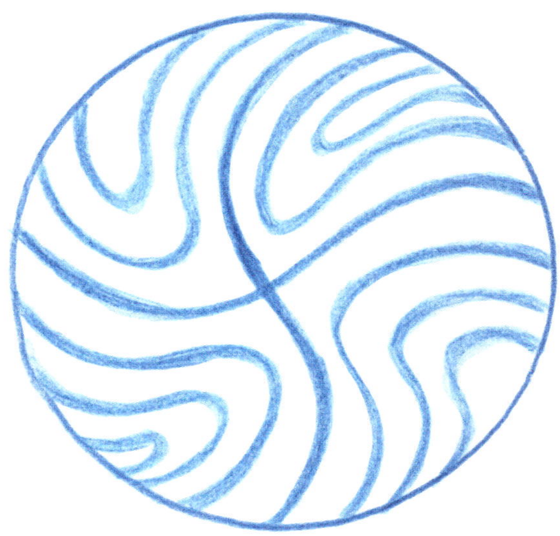

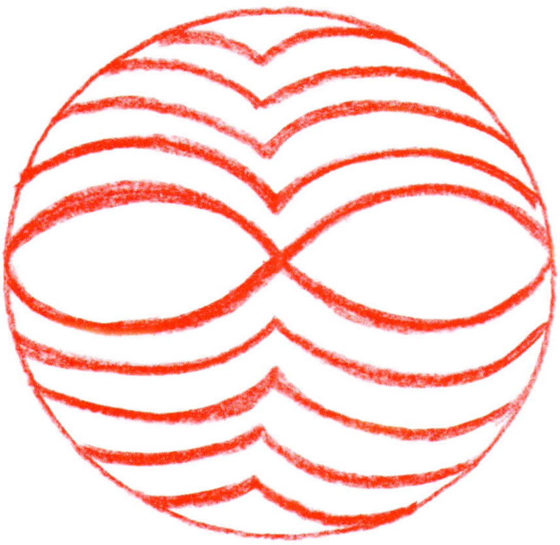

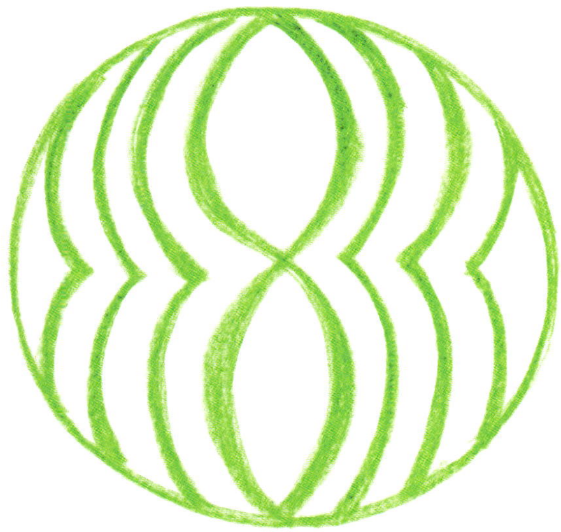

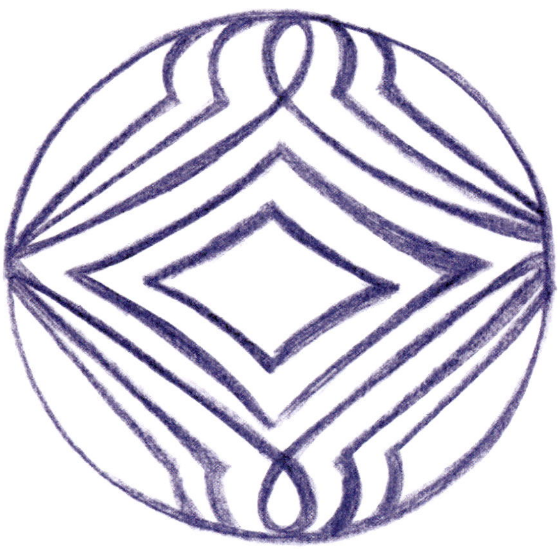

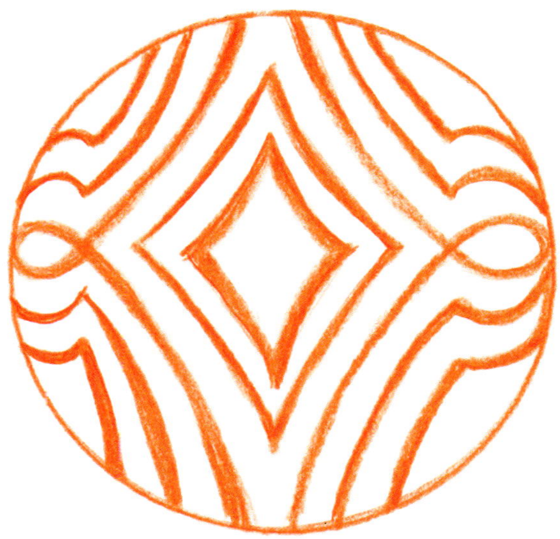

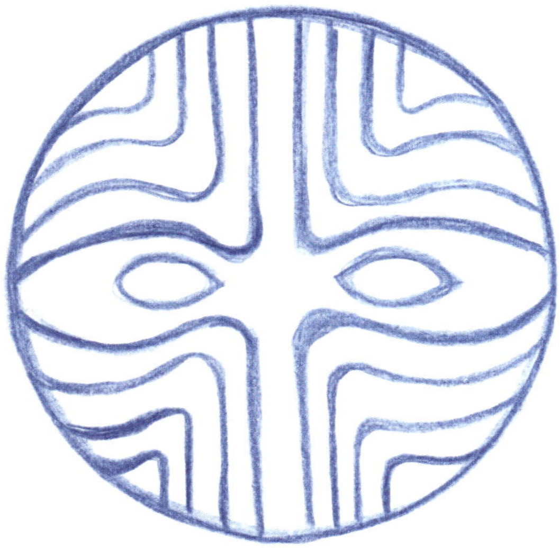
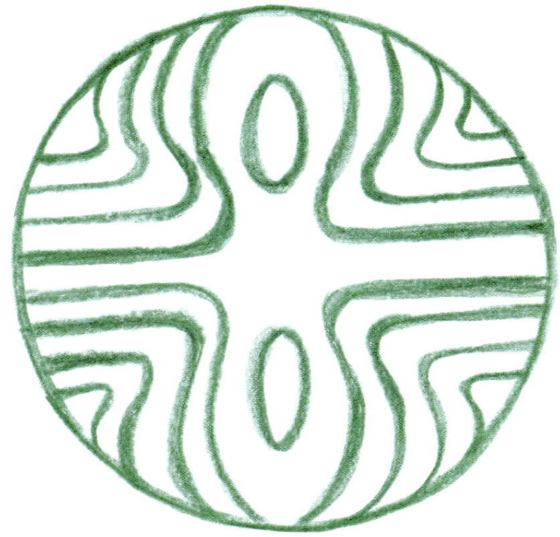
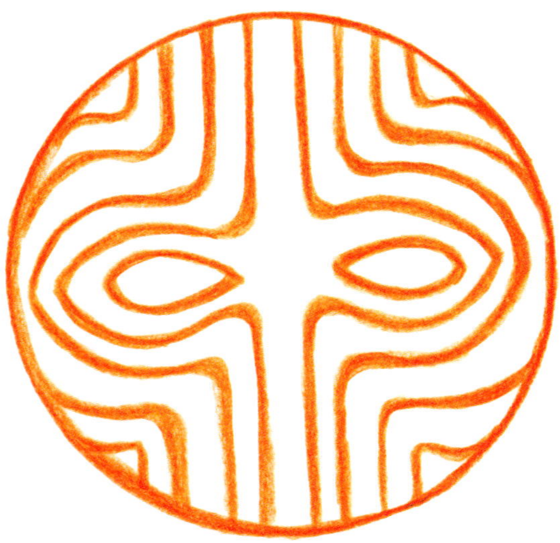
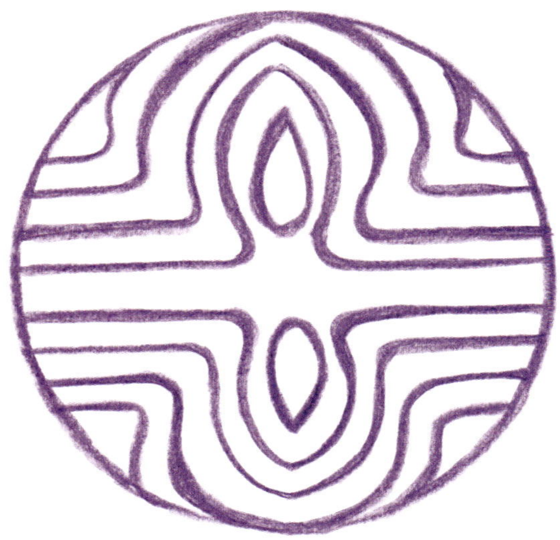

Enhancing forms

Drawing helpful dots will enable the children to balance these crossing-over forms. The crossing can be done in pairs, so that the curves go through the centre point. Then the forms can be enhanced with straight lines, or further curves, then coloured.

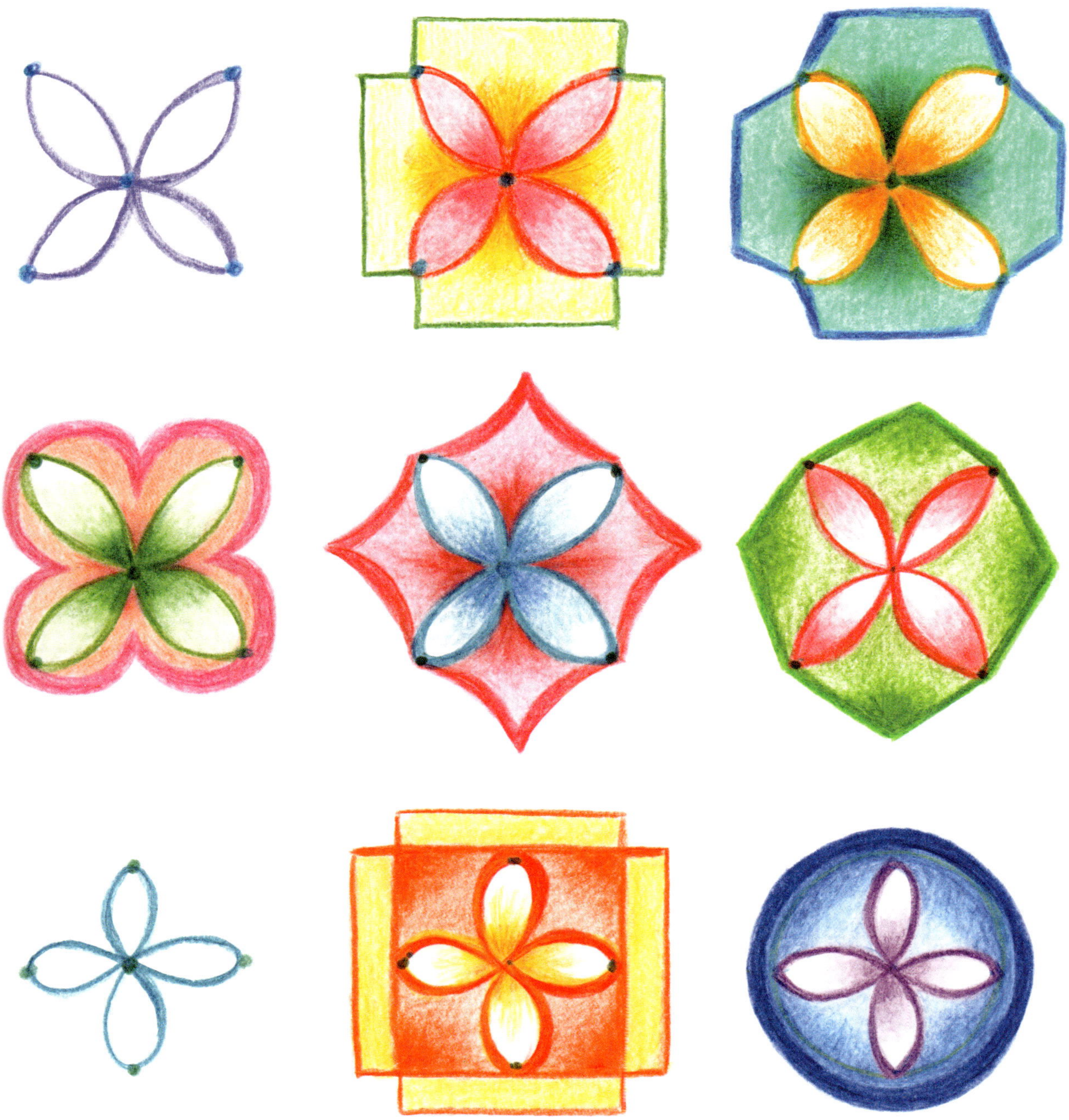

Diamond forms

Using helpful dots will provide the orientation for these structured forms. Lines then connect the dots, drawing very lightly at first, so that adjustments can be made if necessary. The diamond forms can then be added to with curved or straight lines, and coloured.

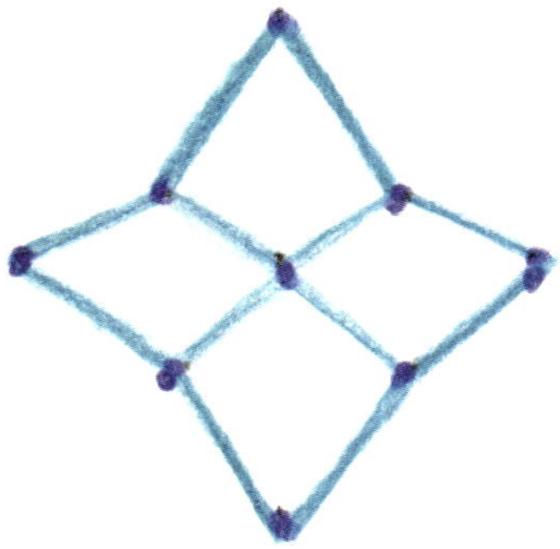

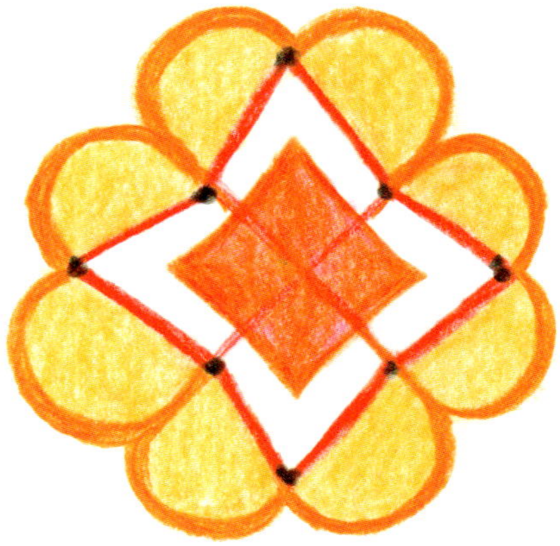

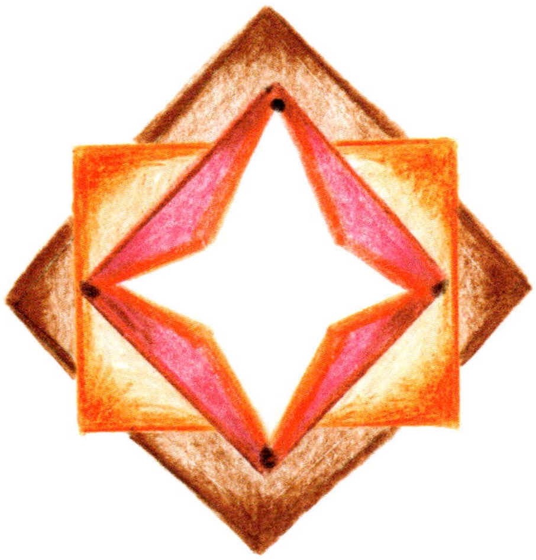

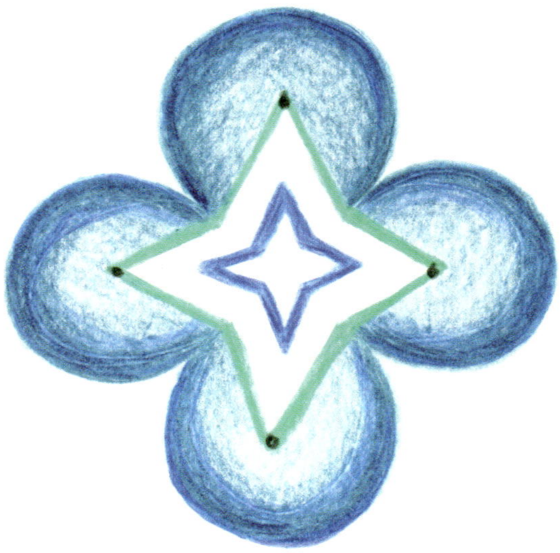

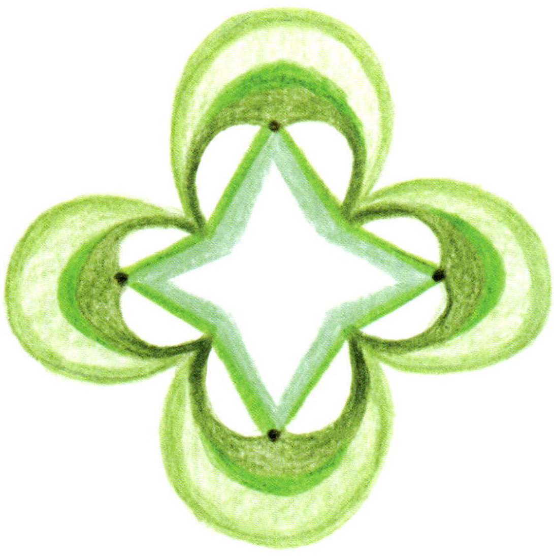

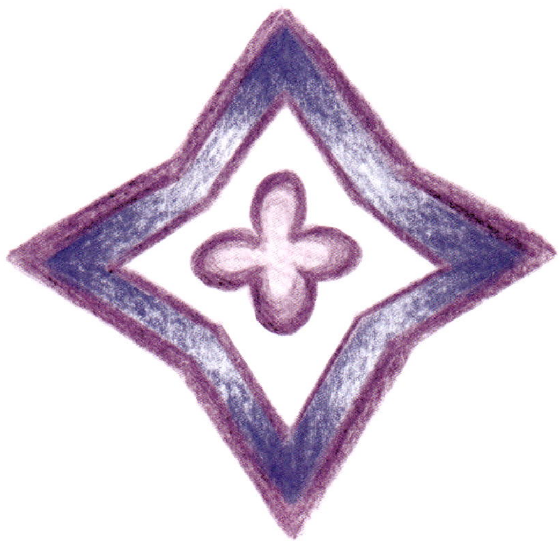

Mirror forms

These mirror forms provide experiences of rhythmical progressions, curved and straight lines, contrasts in size, angles and proportion.

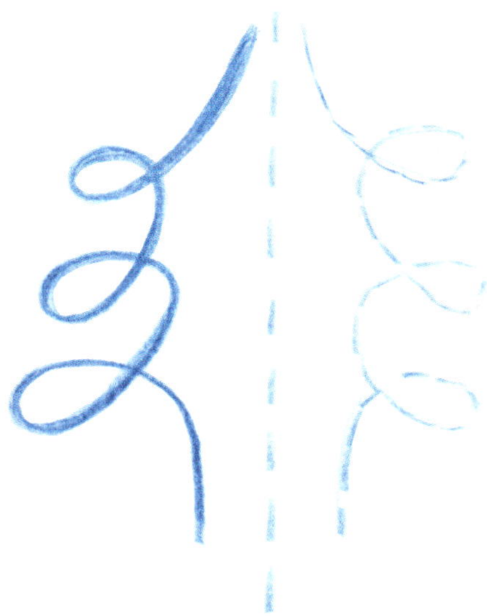

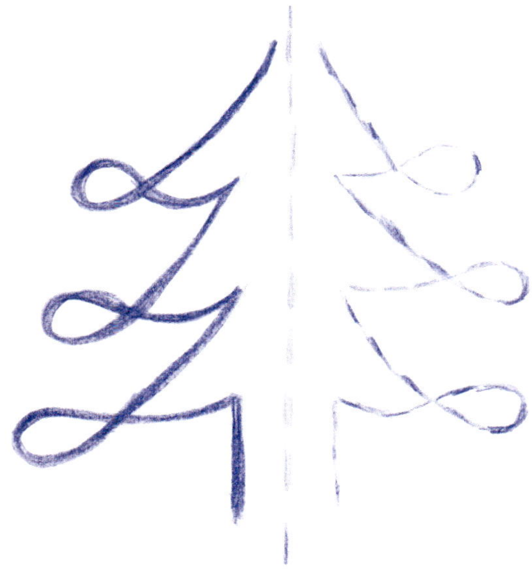

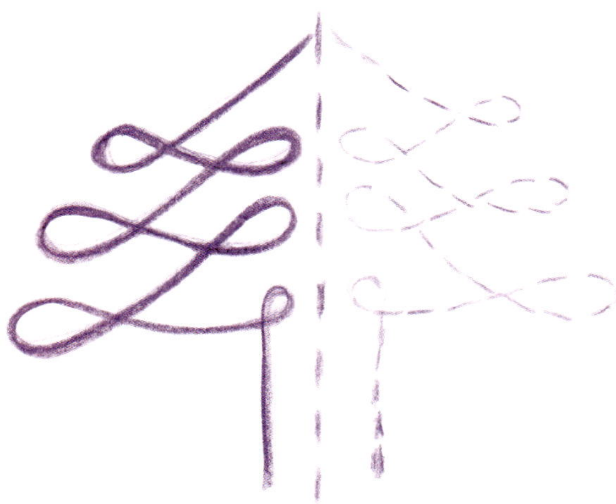

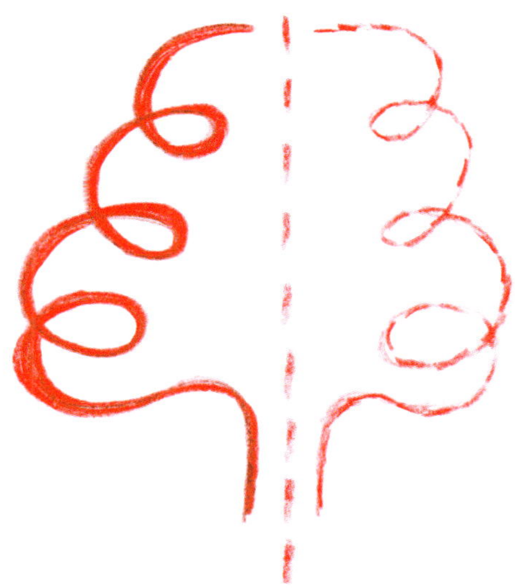

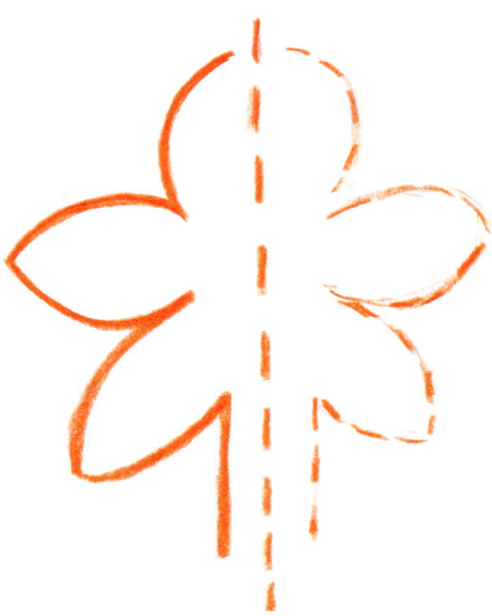

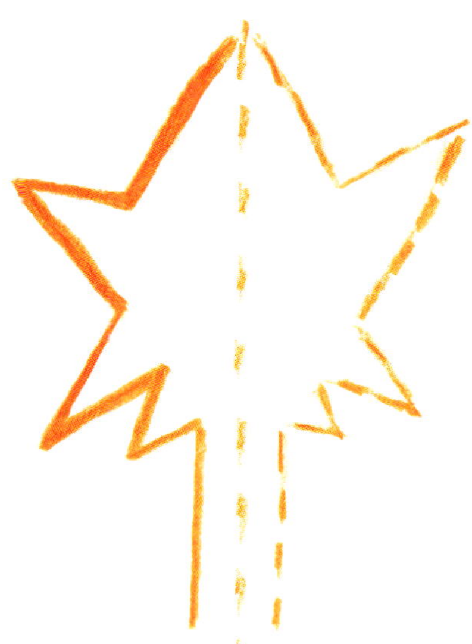

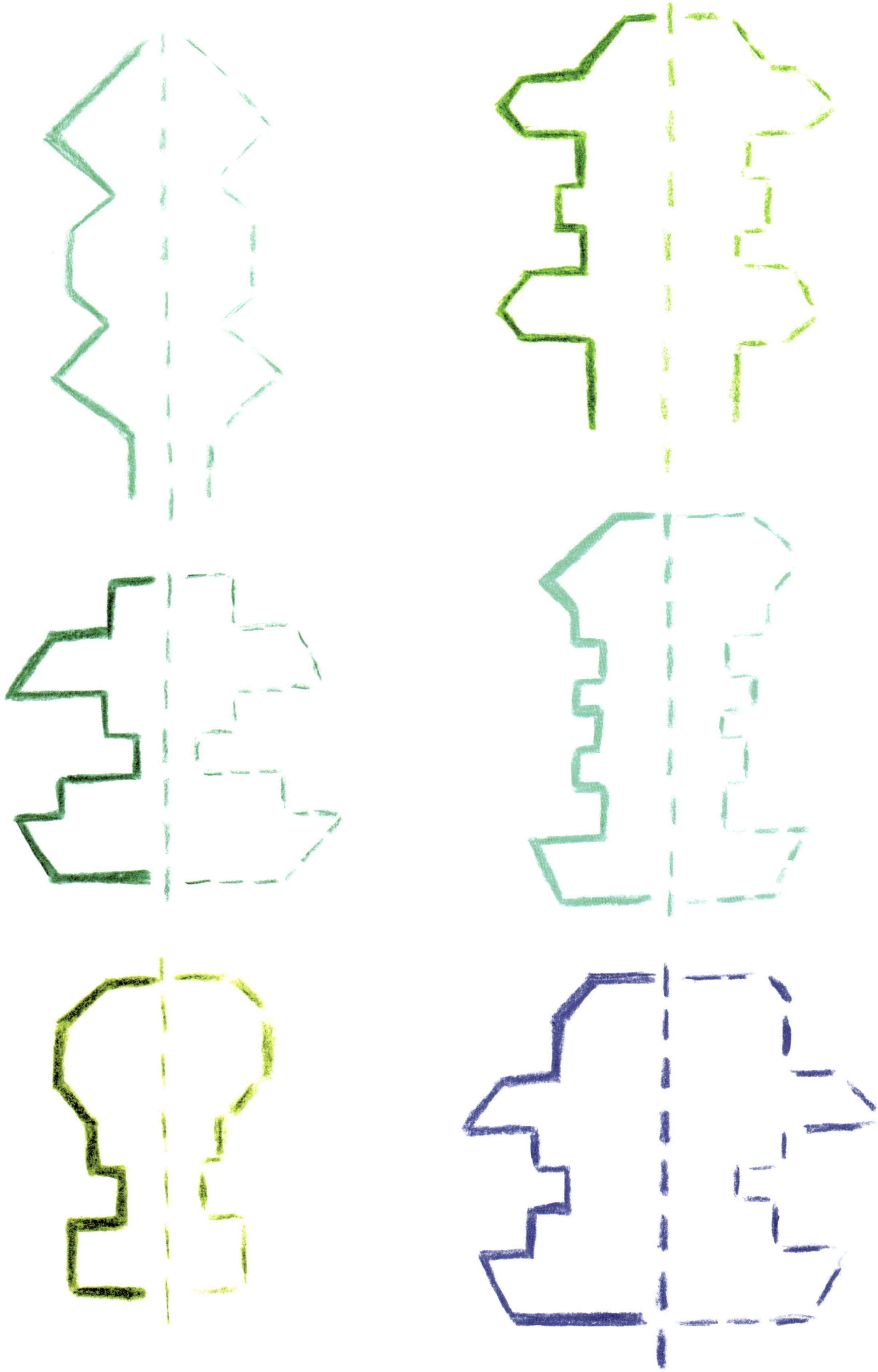

Evaluating the children's work

The children from 9 years onwards will be developing an independent sense of aesthetics, that is, the ability to look on their own work with a slightly more critical eye, in an objective way. They are still in the experience of 'doing', but they begin to evaluate their own work more objectively. They can like their work and feel pleased with their forms, or not be happy with them and feel dissatisified. It may be necessary for the teacher to give individual suggestions: 'You could try this… ' or 'Perhaps something here might look good… '.

At this stage there will be a marked individuality in each child's work, and some distinctive 'styles' will appear. Strengths and weaknesses will also be apparent, and it may be necessary to repeat some exercises in slightly different ways to consolidate their skills, especially with left-handed children.

Some children might begin to copy others. This can indicate an inner sense of insecurity (although this may not be apparent in other lessons, or in general school behaviour). Encourage these children to do something different, so that their work becomes their own. Don't accuse them of copying (this is embarrassing and humiliating for them) but draw their attention to something which looks good in their own form, and help them develop it.

Above all, children should enjoy form drawing and feel secure in their work.They should also appreciate others' drawings. Allow time at the end of the lesson for groups of four or five children to hold their books up for everyone to see.The whole class can take turns at doing this, but remember: No criticising! Enjoy looking! If the class becomes judgemental, or the comparisons become too strong, do this sharing only occasionally.

Quotations from lectures by Rudolf Steiner

The Kingdom of Childhood

August 12th 1924, Torquay, England.

Symmetry exercises: reflecting above/below

With special reference to pictorial thinking, Class 2.

At first the child will be quite awkward doing this work, but gradually he/she will adjust themselves to it and will develop more thoughtfulness in his observations and more imagery in his thinking. Thinking will remain completely within the realm of images. This means that especially in the young child the intellect, the intelligence that works isolated in the soul, should not be yet developed; his thinking should grow by means of the visual, the pictorial.

The development of the intellect

The intellect should not be worked at directly, but rather it should grow out of activity of the will that stems from image-making, so that it emerges as a consequence of the whole human being.

Course for Teachers, Basel, Switzerland, 1924

Lecture 4, July 24th 1924. Pages 73-75.

Forms of the letters must be developed out of the drawing and painting. Of all the arts these must be cultivated first. Everything which introduces the child initially to the forms of the letters, which is quite strange to the child, is quite wrong from an educational point of view.

In an education build up on a knowledge of the human being, learning to write must precede learning to read. After the change of teeth you must as far as possible approach the whole being of the child. When the child is occupied in writing, the whole upper part of the body is active; there is an inner mobility which is quite different from when only the head is kept busy learning the forms of the letters. The children can read what they themselves have written, and in this way an impression is made on them. This is a way to a really health-giving education.

Human Values In Education

Lecture 3. Arnheim, Holland. July 17th 1924. Pages 52–53

Movement

...Observe how a child moves...this reveals the most inward urge of life, the prime life impulse. At the same time the principle of imitation comes to light in gesture, in movement. For gesture is what appears first of all in human evolution, and in the special constitution of the physical, soul and spiritual organism of the human being, gesture is transformed into speech. And an understanding of the world through the senses and through thinking is developed out of speech.

Thought does not produce speech, but speech thought. In the cultural development of humanity as a whole, human beings have first spoken, then thought. So it is also with the child; first out of movement the child learns to speak, to articulate, and only then does thinking come from speech. This sequence is important:

- *movement*
- *speech*
- *thinking.*

The Renewal of Education

Basel, Switzerland, April 26th 1920

Lecture 5 ***Concerning the Curriculum***

...[In the Waldorf Schools]...we do not teach writing straight away, but, with a certain amount of artistry we teach form drawing which can extend into painting. We do this also in order to give the children a living experience of colour and its harmonies for which, at the age of seven or eight, they are especially receptive...While they are engaged in such an activity we can see how, in drawing and painting definite forms and patterns, the children need to make certain movements with their fingers, hands and arms. Thus it is not an intellectual or thinking activity, but practicing manual dexterity which comes at the beginning of our teaching...One should appeal to the whole human being, letting the intellect evolve through the practice of manual skill which, at the same time, is also permeated by a harmonious feeling – life. The less one drills the intellect of young children, the better it will develop later on.

References and recommended reading

Lectures given by Rudolf Steiner

Education as a Social Problem
Anthroposophic Press, New York, U.S.A, 1969.
Six Lectures given in Dornach, Switzerland. August 9th–17th 1919.

The Study of Man
Rudolf Steiner Press, Forest Row, East Sussex, UK.
Lectures given in Stuttgart, August 29th 1919.

Discussions with Teachers
Rudolf Steiner Press, Forest Row, East Sussex, UK, 1967.
Discussions held with the faculty of the Waldorf School in Stuttgart, 21st August–6th September 1919.

The Renewal of Education
Steiner Schools Fellowship Publications, Michael Hall, Forest Row, East Sussex, UK, 1981.
Fourteen lectures given to the teachers in Basel, Switzerland. April 20th–May 11th 1920.

Waldorf Education for Adolescence
Steiner Schools Fellowship Publications, Michael Hall, Forest Row, East Sussex, UK, 1980.
Eight lectures given to the teachers of the Waldorf School, Stuttgart, June12th–19th 1921.

The Younger Generation
Anthroposophic Press, New York, USA, 1967.
Lecture given in Stuttgart, October 12th 1922.

A Modern Art of Education
Rudolf Steiner Press, Forest Row, East Sussex, UK, 1972.
Lectures given in Ilkley, England, August 5th–17th 1923.

The Essentials of Education
Rudolf Steiner Press, Forest Row, East Sussex, UK. First published 1926, revised in 1968.
Five lectures given to the Education Conference at the Waldorf School, Stuttgart. April 8th–12th 1924.

The Roots of Education
Rudolf Steiner Press, Forest Row, East Sussex, UK, 1968.
Five lectures given in Berne, Switzerland, April 13th–17th 1924.

Human Values in Education
Rudolf Steiner Press, Forest Row, East Sussex, UK, 1971.
Ten lectures given in Arnheim, Holland, July 17th–24th 1924

The Kingdom of Childhood
Rudolf Steiner Press, Forest Row, East Sussex, UK.
Lectures given in Torquay, England, August 12th–20th 1924.

There are a number of specific references which Rudolf Steiner gave to teachers concerning form drawing. They are included here in their chronological sequence.

Discussions with Teachers
Stuttgart, August 21st–September 6th 1919.
These discussions were held with the faculty of the Waldorf School in Stuttgart. The third discussion contains suggestions on design in relation to the temperaments.

A Modern Art of Education
August 5th–17th 1923
Lectures given in Ilkley, England, August 5th–17th 1923.

Recommended reading

Creative Form Drawing, Rudolf Kutzli, Work books 1, 2 and 3, Hawthorn Press, Stroud UK, 1985.

Form Drawing, Hans R. Niederhauser and Margaret Frohlich, Mercury Press, Spring Valley, New York, 1984.

Formenzeichnen, Kranich, Juneman, Berthold-Andraw, Buhler, Schubert, Verlag Freies Geistesleben (not translated) 1985, 2nd edition 1992.

Acknowledgements

My thanks to the Shenyang Waldorf Seminar, China, whose participants developed forms suited to the Chinese script (see pages 109, 116, 117, 118 and 128). My thanks also to the Docherty family, Forest Row, East Sussex, whose home-schooling programme welcomed form drawing lesssons, and enabled many forms to be put into practice. Finally I thank Hawthorn Press for requesting a new (and full colour) form drawing book, and extend my gratitude to their team whose assistance, support and attention to detail was much appreciated.

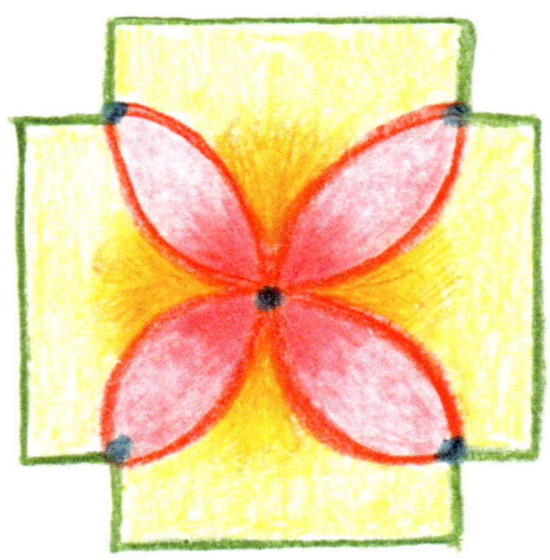

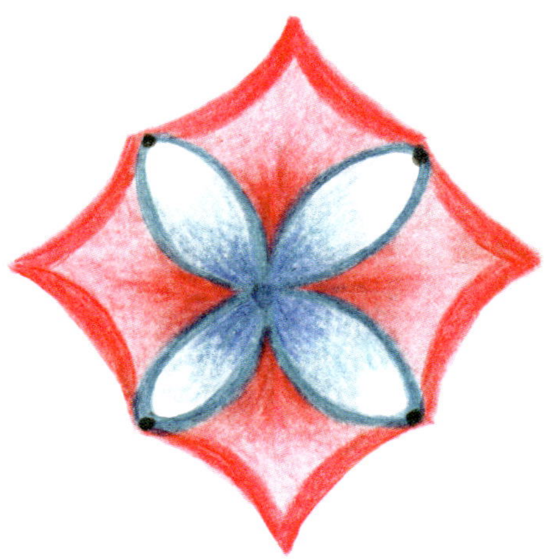

Companion Creative Form Drawing Books

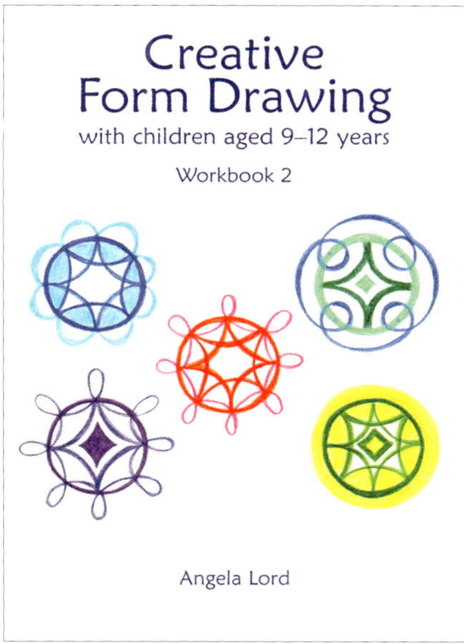

Creative Form Drawing

with children aged 9–12 years

Angela Lord

Creative Form Drawing with children: Workbook 2 is a form drawing resource for teachers working with ages 9–12. It is designed to be used with the Steiner/Waldorf curriculum in classes four and five, although it will also be valuable to home-educating parents using the Steiner/Waldorf ethos as their base. Contents include: Introduction; Using this book; Teaching methods; The adolescent child and art; Part one, Class Four; Part two, Class Five; Quotations from lectures by Rudolf Steiner; References and recommended reading; Acknowledgements.

96pp; 297 × 210mm; paperback; 978-1-912480-08-1

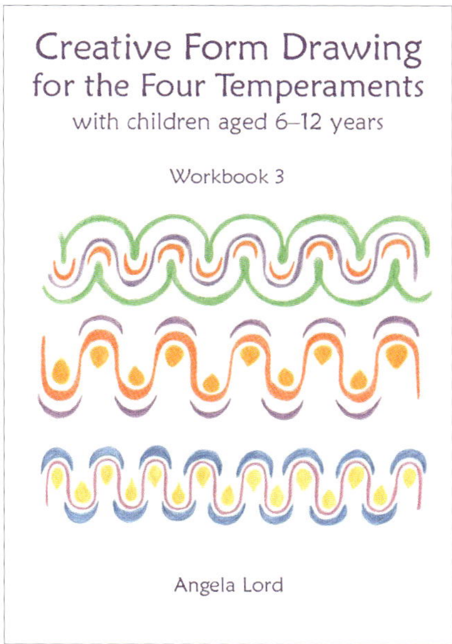

Creative Form Drawing for the Four Temperaments

with Children aged 6–12

Angela Lord

A step by step guide to drawing forms for the four temperaments, a resource to use with children aged 6–12 years. This has a harmonizing, transformative and strengthening effect on child development. Creative form drawing supports many learning capabilities: improved hand to eye co-ordination, spatial orientation, observation skills, focusing attention, confident movement, drawing skills and the foundation skills for handwriting. Designed specifically by Angela Lord for the four temperaments, these exercises also strengthen personal growth. Originally suggested by Rudolf Steiner, creative form drawing is used widely in Steiner Waldorf Schools to support healthy child development and learning.

112pp; 297 x 210mm; paperback; 978-1-912480-04-3

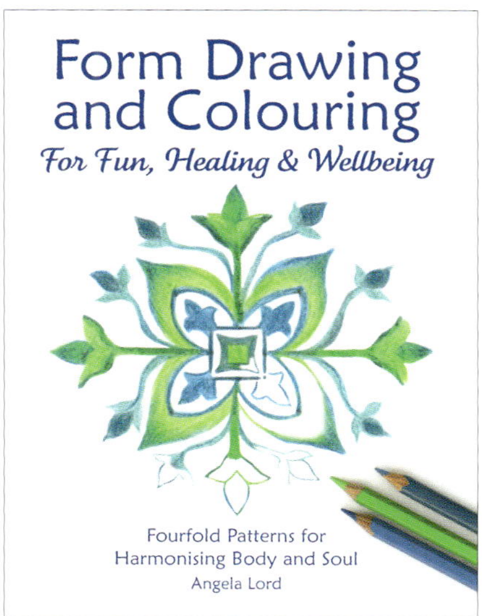

Form Drawing and Colouring

For Fun, Healing & Wellbeing

Angela Lord

Originally developed by Rudolf Steiner, creative form drawing is a fascinating and meaningful artistic activity for health and wellbeing. This book features fourfold patterns of increasing challenge and complexity, providing forms in varying states of completion to copy, experiment with and develop. This approach offers the reader creative freedom, aiming to be both calming and enlivening, and is a valuable aid to harmonising body and soul.

96 pages; 246 × 189mm; paperback; 978-1-907359-78-1

Other titles from Hawthorn Press

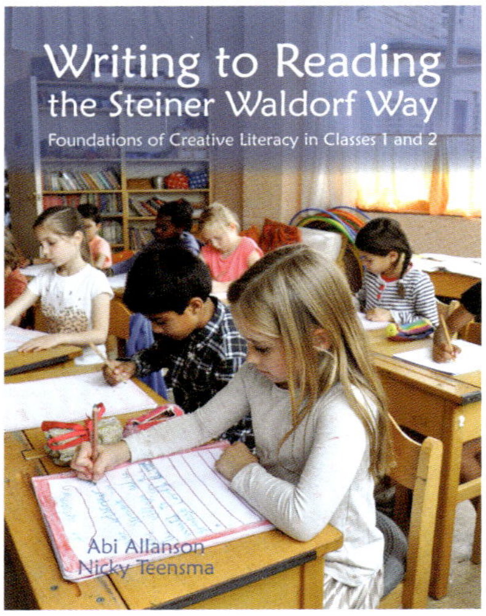

Writing to Reading the Steiner Waldorf Way

Foundations of Creative Literacy in Classes 1 and 2

Abi Allanson and Nicky Teensma

A theory and practice-based book that explores how Steiner/Waldorf pedagogy dovetails with mainstream primary approaches and specialist dyslexia-friendly methods. The child discovers their own voice through movement, form drawing and storytelling. The book includes easy-to-use lesson plans with assessment and feedback tips, movement, games, and activities, also drawings, photos, diagrams, and examples of children's work.

352pp; 246 x 189mm; hardback; 978-1-907359-88-0

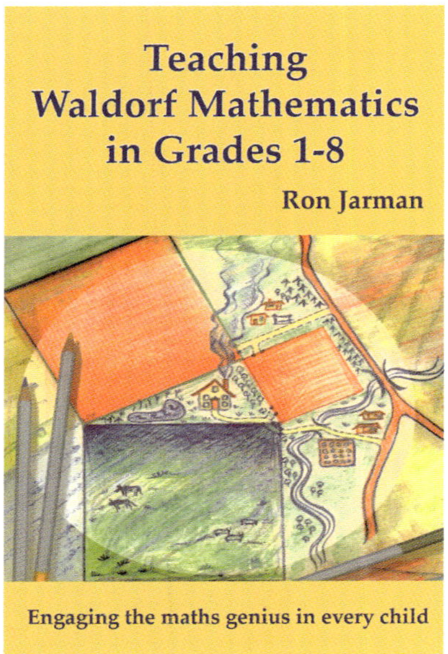

Teaching Waldorf Mathematics in Grades 1–8

Engaging the maths genius in every child

Ron Jarman

The second edition of this time-tested resource for teachers and home educators, back by popular demand. Teach math with imagination and confidence, laying the foundations for life!

Ron Jarman believes there is a maths genius in every child and adult. He shows how children can easily grasp math principles without the drudgery of endless worksheets. Uniquely, Ron draws on Pythagoras, the ancient Greeks, and Rudolf Steiner for re-imagining the vital importance of mathematical learning for human growth. The techniques and exercises in the book have been tried and tested for over a century by Waldorf teachers around the world.

304pp; 234 x 156mm; paperback; 978-1-912489-25-8

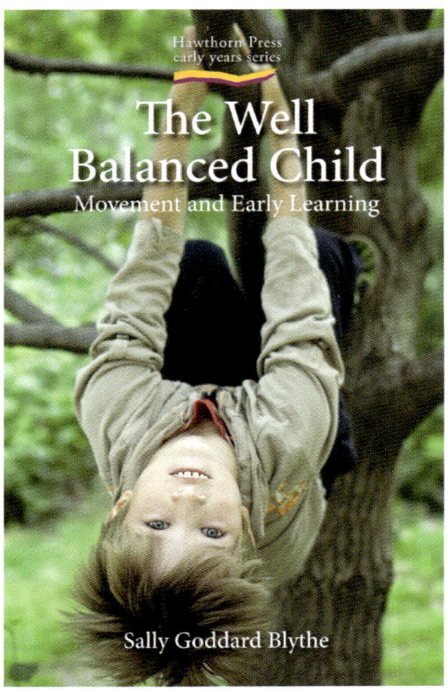

The Well Balanced Child

Movement and early learning

Sally Goddard Blythe

'Learning is not just about reading, writing and maths,' says Sally Goddard Blythe. 'A child's experience of movement will help play a pivotal role in shaping his personality, his feelings and achievements.' Her book makes the case for a 'whole body' approach to learning which integrates the brain, senses, movement, music and play. *The Well Balanced Child* examines why movement matters; how music helps brain development; the role of nutrition, the brain and child growth; and offers practical tips for parents and educators to help children with learning and behavioural problems.

240pp; 216 x 138mm; paperback; 978-1903458-63-1

The Parenting Toolkit

Simple Steps to Happy & Confident Children

Caroline Penney

This is a unique and valuable resource for parents and guardians who wish to give their children the best start in life. Caroline has drawn on her years of experience, facilitating parenting groups and working as a family therapist, to explain clearly how to help your child become confident, capable, caring, and able to reach their full potential. She also offers advice on how to ensure that you are getting all the self-care that you need in order to be a good parent. Illustrated throughout with warm and witty illustrations by Kate Hajducka.

176pp; 250 x 200mm; paperback; 978-1-907359-90-3 78-1

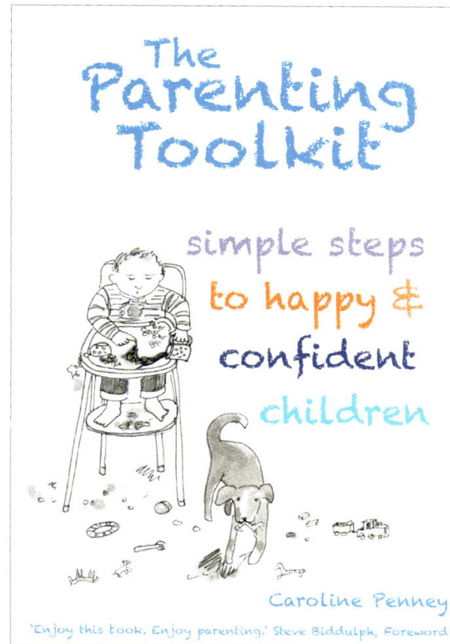

Reclaim Early Childhood

The Philosophy, Psychology and Practice of Steiner-Waldorf Early Years Education

Sebastian and Tamara Suggate

Reclaim Early Childhood presents a lively overview of the philosophical, developmental and educational foundations of Rudolf Steiner-Waldorf early years education as adaptable, creative and dynamic, informed by a profound respect for the uniqueness of each child.

'There is a strong and steady message that education should remove fixed judgements or a static and stuck view of the child or adult learner. Instead, Steiner education is about a state of 'becoming'... I recommend this book wholeheartedly'. From the foreword by Professor Tina Bruce CBE, Roehampton University

200pp; 234 x 156mm; paperback; 978-1-912480-10-4

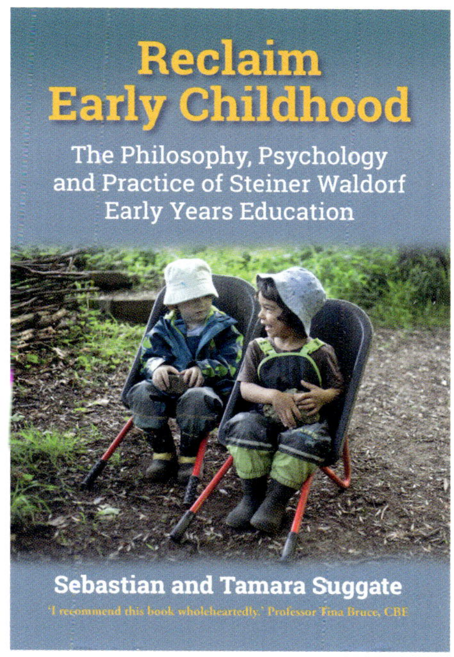

Making the Children's Year

Seasonal Waldorf Crafts with Children

Marije Rowling

Marije Rowling has revised and rewritten the book she originally co-wrote with two friends, *The Children's Year*, bringing new inspiration and ideas to a modern readership. Packed with all kinds of crafts, from papercrafting to building dens, she brings the eye of an artist, a parent, a grandparent and a professional into the home. From beginners to experienced crafters, this book is a gift for parents and adults seeking to make toys that will inspire children and provide an alternative to throwaway culture.

Making the Children's Year reminds us that making things by hand brings inner and outer rewards, and encourages joy in creating and in acknowledging the rhythms of the year.

240pp; 250 x 200mm; paperback; 978-1-907359-69-9

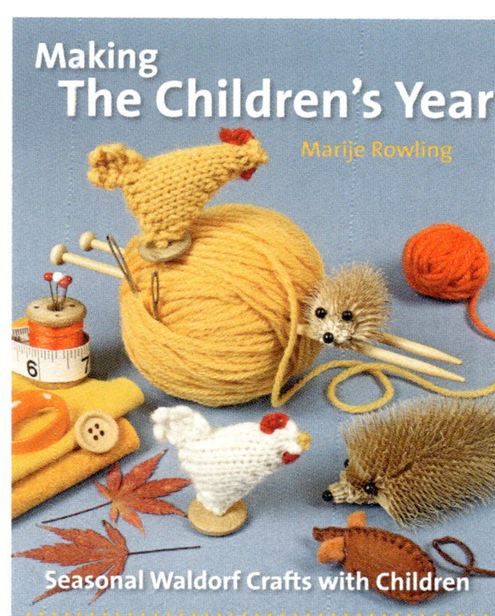

The Children's Forest

Stories & songs, wild food, crafts & celebrations all year round

Dawn Casey, Anna Richardson, Helen d'Ascoli

A rich and abundant treasury in celebration of the outdoors, this book is bursting with colour illustrations and encourages children's natural fascination with the forest and its inhabitants. The authors have produced an enchanting book where imagination, story and play bring alive the world of the forest. Full of games, facts, celebrations, craft activities, recipes, foraging, stories and Forest School skills, *The Children's Forest* is much more than a manual: it is an invitation.

Ideal for ages 5–12 it will also be enjoyed by adults, families and younger children.

336pp; 250 x 200mm; paperback; 978-1-907359-91-0

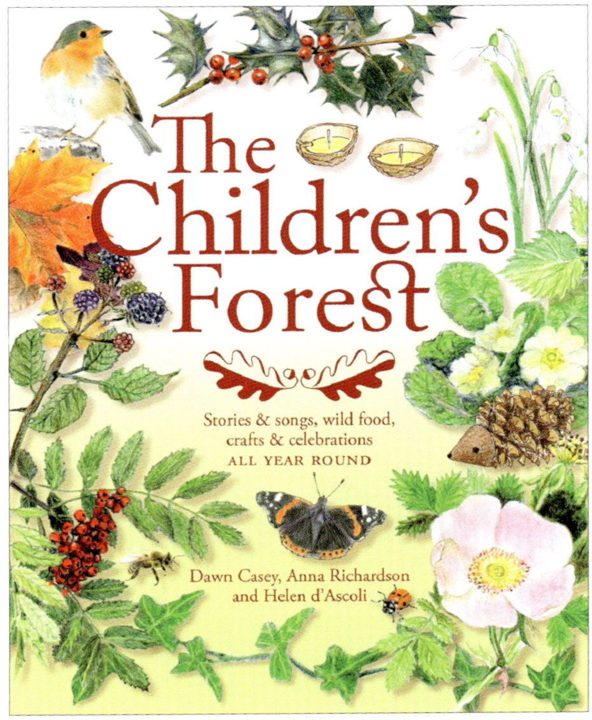

Colour Dynamics

Workbook for Water Colour Painting and Colour Theory

Angela Lord

The book gives an overview of colour through history, watercolour painting and the Steiner Waldorf curriculum, resources, glossary and references. It is a useful resource for beginners, art students, Waldorf teachers, art therapists, architects and interior designers. Steiner Waldorf teachers will find *Colour Dynamics* an up-to-date tried-and-tested educational resource.

128pp; 210 x 260mm; hardback; 978-1-903458-93-8

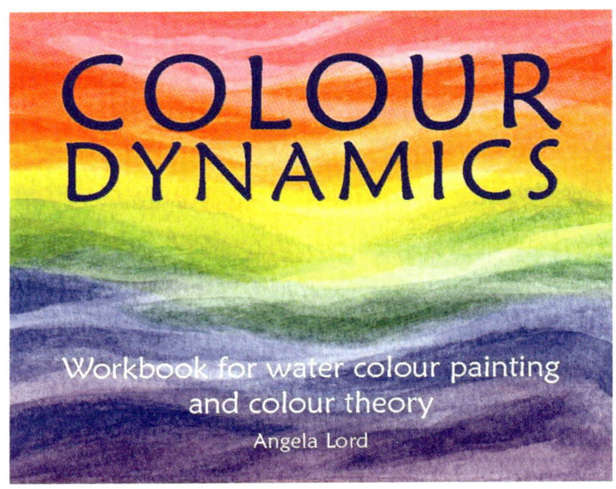

Ordering Books

If you have difficulties ordering Hawthorn Press books from a bookshop, you can order direct from our website www.hawthornpress.com or from Booksource:

Booksource
50 Cambuslang Road, Glasgow
G32 8NB
Tel: (0845) 370 0063
Email: orders@booksource.net

Hawthorn Press
www.hawthornpress.com